TONY   PICARDI

Readings in Urban Dynamics:
Volume I

Readings in Urban Dynamics:

Volume I

Edited by
Nathaniel J. Mass

Wright-Allen Press, Inc.
238 Main Street
Cambridge, Massachusetts 02142

Library of Congress catalog card number: 73-89545
ISBN 0-9600294-7-8

The authors of *Readings in Urban Dynamics* dedicate this volume to the Independence Foundation whose generous and far-sighted support has contributed significantly to the emergence of the field of urban dynamics.

Preface

*Urban Dynamics** was published in the spring of 1969. The book presented a computer model describing the major internal forces controlling the balance of population, housing, and industry within an urban area. Since 1969, a continuing research effort at M.I.T. has sought to extend the original model and to refine the underlying theory of urban interactions. The urban dynamics research program was originally formed under the generous sponsorship of the Independence Foundation of Philadelphia. During a critical interval, Mr. Kenneth J. Germeshausen provided for continuity of the work. More recently, funding by the U. S. Department of Housing and Urban Development has supported work, beyond that reported in this book, to develop policy implications derived from the past four years' study and to apply the urban dynamics approach to analyze the problems of Lowell, Massachusetts.

This volume summarizes the insights gained from the urban dynamics program research at M.I.T. for clarifying the behavior and internal structure of cities. With the publication of *Readings in Urban Dynamics*, it seems important to emphasize that the original *Urban Dynamics* model represented more a viewpoint and a methodology for analyzing urban behavior than a single, finished model. *Urban Dynamics* was a first step in a continuously evolving set of ideas about social systems. The urban dynamics approach has several major distinguishing features. First, it focuses primarily upon the *interrelationships* between economic, political, psychological, and sociological variables rather than analyzing in detail any one subsystem of the urban environment. Second, it deals with the long-term evolution of an urban area; it treats the positive feedback processes that lead to urban growth as well as the nonlinearities and negative feedback processes that arise to limit growth. Finally, it provides a formal means for testing the implications of our collective assumptions about urban behavior.

---

* Editor's note: All references in this volume to *Urban Dynamics* refer to Jay W. Forrester, *Urban Dynamics* (Cambridge, Mass.: The M.I.T. Press, 1969).

In the future, the application of the urban dynamics approach to policy making will require a progression of models from the neighborhood to the metropolitan and regional levels. Individual models will need to focus sharply upon important assumptions and policy questions that are currently uncertain or in debate. Each will form a broad framework wherein individuals in various professions and academic disciplines can contribute toward structuring the overall model. In addition, within each model, new information inputs and questions should lead to continual modifications, clarification, and extension.

This volume serves as a valuable prelude to future, large-scale modeling efforts. It points up many of the current problems and controversies surrounding the construction of realistic urban models. Equally important, it helps to illustrate how the process of urban model building can potentially contribute to improving human judgment and decision making.

Jay W. Forrester

Massachusetts Institute of Technology
Cambridge, Massachusetts
August 17, 1973

Contents

Part One
Overview

Since 1969, the urban dynamics research program at M.I.T. has focused on studying the long-term processes of urban development and the determinants of urban growth and decay. The urban dynamics approach to modeling centers on analyzing the mutual interactions among the various subsystems of an urban area. Readings 1 through 4 provide an introduction to the methodology and perspective underlying this approach. Taken collectively, the papers discuss the value of mathematical models in analyzing social systems and summarize several of the broad policy implications derived from the original urban model and from subsequent work.

1
Managing Our Cities— Can We Do Better?

John F. Collins

In many respects, the structure of urban government is presently geared toward producing a short-term planning perspective. Urban officials are subject to reelection every four years and are thus expected to produce over this period. Moreover, in the preparation of municipal budgets, city agencies are judged according to their recent accomplishments; this leads to an emphasis on short-term results and to heavy discounting of future events.

In the following paper, Professor John F. Collins, former mayor of Boston, describes the implications of cities' past failure to strive toward a set of realizable long-term goals. Primarily, the absence of a long-term outlook in urban decision making has led to conflicts between individual urban agencies and to the ineffectiveness of many urban programs. This paper provides a particularly cogent summary of the potential contribution of the urban dynamics modeling approach in apprising urban residents and decision makers of the long-term implications of proposed urban programs and policies.

1
Managing Our Cities—Can We Do Better?

1.1 Introduction

Our nation is now in the beginning stage of a third round of task forces and ad hoc committees seeking to come to grips with what was called the crisis of our cities, then the urban crisis, and finally our domestic dilemma. By whatever name, the problem has proven intractable, and its symptoms have persisted and indeed by some measures worsened.

Despite the expenditure of billions of dollars by federal and local government and the commitment of 85 billion more, housing in our cities continues to be abandoned at an alarming rate. In many areas, our valuable urban infrastructure, constructed at great cost by the public and private sectors, is underutilized. Nonetheless, we build new infrastructure in concentric rings farther from our decaying core areas even as the wisdom of our throw-away philosophy is widely regarded as imprudent, wasteful, and potentially disastrous.

For decades we believed that the problems of poverty, inadequate housing, crime, unemployment, and overcrowded transportation systems could be solved if only we had the will and the money to match our commitment. Slowly we have learned that these ingredients are not enough. As program followed program, as the symptoms of urban decay worsened and we redoubled our efforts without significant change, disillusionment and doubt followed. How had we failed? Had we not observed symptom after symptom, considered the situation, developed a strategy, and worked conscientiously to implement it? Our dedication to the resolution of urban problems turned to doubt, then despair. In the interim, national urban goals and objectives became more modest as accomplishment lagged behind expectation.

If a city's limited financial and manpower resources are to be effectively marshalled in pursuit of local objectives, plans must be openly arrived at, formally adopted, and published. At the regional level, however, most planning agencies are voluntary in nature, have little power to implement, and are frequently regarded by individual communities as foreign to their own perceived interests.

Even in individual cities that maintain organized planning authorities, these have often proved to be ineffective. Planning agencies have largely been unable to cope with the growing complexity and magnitude of urban ills. The problem is not that urban planners and urban officials individually lack competence or desire; quite the opposite, mayors and urban administrators perceive the current difficulties and endeavor vigorously to deal with them.

The problem does not lie in our motivations or intentions but in the inadequacy of the tools at our disposal. Traditionally, the mayor, the city manager, the city council, and the department heads have been armed with two weapons: common sense and experience. The more successful of our urban administrators have enjoyed the combination of *both* weapons. But as the problems of cities grow more complex, the limitations of our traditional approaches become more apparent. Today's problems take new shapes; they seem to be more persistent than before. Most important, it is becoming clear that the problems are interconnected.

The interconnections between problems lie at the heart of our inability to deal with them effectively. Efforts to alleviate one problem tend to aggravate another. For example, when a city yields to pressure from developers or residents to build more roads, the city will ultimately confront new community pressures. With improved transportation, extra housing will be built and the population may expand outward as new land becomes accessible to the central city. This will create demands for more sewer lines, waste disposal facilities, classrooms, parking, and police services. The quality of these services may suffer as a result. If the city expands its services to meet the increased needs, it may find itself right where it began—with increasing pressure to build more and wider roads. In this situation, as the urban area expands, its problems may expand, too.

Unfortunately, it appears that many decisions can produce chains of events that actually worsen the city in the long run. Why does this occur? One reason is that city decision makers are unable to anticipate the many side effects that may stem from their actions. These side effects often outweigh and negate desired results. Decisions to build more roads, rezone land, increase services, or build new schools set off waves in many directions—both positive and negative. Will the final outcome of a proposal be a net gain or loss? As urban administrators attempt to predict the changes that may result, it is all too easy to distort the projections so that the desired impacts receive emphasis and the negative ones are ignored.

The urban decision maker collects relevant data, consults his advisers, listens to his constituents, draws on his own experience, and makes his decision. The inputs to the decision are many, yet they often conflict more than they convince. In general, very few important decisions are made with total confidence. The present state of our cities suggests that this lack of confidence has been justified.

In several respects, the proliferation of city administrative agencies is clear testimony to the increasing size and complexity of city problems. As the problems have become visibly more complex, so too has city government. Although some could argue that municipal government itself has become sufficiently cumbersome and inefficient to qualify as a part of the overall problem it is important to point out that growing city problems generally preceded the expansion of city government. The urban system was complex, and its problems interconnected, long before we began conceiving complex urban governments.

1.2 Urban Dynamics: Viewing the City as a System

The theory of urban dynamics was developed in the belief that the key to improving a city lies not only in isolating its many problems but also in identifying the network of connections that exist between problems. The first urban dynamics model was an attempt to describe the causal connections between such major problems as underemployment, housing inadequacies, increasing tax rates, inefficient land use, industrial disinvestment, low upward economic mobility, and overcrowding. Instead of looking at one city problem at a time, urban dynamics views the city from an overall perspective.

Urban dynamics is clearly a technical approach to understanding and improving cities, but the approach itself is based on some very simple concepts. The attractiveness principle and the orientation toward problem interconnections combine to form the basis of the model. I believe that these concepts lead directly to some major implications for urban management. Even for those without access to computers or programming experts, these concepts produce a new kind of thinking about cities; for example, the concepts of problem interconnectedness and urban attractiveness appear to explain why many past urban strategies have failed, and they provide some new directions for policy. Let me summarize some of the practical implications.

1.3 Urban Utopia

Professor Jay W. Forrester developed, in the text of *Urban Dynamics*, the argument that there can be no utopian city. He proposes that we try to imagine the "perfect" city: no crime, no unemployment, excellent transportation, little congestion, plenty of good housing, and a showcase school system. What can we say about such a perfect city? The attractiveness principle suggests that we can say a good deal.

First, people will begin moving into the perfect city, much as people move to the younger, growing cities of today. But as the population of the city increases, the elements of attractiveness become strained. Schools become crowded, traffic jams become frequent, crime may rise. As taxes rise to meet increasing city costs, new construction is discouraged, and jobs and good housing become scarcer.

The attractiveness principle assures us that people will continue to move to a perfect city until its overall attractiveness falls to the level of other cities. Whether one interprets this to mean that all cities tend to be equally good or equally bad is only a matter of semantics. The important point for the urban manager is that all cities must tend to become equal in attractiveness. Hence each city, as viewed on average by those who might move to it, will always tend toward being no more perfect as a place in which to live than other cities.

Most cities, meanwhile, are making every effort to become perfect. Laws are passed, money is spent, and decisions are made with the goal of improving every part of the city. Clearly, such efforts will fail in their total purpose; waste, frustration, and confusion are the only guaranteed results. Plans that call for "more of everything for everyone" have failed and will inevitably continue to fail. The attractiveness principle suggests that we begin looking for a more realistic approach to urban planning and decision making.

Cities harbor a diverse number of constituents—blacks, whites, tenants, landlords, industrialists, environmentalists—and each of these strives for attention to its own interests. A single individual may be part of several such constituencies as his concerns overlap those of other urban residents. Still, in the face of many competing interests, how does a mayor or a planning commission decide a city's goals and priorities? Because any city's resources, and therefore the money and effort that can be expended in dealing with any one set of problems, are finite, cities can never be everything to everyone. However, faced with the pressures created by perceived needs that rival one another, cities have tended either to eschew an explicit statement of goals or to shift progressively from one set of goals to another and from one set of problems to another. In this way, major conflicts are avoided to the greatest possible extent. Without goals, conflicts are fewer, but measurable progress is nearly impossible to achieve. Cities cannot expect to improve by accident. Instead, they must create and strive toward a well-defined set of goals.

In the past, even in cities that have prepared explicit goal statements, the value and realism of those goals are often subject to question. City planning reports have all too frequently emerged as consensus documents that urge more and better housing, jobs, transportation, education, parks, and municipal services for all city residents. However laudable these objectives may be, their accomplishment seems beyond the range of reality for cities. Efforts to promote economic development may, consciously or otherwise, lead to environmental degradation. Construction of a new road depletes funds that would otherwise be available for construction of a new library or arts center. Increased provision of jobs leads to increased population levels and increased rents. From the standpoint of the city government, such trade-offs and compromises are inevitable; they cannot readily be put aside.

We can no longer afford to manage our cities according to a set of utopian objectives. We must come to recognize that efforts to improve a single dimension of urban life may cause other elements to deteriorate. In the past, cities have attempted to deal with individual problems in isolation as they arise. Lately, the shortcomings of the "crisis management" mode of operation have become more evident. Instead of solving all problems, crisis management prevents the city from taking a broad view of its problems and their causes. As a result, many cities now find themselves entangled with problems that seem to be totally out of control.

In addition to the financial crisis of cities, even more serious by-products of our urban decision patterns are becoming visible. We may be inadvertently trading solutions to the physical problems of cities for worsening psychological and social problems. Cities have continued to work on the problems that our society has traditionally been able to solve—the kinds that yield to money, technology, and manpower. New transportation systems have increased city capacity; energy generation equipment has expanded development potential; and high-rise structures allow far more intensive use of city land and place greater demands on roads and mass transit.

But the problems that have no simple physical or technological solutions have gotten measurably worse—problems such as drug addiction, crime, poverty and alienation. The list of urban problems is now being reordered, with the most insoluble moving to the top of the priority list. The total amount of internal urban pressure still remains about the same. City decision makers should begin to consider whether their actions to ease the physical problems and pressures have in fact given rise, through the interconnected urban network, to problems and pressures in the social section of the urban system.

Some readers may infer from the arguments presented thus far that nothing can be done—that while I am describing why cities are in trouble, I am also building up to the conclusion that there is no way for the cities to be improved. In fact, the conclusions are far more optimistic. I believe that the forces that lead cities into their decline can be controlled—that we can prevent and even reverse their decline. It is within our ability to understand the major forces that lead to trade-offs between urban pressures. When one understands the real constraints of the urban system, feasible solutions can be separated from the infeasible. To the urban manager, no tool can be more useful and optimistic than one that separates feasible improvements from utopian failures.

To guide their long-term development, cities require more sensible means for making decisions and for accepting trade-offs. Many of our cities' problems are lodged in a failure to focus on identifying goals that are both feasible and desirable. While there may never be full consensus within a single urban area on which elements are most valued by local residents, we cannot presume to satisfy all needs; nor can we successfully revitalize our cities until we have decided what is achievable and what is desirable.

The wide gap between planning and management in today's cities is evidence that planning has not been responsive to the needs of decision makers. A unique feature of the urban dynamics approach is its potential for bridging the gap. The modeling approach can be used not only for identifying feasible long-term goals but also for assessing which of today's decision alternatives can best achieve those goals. The model translates future goals into current actions.

1.4 The Fundamental Alternative: Whether to Be Different

The model described in Professor Forrester's *Urban Dynamics* shows how initial improvements in a city raise its attractiveness and cause increased population and crowding. As a consequence, in the long run, the city's initial gains may be offset by a lower overall quality of life for its residents.

On the other hand, there may be many programs that regulate a city's population size but do not harm the quality of life for those within the city. Stated more simply, if a city can deliberately choose to sacrifice one element of urban attractiveness in order to constrain excessive in-migration, then improvements in other parts of the city are possible. To those outside the city, the net attractiveness of the area then stays the same, while the quality of life has been improved for those inside the city.

In a sense, many suburbs have followed this principle and used it to their perceived advantage. The more affluent suburbs generally have an acute shortage of low-income housing. Few suburbanites view this as a major problem. Inner-city residents, however, view suburbia with envy.

The urban system contains a broader constituency and a more complex set of problems than the suburbs. Yet there appear to be trade-offs that even whole cities will prefer over others as the price to be paid for a higher quality of life. Once it becomes clear to a city that the real improvements can be gained only through trade-offs, agreement among city residents on the choice of counterpressures becomes even more likely.

That cities are and will remain different from one anther does not invalidate the preceding argument. Instead, it suggests the need to find different counterpressures for different cities. The resort city might choose to discourage manufacturing jobs in order to prevent the buildup of manufacturing-oriented services, worker housing, pollution, and urban change. The manufacturing city might discourage additional low-income housing to prevent the threat of an imbalance between total jobs and workers. The educational city, to keep the cost of school expansion low and to preserve aesthetics, might discourage high-rise construction and small-lot zoning. The long-term needs of the community should be the prime criteria in the selection of pressures to be applied.

Differences between cities can improve the quality of life within each. Although two cities may be equally attractive in terms of the preceding discussion, they may differ in such a way that one city is perceived to be substantially more perfect by its residents. One city may stress the qualities that are important to its residents by suppressing the qualities that are less important. Another city can stress a different set of qualities that are most valuable to *its* residents. Viewed by those outside, neither city is better than the other; yet for those inside each city, the character of the city best meets the needs of its residents. Focusing attention on making our cities different may be the most viable approach to making them better.

If this country can achieve a diversity of types of cities, it will have moved far closer to a democratic urban environment. Today, cities are becoming more alike, not more different. The range of alternative living conditions open to our society is limited. Differences among cities, if established and sustained, foster the very freedom of choice in migration that produced this great nation. Each of us will gain if there is a wide variety of interesting, safe, and accessible places to live.

1.5 Conclusions

Translating these general implications from urban dynamics into specific programs will be an immense but exciting task. Fortunately, the time for new ideas is at hand. There is widespread uncertainty in Washington about the proper role of the federal government in urban affairs. The massive programs of the past have failed to meet their desired objectives. A growing attitude, evidenced particularly by the progress of revenue sharing, is that local governments can and should deal with their own problems. Although many local officials will view this trend only as symbolic of federal defeat rather than local strength, the trend toward greater local autonomy may be a healthy one.

The forces of urban decline were at work long before the federal government took an active role in urban problem solving. Since the causes of urban decline are not at the federal level, we should not necessarily expect the solutions to be there either.

Urban dynamics builds a strong, logical argument that many urban problems have evolved as a consequence of decisions and actions taken within the city itself. By failing for many years to recognize the physical and social constraints that govern urban development, cities have created many of their own major problems.

The tendency over the past three decades to look toward federal and state governments for help was understandable. Having now explored the possibilities and problems of outside solutions, it is time for cities to recognize the imperatives for self-renewal. The more the city looks to outside sources for answers, the less it will feel compelled to understand and treat its problems with internal resources. Federal and state support to cities has relaxed local problem-solving forces. Cities waited for answers that never came, and merely became older, weaker, and more discouraged in the process. General and special revenue-sharing measures will restore self-determination to local administrations. Problems to be attacked will no longer be directed from the federal level. The city can use the money to meet its own special needs rather than spend it according to a formula that makes each city look and become more and more like the rest. Revenue sharing may not be the total answer, but it makes resources available for the city to take bold and innovative approaches that until now have been unfeasible. It sets the stage for an important local challenge.

The problems of cities will not wait for us to provide perfect solutions. Decisions on important issues must be made today within our present understanding and with our best available information. Yet it is also clear that there are serious shortcomings in our traditional approaches to urban decision making.

In the future, urban decisions will need to be made with greater recognition of the long-term consequences emanating from policy actions. We must develop a generation of knowledgeable urban statesmen who will be insulated from daily pressures and short-term demands and dedicated to understanding the long-term effects of important decisions.

It is time to learn from the past failures of urban management. If we can redirect the focus of urban decision making toward understanding the trade-offs between urban qualities, we will have moved significantly toward improving the economic and social environment of our cities.

2
Systems Analysis as a Tool for Urban Planning

Jay W. Forrester

The development of high-speed computers and modern methods of systems analysis has led in recent years to renewed efforts to understand urban behavior and policy. In this paper, Professor Jay W. Forrester identifies many of the characteristics of complex systems that necessitate the use of formal, quantitative models to analyze social behavior. In particular, Professor Forrester effectively illustrates the merits of formal models such as that described in Urban Dynamics *over the "mental models" that have traditionally guided urban policy analysis.*

This paper provides an introduction to several of the principal concepts embodied in Urban Dynamics—*urban attractiveness and the aging of industrial and residential structures. The paper was originally prepared for the symposium on "The Engineer and the City," sponsored by the National Academy of Engineering, held in Washington, D.C., October 22–23, 1969.*

New ways are becoming available for analyzing our social systems. These permit the design of revised policies to improve the behavior of the systems within which we live. Many of the ideas discussed here are treated more fully in my book *Urban Dynamics*, which shows the city as an interacting system of industry, housing, and people. The book presents a theory, in the form of a computer model, that interrelates the components of a city. It shows how the interacting processes produce urban growth and cause growth to give way to stagnation. Various changes in policies are examined with the laboratory model to show their effects on an urban area. A number of presently popular proposals are tested—a job training program, job creation by busing to suburban industries or by the government as employer of last resort, financial subsidies to the city, and low-cost housing programs. All are shown to lie between neutral and detrimental in their effect on a depressed urban area. The evolution of an urban area from growth to stagnation creates a condition of excess housing. Housing is excess compared with both population and the availability of income-earning opportunities. To reestablish a healthy economic balance and a continuous process of internal renewal, it appears to be necessary to reduce the inherent excess housing of depressed areas and to encourage the conversion of part of the land to industrial use. By so doing, a large enough wage and salary stream can be brought in from the outside economy to make the area self-sustaining.

As you can see, these results are controversial. If they are right, most of the traditional steps taken to alleviate the conditions of our cities may actually be making matters worse.

Urban Dynamics is based on methods for studying complex systems that form a bridge between engineering and the social sciences. Although I shall present here some results from the book, my principal emphasis will be on the importance of the methods to all social systems.

Over a decade ago at MIT we began to examine the dynamic characteristics of managerial systems. The field known as "industrial dynamics" resulted.[1] Industrial dynamics belongs to the same general subject area as feedback systems, servomechanisms theory, and cybernetics. It is the study of how the feedback-loop structure of a system produces the dynamic behavior of that system. In managerial terms, industrial dynamics makes it possible to structure the components and policies of a system to show how the resulting dynamic behavior is produced. In terms of social systems, it deals with the forces that arise within a system to cause changes through time.

A design study of a social system seeks changes in structure and policies that will improve the behavior of the system. Some people recoil at the thought of designing social systems. They feel that designing a society is immoral. But we have no choice about living in a system that has been designed. The laws, tax policies, and traditions of a society constitute the design of a social system. Our available choice is only between different designs. If we lament the functioning of our cities, or the persistence of inflation, or the changes in our environment, we mean that we prefer a social system of a different design.

The design process first observes the behavior modes of a system to identify the symptoms of trouble. Second, the system is searched for the feedback structures that might produce the observed behavior. Third, the level and rate variables making up that structure are identified and explicitly described in the equations of a computer simulation model. Fourth, the computer model is used to simulate in the laboratory the dynamic behavior implicit in the identified structure. Fifth, the structure is modified until its components and the resulting behavior agree with the observed conditions in the actual system. Sixth, modified policies can then be introduced into the simulation model in search of usable and acceptable policies that will yield improved behavior.

This design process brings the essential substance of a social system into the laboratory where the system can be studied. Laboratory representation of a social system can be far more effective than most people would expect. Anything that can be stated or described about a social system can be represented in such a laboratory model. The major difficulty is the rarity of skilled professional talent. There are very few men with a knowledge of the proper guiding principles and with experience in perceiving the pertinent feedback structure of complex, poorly defined systems. Whatever one may say about the shortcomings of the process, there is no comparable effective substitute.

Surprising discoveries come from this combination of theory and laboratory experimentation. We observe that relatively simple structures produce much of the complex behavior of real-life systems. We find that people's skills in perception are very different from those commonly supposed. It is often asserted in the social sciences that people are unreliable in analyzing their own actions, yet time and again we find that the policies and practices that people know they are following are the ones that interact to produce the most troublesome consequences. Conversely, it can be clearly demonstrated that the vaunted powers of judgment and intuition usually deceive the person who tries to guess the time-varying consequences that follow even from a completely known system structure. We find that the most conspicuous modes of behavior in managerial, urban, and economic systems are produced by nonlinearities within those systems. The linearized models that have been used in much of engineering and in the social sciences cannot even approximate the important modes of behavior in our social systems. The most visible and troublesome modes are manifestations of nonlinear interactions. We find it relatively straightforward to include the so-called intangible factors relating to psychological variables, attitudes, and human reactions. Again, if the influences can be discussed and described, they can be inserted in the policy structure of a model. Any person who discusses why people act the way they do, explains a past decision, or anticipates a future action is relating the surrounding circumstances to the corresponding human response. Any such discussion is a description of decision-making policy. Any such policy statement can be put into a system model.

A body of dynamic theory and principles of structure is emerging that allows us to organize and understand complex systems.[2] For example, the feedback loop becomes the basic building block of systems. Within the feedback loop there are two and only two kinds of variables. One is the level variable produced by integration; the other is the policy statement or rate variable that governs the changes in a system. The level variables are changed only by the rates of flow. The rate variables depend only on the levels. Any path through a system network encounters alternating level and rate variables. These and many other principles of structure are universal in the entire sweep of systems that change through time. Furthermore, the structure of a system determines its possible modes of behavior. Identical structures recur as one moves between apparently dissimilar fields. These identical structures behave in identical ways wherever they are found.

The same principles of structure and the same relationships between structure and behavior apply to a simple swinging pendulum, a chemical plant, the processes of management, internal medicine, economics, power politics, and psychiatry. A universal approach to time-varying systems is emerging that seems to be capable of dealing with systems of any complexity. We observe that students, as they master the principles and practice of dynamic analysis, develop a remarkable mobility between fields of endeavor. The same person can clarify the dynamics of how a transistor functions, organize the processes of a public health epidemic, design new management policies to avoid stagnation in product growth, discover the sensitive factors in ecological change, and show how government policies affect the growth and decline of a city.

Some diagrams showing urban behavior will illustrate these ideas. Figure 1 shows the central structure of an urban area. The nine rectangles represent the

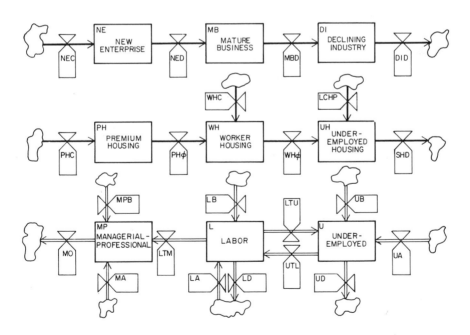

Figure 1 Urban structure

selected level variables. The twenty-two valve symbols represent the rates of flow that cause the nine system levels to change. Engineers often refer to these level variables as the state variables of a system. The distinction between level and rate variables is also familiar to anyone who examines financial statements. Balance sheet variables are always separated from variables on the profit-and-loss statement. These two types of accounting variables are conceptually quite different. The balance sheet variables are system levels. They are created by accumulating financial flows. The profit-and-loss variables are system rates. This sharp distinction between level variables and rates of flow is found in all systems.

In the simplified urban system of Figure 1, nine levels are grouped into three subsystems. Across the top the industrial sector contains commercial buildings in three categories distinguished primarily by age. Across the center are residential buildings in three categories, also distinguished by age and condition. Across the bottom are three economic categories of population. Because of their complexity, the information linkages connecting the system levels to the system rates are not shown on this figure. In this figure one can begin to detect the reasons for urban decline. The age of a building tends to determine the character of its occupants. A new commercial building is occupied by a healthy, successful commercial organization that uses relatively more managers and skilled workers than unskilled workers. As the building ages, it tends to house a progressively less successful enterprise with lower employment skills. In addition to the changing employment mix as the industrial building ages, there is a tendency for total employment per unit of floor space to decline. On the other hand, as residential buildings age, there is a tendency for occupancy to increase as well as to shift to a lower economic category of population. One then perceives a condition in which the aging of buildings in an urban area simultaneously reduces the opportunities for employment and increases the population. The average income of the community and standard of living decline.

Figure 2 shows the same nine system levels and one of the twenty-two flow rates. The dotted lines are the information linkages from the system levels to control the one flow rate—here the arrival of underemployed population into the urban area. The various levels of the system combine to create a composite "attractiveness" that determines the inflow rate to the area. If the area is more attractive than those from which people might come, a net inward population flow occurs. If the area is less attractive, an outward flow dominates. Five components of attractiveness are shown in Figure 2. In the upper right corner UJM is the underemployed/job multiplier, which relates the population to the available jobs and represents the income-earning attractiveness of the area. The circle UAMM generates the attractiveness created by upward economic mobility. In other words, an area with high upward economic mobility is more attractive than one offering no hope of advancement. The circle UHM relates the underemployed population to the available housing. The area becomes more attractive as housing becomes more available. UHPM represents the attractiveness of a low-cost-housing program if one exists. And in the lower right corner

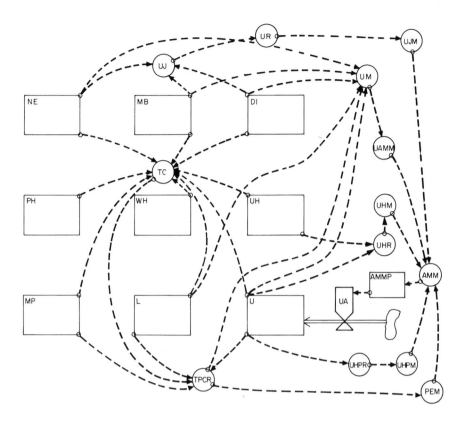

Figure 2 Information links to the underemployed-arrival rate

PEM is the influence on attractiveness of the public expenditure per capita. Rising per capita expenditure means better public services, better schools, and higher welfare budgets.

The concept of attractiveness is fundamental to the population flows. All the characteristics that make an area attractive—these five and many more—combine to influence migration. An attractive area draws people. But almost every component of attractiveness is driven down by an increase in population. If there is an excess of housing, the area is attractive, but a rising population crowds the housing. If there is an excess of jobs, the area is attractive, but the incoming flow of people fills those jobs. In other words, migration continues until the attractiveness of the area falls and becomes equal to that of all other places from which people might come.

An important idea follows from examining these components of attractiveness. In a condition of population equilibrium, all areas must be equally attractive to any given population class; otherwise, net migration would occur. If one component of attractiveness is increased in an area, other components must necessarily fall to establish a new equilibrium. Compensating changes in the components of attractiveness explain many past failures in our cities; frequently we have attempted to improve one aspect of the city only to discover that other aspects have become worse.

In making a laboratory model of a social system one should not attempt straightaway to solve a problem. Instead one should generate a model that will create the trouble symptoms. Only if one fully understands the processes whereby difficulties are created can he hope to correct the causes. This means that we want a model of an urban area that can start with empty land, grow a city, and show the processes whereby economic health falters into stagnation and decay.

As another guide to modeling, one should not start by building a model of a particular situation, but instead should model the general class of systems under study. This may seem surprising, but the general model is simpler and is initially more informative than a model of a special case. Here we wish to model the general process of urban growth and stagnation. It should be a model that, with proper changes in parameters, is good for New York, Calcutta, a gold-rush camp, or West Berlin. These all seem to have very different characteristics, but they have certain elements in common that describe their urban processes. There are fewer concepts that are common to all than are to be found in any one. The general model can strip away the multitude of detail that confuses any one special situation. The general model identifies the central processes and is a statement of the theory for the entire class of systems.

Figure 3 shows the behavior of the laboratory model of an urban area. It presents the nine system levels over 250 years. The first 100 years are a period of

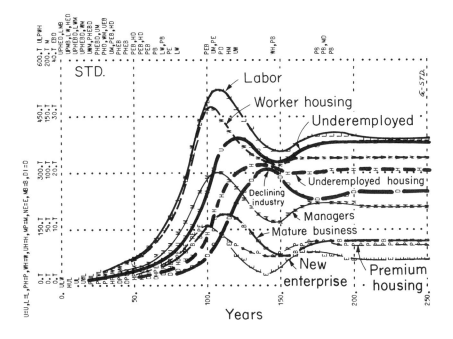

Figure 3   Growth and stagnation

exponential growth, but then the land area becomes filled, growth ceases, and the aging process begins. At year 100, near the end of the growth phase, the labor population is almost double the underemployed population. This is a healthy mix that is well matched to the job distribution in the area and gives a high upward economic mobility to the underemployed population. But by year 150 the labor population has fallen and the underemployed population has risen until the two groups are almost equal; business activity has declined, and the area has taken on the characteristics of a depressed city.

Figure 4 shows other variables during the same 250 years. Notice especially the underemployed/job ratio and the underemployed/housing ratio. During most of the first 100 years of growth these two ratios were almost constant. The underemployed/housing ratio was high (above the center of the figure), meaning that the population is large compared to the housing. In other words, during the first 100 years there was a housing shortage for the underemployed population. On the other hand, the underemployed/job ratio was low, meaning that the population was below the job opportunities, jobs were readily available, economic opportunity was good, and upward economic mobility was high. During this early period of growth and high economic activity, the underemployed population was being effectively adjusted in relation to other activity by balancing good economic opportunity against a housing shortage.

But between 90 and 140 years, notice the sharp reversal of the curves for the underemployed/job ratio and the underemployed/housing ratio. Within this 50-

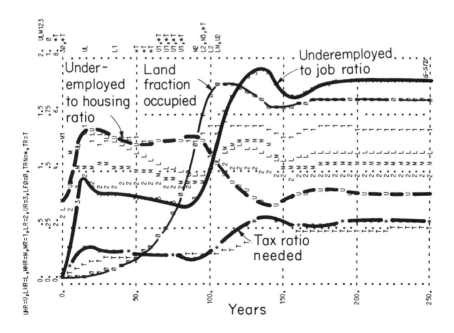

Figure 4 Compensating changes in housing and employment

year span, the underemployed increased while available jobs decreased; the result is a precipitous rise in unemployment. But in this same period, the housing that is aging and becoming available to the underemployed is rising even more rapidly than the underemployed population. Jobs have become scarce while housing has become surplus. The model is behaving the way our cities do.

Many people seem not to realize that the depressed areas of our cities are areas of excess housing. The economy of the area is not able to maintain all the available housing. Because of low incomes, people crowd into some dwelling units while other buildings are abandoned, stand idle, and decay.

Recall the earlier comments about compensating movements in the components of attractiveness. Here, as housing becomes more available, jobs become more scarce. The stagnating urban area has become a social trap. Excess housing beckons people and causes inward migration until the rising population drives the standard of living down far enough to stop the population inflow.

Figure 5 shows 50 years, beginning with the conditions found at the end of Figure 3. At time 0, a low-cost-housing program is introduced, which each year builds low-cost housing for 2.5 percent of the underemployed population. Observe what happens. Underemployed housing, which is being actively constructed, rises 45 percent but premium housing falls 35 percent, and worker housing falls 30 percent. New enterprise declines 50 percent and mature business declines 45 percent, all in the 50-year period. Economic conditions become sufficiently worse so that even the underemployed population, although it rises initially, eventually falls to slightly less than its beginning value. These changes are a result of the low-cost-housing program.

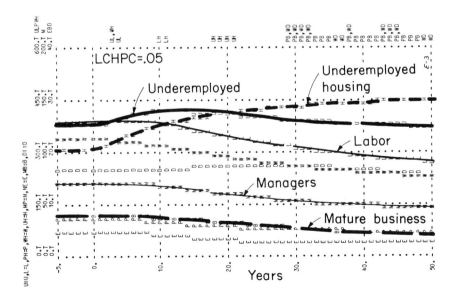

Figure 5 Decline of urban area caused by low-cost-housing construction each year for 2.5 percent of the underemployed

In Figure 6 the corresponding underemployed/job ratio has risen 30 percent, indicating substantially higher unemployment, while the underemployed/housing ratio has fallen 30 percent, indicating a still higher excess of housing. Again, the two components of attractiveness compensate for one another with better housing and a falling standard of living. In the long run, the low-cost-housing program has not served the interests of the low-income residents. Instead, it has intensified the social trapping characteristic of the area. Over the period, the tax levies rise 35 percent. The area has become worse from almost all viewpoints.

Job training programs, job creation programs, and financial subsidies were examined in this same manner. All lie between ineffective and harmful. The low-cost-housing program was the most powerful in depressing the conditions of a stagnant urban area.

The depressed areas of our cities seem to be characterized by excess housing compared to jobs and by an excessive concentration of low-income population. These conditions, created by aging industrial and dwelling buildings, interact to drive out the upper-income population and business activity and to reduce the tax base. Once the decline starts, it tends to accelerate. Unless one can devise urban management policies that produce continuous renewal, difficulties are inherent.

Figure 7 shows an urban condition that begins with stagnation and then changes toward revival. Here 5 percent of the slum housing is removed each year and the incentives for new-enterprise construction are increased somewhat. The result is a cascading of mutual interactions that raise the economic activity of the area, increase upward economic mobility for the underemployed population, and shift the population internally from the underemployed to the labor class. This is

Figure 6 Rising unemployment and falling occupancy of housing

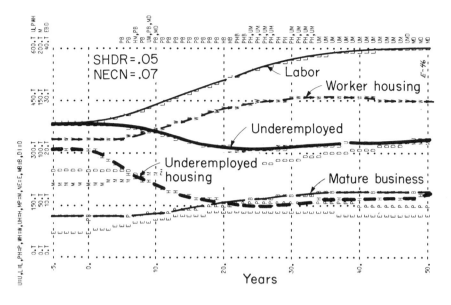

Figure 7   Revival caused by removing 5 percent of underemployed housing each year and encouraging business construction to generate jobs

done without driving the existing low-income population out of the area. Underemployed housing is reduced. Initially, this reduction comes largely from the empty housing. The resulting housing shortage restrains the population inflow that would otherwise defeat the revival of the area.

Figure 8 shows the same 50-year span as the preceding figure. Here again, employment and housing move in opposite directions. The underemployed/job ratio falls, which means more jobs and lower unemployment. On the other hand, the underemployed/housing ratio rises, which means a tighter housing situation. If the economic circumstances are to be improved, we must accept some compensating change in other components of attractiveness. Here it is the increased tightness of housing that allows job opportunities to increase faster than population until a good economic balance is reached. I stress economic revival as the first stage of rebuilding a depressed area because it appears that an economic base must precede social and cultural development.

It is simply not possible to increase all of the attractiveness components of an area simultaneously. Attractiveness is here defined in a very broad sense. For example, legal restrictions like an immigration barrier into a country can produce enough "unattractiveness" for inward migration so that other components might be maintained at a high level. But wherever one component of attractiveness is high others will be found to be low.

Engineers, especially, should consider the compensating changes that will occur in the attractiveness components of an area because engineers tend to deal with economic considerations and technology. Economic and technical factors

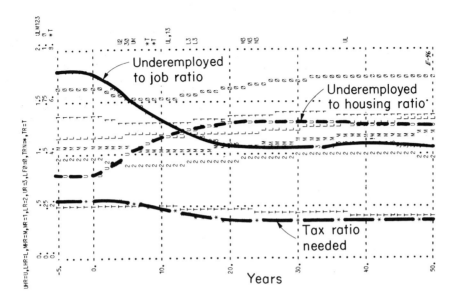

Figure 8 Falling unemployment and rise in housing occupancy

are more concrete than the intangible "quality-of-life" variables. The economic and technical aspects of a city are the ones we most easily see how to improve. Our technological society tends, therefore, to observe, react to, and improve the economic and technical aspects of a city. Such improvements increase the technical and economic components of urban attractiveness. But as a result, population density rises until the urban area once again reaches an attractiveness equilibrium with its environment. The burden of forced reduction in other components of attractiveness falls on the quality of life variables—crowding, pollution, and psychological stress. These less tangible variables have been weak, hard to measure, and have been defenseless against the persuasiveness and the certainty of improvement shown by the technical and economic considerations. But we are entering a time when a reversal will occur between the formerly weak and strong variables. For a substantial fraction of our population, the standard of living is already high enough so that more gain in the economic and technical areas will come at too high a price in the quality-of-life components of our environment. The engineer, if he continues to serve society, must balance a greater number of social needs against one another. At one time his task was simply to balance the financial cost against the economic performance of his technology. Now the product and also the medium of payment are both expanding. Social value and quality of life become part of the product. Psychological stress, ugliness, and crowding become part of the cost. Engineers who fail to recognize this broadened role will be vilified and castigated by a society that perceives them as narrow and insensitive to the demands of the times.

When a system misbehaves, we should ask ourselves what policies within that system cause the undesirable characteristics. If we examine the laws under which a city operates, we see a structure of regulations that could hardly be better designed to create stagnation and decline. The aging and decay of buildings are central to the urban decline process, yet we see throughout our tax laws and regulations numerous incentives to keep old buildings in place. As the value of a building decreases, so do the assessed taxes. The reduced expense makes it possible to retain the old building longer. For income tax purposes under some circumstances the value of a building can be depreciated several times. This produces incentives to keep an old building in place. Here is not the place for detail, but it seems to be clear that a different set of tax laws and city regulations could be devised to produce the individual incentives necessary for continuous renewal. As an example, I recently saw a suggestion that each building have a mandatory trust fund into which the owner must pay a levy each year. At anytime, whoever owns the building can draw out the money in the trust fund if he demolishes the building and clears the land. This would create an earlier incentive for replacement. Property tax levies and income tax accounting could both be changed to produce pressures in the same direction.

Our studies of managerial, urban, and other social systems have uncovered many general characteristics of complex systems to which we must be alert if we are to avoid continuing to create detrimental modes of behavior.

First, complex systems are counterintuitive. They behave in ways that are opposite to what most people expect. They are counterintuitive because our experience and intuition have been developed almost entirely from contact with simple systems. But in many ways, simple systems behave exactly the opposite from complex systems. Therefore, our experience misleads us into drawing the wrong conclusions about complex social systems.

Second, complex systems are strongly resistant to most policy changes. A new policy tends to warp the system so that slightly changed levels present new information to the policy points in the system. The new information, as processed through the new policies, tends to give the old results. There are inherent reasons within complex systems why so many of our attempts at correcting a city, a company, or an economy are destined to fail.

But, third, the converse is also true. There are points in systems from which favorable influences will radiate. Often these points are difficult to perceive. Often the action required is the opposite to that which might be expected. But when these points are found, they tend to radiate new information streams in such a way that the new circumstances, when processed through the old attitudes and policies, produce a new result.

Fourth, complex systems tend to counteract most active programs aimed at alleviating symptoms. For example, Chapter 4 in *Urban Dynamics* shows how a job training program can increase the number of underemployed in a city. When outside action tries to alter the condition of a system, the system relaxes its own internal processes aimed at the same result and throws the burden ever more onto the outside force that is attempting to produce a correction. The internal need for action is reduced and the external supplier of action must work ever harder.

Fifth, in complex systems the short-term response to a policy change is apt to be in the opposite direction from the long-term effect. This is especially treacherous. A policy change that improves matters in the short run lays a foundation for degradation in the long run. The short tenure of men in political office favors decisions that will produce results quickly. These are often the very actions that eventually drive the system to ever-worsening performance. Short-run versus long-run reversal processes are all around us. If an agricultural country is to industrialize, it must accumulate railroads, factories, and steel mills. This capital accumulation can only be done by foregoing consumption and reducing the standard of living first so that the standard of living may rise at a later time. If a company faces declining earnings because its products are obsolete, it must invest more heavily in product research and incur even deeper short-term losses if it is to recover in the more distant future to a profitable product stream. A student foregoes short-term earning opportunities by attending college to increase his longer-term earning capability. This reversal between the short run and the long run occurs repeatedly.

Sixth, a system contains internal dynamic mechanisms that *produce* the observed undesirable behavior. If we ignore the fundamental causes and simply try to overwhelm the symptoms, we pit two great sets of forces against one another. In general, our social systems have evolved to a very stable configuration. If the system is troublesome, we should expect that the causes of the trouble are deeply embedded. The causes will outlast our persistence in overwhelming the symptoms. Furthermore, the internal pressures usually rise to counteract a corrective force from the outside. We can expend all our energy to no avail in trying to compensate for the troubles unless we discover the basic causes and redesign the system so that it will spontaneously move to a new mode of behavior.

And as the last of these characteristics of complex systems, we must recognize that a certain ensemble of conditions goes with each possible mode of a system. More specifically, each mode of a system is accompanied by a set of pressures characteristic of that mode. We cannot sustain a particular mode unless we are willing to accept the corresponding pressures. For example, contrast the depressed mode of a city in Figures 5 and 6 with the revived mode in Figures 7 and 8. The depressed mode is characterized by the pressures that come from decaying buildings, low incomes, and social disorientation. But the revived mode also contains pressures. The revived mode is sustained by the housing shortage and by the legal and tax pressures that generate a steady demolition and replacement of old buildings. But everyone in the system will want to alleviate the pressures. Active industry will want more employees; residents will want more floor space; and outsiders will want housing so they can move to the attractive job opportunities. Rents will be high. These pressures are easy to relieve by increasing the fraction of the land area permissible for housing, by keeping old buildings in place longer, and by allowing taller apartment buildings. But such moves will start the area back toward the depressed mode. We must decide the kind of system we want with knowledge of and acceptance of the accompanying pressures. Instead, much of our social legislation of the last several decades has consisted of trying to relieve one set of pressures after another. The result is a system mode characterized by inflexibility, conformity, crowding, frustration, supremacy of the organization over the individual, and a choking of the environment. And the resulting pressures, acting through the counterintuitive and short- versus long-term reversal characteristics of complex systems, may well move us further in the same direction.

I am suggesting that the time is approaching when we can design social systems to obtain far better behavior. Different policies could change our urban areas from ones designed to deteriorate into ones designed for self-renewal. One can foresee a time when we will understand far better the relationships between monetary policy, interest rates, unemployment, and foreign exchange. Studies have already thrown new light on the processes of corporate growth, on the reasons for product stagnation and loss of market share, and on the growth and decline of cities.

But to design new policies for social systems requires a level of skill that is rare. The kind of system modeling and policy design I have been describing requires a professional training at least as extensive as that in any of the established professions. The proper training requires theory, laboratory, case studies, apprenticeship, and practicing experience.

But in the area of designing the dynamic behavior of social systems, there are as yet no adequate professional schools. The educational materials are still in the development stage. The few who show skill in this area have learned by apprenticeship and by trial and error.

Those interested in the long-run improvement of society, can make a valuable contribution by encouraging research and educational programs aimed at developing a high level of talent. Again, the long run competes with the short run. Creating educational materials and teachers will at first absorb money and talent that in the short run might instead be devoted to solving particular present social problems. Unless a proper balance is maintained, with substantial energy devoted to establishing an educational capability for enlarging the future pool of skills in social system design, the time when we can master our own systems will be further delayed.

Notes

1. See Jay W. Forrester, *Industrial Dynamics* (Cambridge, Mass.: The M.I.T. Press, 1961).
2. See Jay W. Forrester, *Principles of Systems* (Cambridge, Mass.: Wright-Allen Press, 1968).

3

Understanding *Urban Dynamics*

Gerald O. Barney

This paper deals with several questions that have been raised concerning the boundary definition in the Urban Dynamics *model and the impact of policies on the economic health of an urban area. Gerald O. Barney explains how population interchange between a city and its external environment regulates the local availability of housing and jobs, and describes the feedback mechanisms controlling migration, which have led to the failure of many traditional urban programs. Barney further summarizes the potential benefits accruing to a city from the application of Forrester's revival policy of new-enterprise construction and slum-housing demolition.*

A version of this paper was published in the proceedings of the 1971 Fall Joint Computer Conference.

3
Understanding *Urban Dynamics*

3.1 Introduction

As indicated by published reviews and unpublished criticisms, some readers have had difficulty in understanding several of the most important points of *Urban Dynamics* by Professor Jay W. Forrester. The book contains several stumbling blocks. For example, certain pet theories that for years have been thought to be important in the dynamics of an urban area are scarcely even mentioned (for example, transportation, crime, pollution, discrimination, and suburbs). Also, several measures of urban characteristics appear to be sufficiently different in the model from those found in real urban areas to distract one's attention from the main points of the book. But there is a message in *Urban Dynamics*, and when it is comprehended these stumbling blocks become less significant. This paper is intended to help the reader of *Urban Dynamics* to understand the message of the book and to see beyond many of the criticisms that have been made.

3.2 What Is *Urban Dynamics*?

Urban Dynamics is an analysis of how the urban system operates and how it can be more effectively managed. The development of large concentrations of relatively unskilled persons and the adverse effect these concentrations have on our people and cities are the primary issues discussed in the book. The analysis is based on a computer model that, in the most general terms, simulates the interactions among population, housing, employment (industry), and municipal services.

The urban system is an example of a "complex system"—a system whose behavior is dominated by multiple-loop, nonlinear feedback processes. Mathematical analysis is not very helpful in understanding complex systems since their nonlinear properties are as yet very difficult to treat analytically. Currently, the only successful method of dealing with systems as complex as the urban system is experimentation—with the actual system or with some representation of the actual system. In the case of the urban system, most of the experimentation is done with a mental representation—the mental image (or model) we each have of how the urban system operates.

Our public officials are constantly performing experiments with their mental models as they evaluate proposed changes and additions to laws and policies. Although most public officials are probably not explicitly aware of it, their experiments involve three separate and distinct steps. The official first brings to mind his latest mental image of how the system operates; he then uses his mental model to deduce the effects of the proposal; and finally he judges his deduction of the effects against his set of values and goals. In the past, it has not been too important to distinguish these three steps, but as policy and legislative issues become more complex, it is increasingly important to know whether disagreements over a given proposal stem from different conceptions of how the system works, from inaccurate or inconsistent deductions of effects, or from more basic differences of values and goals.

In turning to the computer for assistance, we are forced to consider each step separately. Our mental image must be developed and expressed in a language that can be used to instruct the computer. Any consistent, explicit mental image of any system can be so expressed. Our mental images are the results of our experiences and observations; formulating these experiences explicitly for the computer permits others to examine, correct, and comprehend our mental images and to contribute to a broader understanding through their different perspectives. Given the expression of our mental images, the computer can point out inconsistencies, determine sensitivities, and deduce implications much more accurately than can the human mind—and without changing the ground rules part way along as the human mind is so prone to do.

But probably the most important contribution the computer makes is that it forces us to give separate consideration to questions of values and goals. Given the implications of a proposed change in a law or policy, we are forced to ask if this is what we want, if this is consistent with our values, and if this brings us any nearer our collective goals. With finite resources, cities can't be everything to everyone. Given a better understanding of the options available and the effects of any given proposal, debate must then center on the desirability of the effects and the values necessary for judging desirability.

By passing laws and changing policies, our public officials are making changes in the very structure of our society. To assist in analyzing the questions they face, a model must not only reproduce the behavior of a city in a general sense; it must also correctly reflect the basic causal mechanisms at work within the city. Many different models could potentially reproduce urban history, but a model that is to be used to examine the effects of change in policy must embody all of the important causal mechanisms—some of which are not yet easily measured or quantified. This is a formidable requirement, and success for now must be measured not against an absolute standard of accuracy but rather against our only alternatives—inexplicit mental models or intuition.

3.3 The Heart of The Model

The *Urban Dynamics* model is an explicit distillation of several mental images. Its subject is the causes of urban decay—the concentration of large numbers of relatively unskilled people in urban areas, and all the attendant problems. In the model, just as in real cities people migrate in and out and move among the socioeconomic classes (Forrester defines three such classes: underemployed U, labor L, and managerial-professional MP) in response to a variety of conditions, including population, housing, employment, and municipal services. The heart of the model is the explicit representation of the network of forces that together determine urban migration and economic advancement.

The concept of "attractiveness," the central idea behind Forrester's description of migration, is frequently misunderstood. Attractiveness is not an indication of a city's beauty but rather a measure of a city's drawing and holding power for people in the three socioeconomic classes. Although a city's attractiveness is generally different for the underemployed, labor, and managerial-professional populations, there is an attractiveness for each of the three classes determining the rates at which they are drawn to the city and how effective the city is in holding them there once they arrive. Forrester inadvertently confuses many readers when he gives the attractiveness indicators the following three apparently unrelated names: attractiveness-for-migration multiplier AMM, labor-arrival multiplier LAM, and manager-arrival multiplier MAM. The identical modeling function of the three attractiveness multipliers is indicated in Figure 1.

The attractiveness multipliers are especially important in that they reflect the population's response to a variety of "incommensurables." Population, housing, housing programs, economic advancement potential, public expenditures, and employment opportunities are reduced to a common scale or commensurated (differently for the three classes) to give a composite attractiveness for each class. For example, attractiveness for the underemployed population increases with increased housing programs, economic advancement potential, public expenditures, and employment opportunities but decreases with increased underemployed population (reflecting more competition for jobs, housing, and so on). Whenever differences in attractiveness exist between areas, people gradually migrate to the more attractive area, and the changed population distribution gradually reduces the initial difference in attractiveness. For example, as people move to an urban area, they compete with local residents for jobs and housing,

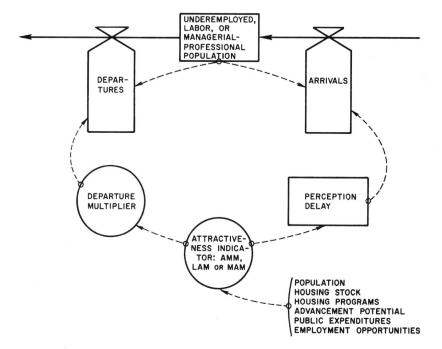

Figure 1 A flow diagram summarizing how the attractiveness indicators are used to influence the arrivals and departures for the three socioeconomic classes (See *Urban Dynamics*, pp. 134, 160, 165)

and they place increased pressure on existing schools and transportation facilities. All these effects tend to lower the attractiveness of the urban area for further migration.

The attractiveness concept suggests that, in the long run, all cities must be equally attractive for any given socioeconomic group. Different cities may still differ in their components of attractiveness; for example, one city may offer excellent job opportunities while another features good climate and geography. But when all components of attractiveness are considered, New York City, Chicago, Colorado Springs, and Bend (Oregon) must have very nearly equal attractiveness for all socioeconomic classes.

Another important part of the model is the description of the factors that determine how fast people advance from underemployed to labor and from labor to managerial-professional. The rate of advancement from underemployed to labor UTL is particularly important, since it is only through this transition that the underemployed can improve their economic living standards. The conditions that influence UTL are total labor and underemployed jobs, labor availability, educational level of the underemployed, job training programs, and the ratio of labor to underemployed.

3.4 The Failure of Current Urban Programs

The importance of the advancement and attractiveness concepts can be seen in Forrester's analysis of current urban programs. In actual practice, these programs generally have a similar and characteristic development pattern: an initial period of slight improvement and generation of hope, followed within a few years by readjustments within the urban system that result in a loss of gained ground. The net result has been increased concentrations of underemployed, continually decaying conditions, and growing hostility of the underemployed toward the "System" and toward the "Establishment" that they think controls the "System." Actually, as Forrester's analysis shows, the failure of our urban programs is due not to the control of the establishment, but rather to a collection of feedback processes that are at work within the system and are almost beyond the influence of the establishment. The advancement and attractiveness concepts are important in understanding the operation and effects of these feedback processes.

There are many interacting feedback processes that cause urban problems to feed on themselves and make failures of our urban programs but, in a highly simplified way, two of the most dominant interactions are illustrated in Figure 2. Shortly after the initiation of any given program (housing, food, health, job training, etc.), conditions for the underemployed do measurably improve, and the improvement encourages continuation of the program. In time, the increased attractiveness of the area is evident to the underemployed; as a result, a somewhat larger number move into the area and a somewhat smaller number leave than would have, had the attractiveness not increased. There follows a period of somewhat expanded growth of the underemployed population in the area, and this population growth increases the pressures on the available schools, housing, employment opportunities, shopping and recreational facilities, and transportation systems. The effects of this first feedback loop are felt within a few years when the increased crowding and congestion begin to drop the city's relative attractiveness back toward what it was before the program was started.

The effects of the second feedback loop are delayed by another few years. The enlarged underemployed population, which resulted from the initial success of the program, increases the demand for underemployed housing. As a result, underemployed housing competes more and more vigorously for available land. This competition not only takes vacant land but preserves decayed housing that might otherwise be demolished to permit an alternative land use. The increased demand for underemployed-housing land use drives up the cost of land for labor and managerial-professional housing—thus tending to reduce the attractiveness of the area for these two populations. This reduced attractiveness for labor and managerial-professionals, combined with the more intense competition for land, implies more business expenses, fewer business opportunities, and increased difficulties for all forms of business activity. Declining business activity reduces the advancement potential for the underemployed. The lowered advancement potential in turn diminishes the chances of the underemployed escaping from the urban poverty trap, destroys their chances of improving their living conditions, and increases their frustration and hostility.

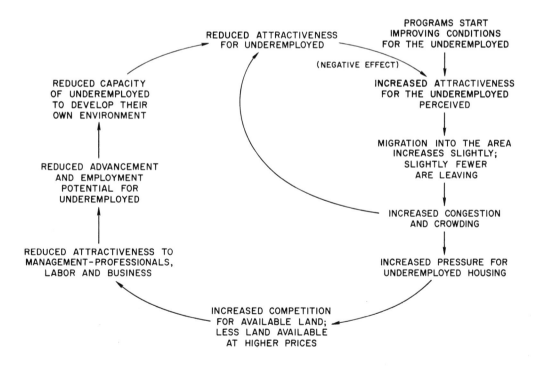

Figure 2 Illustration of two negative feedback loops that tend to undermine the effects of direct aid to the underemployed

3.5 The Problem and Forrester's Solution

The really basic problem is this: given the existence of feedback processes that tend to counter the effects of direct improvements, how can a city best improve the lot of its underemployed with the limited resources it has available? Forrester's approach to this problem is significantly different from many approaches used in the past. He does not start by stating what cities should be like but rather asks the very practical question: in what ways can the urban system be made to operate differently? The effects of changing the way the system works are then investigated with the model, and the "best" alternative is recommended.

But "best" for whom: the rich, the poor, the absentee landlords, the stockbrokers? What values are to be used in judging the possibilities? Forrester does not explicitly discuss the values he uses to evaluate policies, but implicit in his discussions of the alternatives are two values: the solution must be lasting (decades at least) as opposed to temporary (a few months to a few years), and the solution must lead to increased upward economic mobility for the underemployed. Others (slumlords, for example) might have different objectives and values to use in evaluating the results of the computer runs, but the values behind Forrester's discussions deserve careful consideration. Temporary solutions have produced much disillusionment, frustration, and resentment among the urban poor; also, while the poor may not be able to agree on which particular urban conditions are most in need of improvement, increased upward economic mobility provides them with both hope and freedom of choice.

Forrester's choice for the best way to revive a decayed urban area is to demolish 5 percent of the slum housing stock (some of which would have been destroyed anyway and much of which is already vacant) each year to provide business encouragements that increase new-enterprise construction 40 percent over what would have occurred under the same conditions without the added incentives. The demolition need not involve active intervention by the city; it is probably best accomplished through changes in tax laws and zoning. The increased availability of land improves the attractiveness of the area to business, labor, and managerial-professionals. This in turn produces an upsurge in the demand for labor and increases the opportunities for upward economic advancement for the underemployed. As the area becomes more of a place for the underemployed to get ahead, its attractiveness to the underemployed begins to increase, and if unchecked, a new underemployed in-migration (and a resulting demand for underemployed housing) would within a few years increase competition for the available land to the point that business opportunities (and the associated advancement potential for the underemployed) would again be decreased. In Forrester's solution (*Urban Dynamics*, Section 5.7), attractiveness and migration are regulated by controlling the housing stock available to the underemployed.

3.6 Common Misunderstandings

Forrester's proposed program of slum-housing demolition provides an interesting demonstration of the need for more than intuition in predicting the dynamics of urban systems. Intuitively it would seem that slum-housing demolition could do nothing but make housing scarcer and ultimately drive the underemployed out of the area. At first glance, the analysis from the model also seems to support these conclusions, in that the underemployed population of the area decreases significantly. But something else is happening. The net in-migration of the underemployed *increases* by almost 4,500 persons per year, a factor of approximately 450. Why does this occur? Because even though housing is tighter, the increased availability of jobs draws in many underemployed.

Under Forrester's revival policies, many underemployed migrate into the urban area, attracted by job opportunities and economic potential. In spite of the increased influx, the underemployed population actually decreases by 10 percent because many more are advancing into the labor class. The net annual advancement rate from underemployed to labor rises from about 5,500 to just over 9,000 persons per year, 165 percent of the old rate. In contrast to the urban renewal programs of the fifties, this program works slowly and does not disrupt whole communities. In Figure 3, the effects of the program on population movements to, from, and within the urban area are illustrated. In addition to being economically viable, the urban area is now an efficient upgrader of the population. The overall effects of Forrester's revival policies are indicated in Figure 4.

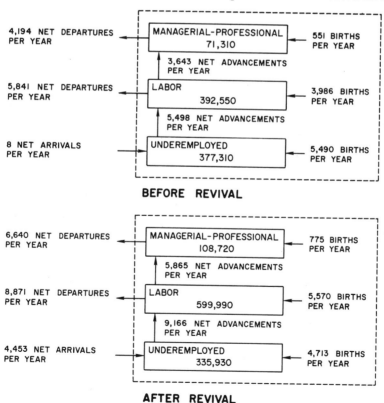

Figure 3 Equilibrium population flows before and after revival. The dashed lines represent the boundary of the urban area.

	Original Equilibrium[1] Mode	Revival[2] Mode	Percent Difference
Land use for income-producing activities (acres)	5,800	8,600	+50%
Land used for housing (acres)	75,700	77,900	+ 3%
Ratio of housing land to business land	12.96	9.05	−30%
Managerial-professional population	71,000	109,000	+50%
Labor population	393,000	600,000	+50%
Underemployed population	377,000	336,000	−10%
Total population	841,000	1,045,000	+25%

[1] This is the starting point for all runs in Chapter 5 of *Urban Dynamics*.
[2] See ibid., Section 5.7

Figure 4 Changes in population mix and land-use distribution resulting from slum-housing demolition and industry encouragement

3.7 Omissions?

The *Urban Dynamics* work has been criticized for the omission of a variety of factors that are alleged to be central to the urban problem. Influences of the suburbs, transportation systems, discrimination, pollution, and "external driving forces" are among the factors frequently cited. Although some of these factors are very important to certain urban phenomena, the urban dynamics model already contains enough detail to produce the urban phenomenon about which the book is written: the concentration of large numbers of low-income and unskilled people in decaying sections of our cities. Additional details are likely to make an already complex model more confusing; unless they are required to produce the problem under study, extra details are probably best left out. Some comments on several of the frequently noted "omissions" are given in the following paragraphs.

First, *Urban Dynamics* does not assume (as has been asserted) that the dynamics of urban areas are independent of depressions, world wars, technological change, earthquakes, and other "external driving forces." What *Urban Dynamics* does assume is that the management of a given urban area has little or no influence on the external forces acting on the area, and that, come what may, urban areas must be managed as effectively as possible. Although uncertainties may dictate a more or less cautious advance, *Urban Dynamics* asserts that effective urban management is possible in spite of uncertainties. The effectiveness of urban management seems to be limited not so much by an inability to predict the future course of external driving forces as by an inadequate understanding of the time-dependent consequences of the many nonlinear feedback processes at work.

Concerning suburbs and their effects, it should be noted that every city is in competition with its environment (that is, the remainder of the nation) for people and industry. A city's suburbs are a part of its environment, and this basic competitive influence of the suburbs on a city is included in the attractiveness and migration concepts of the model. A city's suburbs are different from the remainder of its environment only in that they are close enough to the city to allow suburbanites to commute to jobs in the city without actually living in the city.

The definitions of the attractiveness indicators and the system boundary are closely related to the suburb question. In defining the term "urban area" and in specifying the system boundary, *Urban Dynamics* assumes that the population both lives and works in the "urban area" inside the system boundary. In determining the migration rates, the attractiveness of the area as a place to work is not differentiated from the attractiveness of the area as a place to live. Daytime and nighttime populations are implicitly assumed to be equal. Some very important urban phenomena have been studied in this approximation, and *Urban Dynamics* is clearly one such study. It is interesting to note, however, that the conditions resulting from Forrester's solution (good business activity, many job opportunities, a shortage of housing—especially for labor, where the housing ratio equals 1.33) are a combination of conditions that often lead to highway-expansion programs and suburban growth (i.e., just outside the model boundary). Under the approximations of the model, migration (movement across the model boundary) takes people out of both the city's housing and job markets. In practice, however, migration takes many people to residences just beyond the boundary so they leave the area's housing market but not its job market. An expanding suburban population that is allowed to enjoy the attractiveness of the city as a place to work and enjoy the attractiveness of the suburbs as a place to live might have a significant impact on Forrester's recommended solution. Without expansion to include a more explicit representation of suburbs (including their political effects), the model cannot analyze this impact. The book does, however, suggest ways of minimizing the effect (for example, by adopting policies designed to discourage commuting). *Urban Dynamics* also provides a very useful framework around which an expanded model of city-suburb relations could be developed.

3.8 The Message

In spite of its first appearance, much of what *Urban Dynamics* says closely resembles what urban experts have been saying for years. There is nearly complete agreement, for example, that the fundamental characteristics of a decayed urban area are an inappropriate population mix and an economically unsatisfactory distribution of land use. Without managers and professionals to recognize opportunities and to organize income-producing activities, and without a large labor population from which skills can be learned, it is not surprising that the economic advancement of the underemployed living in decayed urban areas is rather limited. Yet relatively inexpensive shelter, welfare income, public transportation, and municipal services attract the underemployed into our inner city areas. As the number of underemployed in an area increases, many small changes interact to shift land use toward housing and away from income-producing activities. This is another way of describing what Forrester calls excess housing. This mode of operation in which problems feed upon themselves and in which the underemployed are trapped for generations is widely agreed to be *the* urban problem.

The new and important contributions that *Urban Dynamics* makes are in three areas. First, it describes the basic mechanisms at work in the urban system that cause decay to feed on itself. These mechanisms are complex and not easily summarized, but a particularly important element is the close coupling between land use and population mix. As is very clearly illustrated in the book, neither land use nor population mix can be managed independently. A change in one always produces a change in the other. Municipal responsibility for land-use management has long been recognized, but the fact that every land-management and municipal-service decision affects the relative attractiveness of the area to the various socioeconomic elements of the population (and thus determines the population mix) has only rarely been openly discussed. *Urban Dynamics* discusses this point quite openly and points out how land-use policies, tax laws, assessment practices, and zoning procedures play a major role in bringing together the population mix we find in our slums.

A second and related contribution is the analysis of the failure of past urban programs to achieve any lasting impact on the basic problem. Urban renewal (as practiced in the fifties) and the relocation of underemployed in low-rent suburban housing have destroyed communities and transplanted the underemployed to new locations where they are needed and wanted no more than they were before the relocation. These brute force solutions do not recognize and deal with the basic causes of the difficulties and can lead to nothing more productive than localized temporary improvements.

The final and most significant contribution of *Urban Dynamics* is that it provides an approach through which even a single city, acting alone, can make a lasting and significant impact on the distribution of land use and the population mix in its blighted urban areas. The solution does not involve pushing the underemployed out but rather gradually attracting management, labor, and business back. This approach requires patience, tenacity, and understanding, but it treats the problem rather than the symptoms. Lasting solutions will be achieved only when the underlying feedback processes are recognized and dealt with. Some basic changes and new responsibilities for municipal management are required; but only if we establish as our goal the rebalancing of both the population mix and the distribution of land use to enhance the upward economic mobility of the underemployed can we hope to eliminate the frustrations of our inner-city underemployed and the explosive atmosphere that accompanies their disillusionment. In that cities have open to them an effective, independent, and imperative course, they are truly "masters of their own fate."

A Systems Approach
to Urban Revival

Louis Edward Alfeld and Dennis L. Meadows

In most American cities, administrative authority is distributed vertically, according to specialized tasks and responsibilities. Different agencies oversee economic development, environmental protection, code enforcement, and public assistance. Because of this delegation of authority, the traditional approach to urban problem solving has been one of individual agencies working to contain problems arising within their jurisdictions.

In several respects, Urban Dynamics *has shown that vertical forms of municipal government may be relatively ineffective because urban functions administered by separate agencies are in fact highly interconnected. The attractiveness principle in* Urban Dynamics *implies that all cities tend toward an attractiveness equilibrium with their external environments. Because people migrate to areas that they perceive as being relatively attractive, efforts by local government to improve a single component of urban attractiveness (such as housing availability) always lead to a rising urban population and the degradation of other components of attractiveness (such as job availability). The following paper by Louis Edward Alfeld and Dennis L. Meadows begins to demonstrate how cities can operate within the attractiveness principle and more effectively coordinate individual policy measures to enhance the quality of urban life.*

A version of this paper was presented at the Fifth Systems Symposium, "Systems Approach and the City," Case Western Reserve University, November 9–11, 1970.

4
A Systems Approach
to Urban Revival

New programs touted as the answers to America's urban problems are announced one after another in the newspapers. Nearly every day somewhere in the United States a new urban program is initiated—a program designed to eliminate poverty, to rehabilitate slums, to decrease traffic jams, to solve parking problems, or to alleviate some other aspect of our current "urban crisis." A mayor promotes tax relief for new housing; a law enforcement officer seeks to hire hippies to fight against the spread of drugs on his community; a transportation department announces plans for a new or improved mass transit system. To many Americans, the proliferation of new urban programs at the federal, state, and local levels in recent years must be staggering.

By 1970 there were more than 600 federally funded urban programs alone, administered by 78 different agencies. Some 15 percent of the federal budget was going into these programs, and the dollar amount was increasing at a rate of 12 percent per year.[1] These programs include public assistance, highways, education, antipoverty, food distribution, public health, urban development, public works, unemployment insurance, vocational rehabilitation, and business development. A similar phenomenon exists at state and local levels.

Behind each program there is someone who believes that a problem has been identified and that it can be solved through direct action. These programs are based upon a common premise: through the solution of individual problems the city will become a better place in which to live and work.

Yet the quality of urban life in American cities was not raised during the 1960s. By any objective measure, the individual problem-solving approach seems to have failed. Reports and statistics on urban crime, pollution, slums, traffic, taxes, and welfare attest to this fact.[2] Most observers of the urban scene would agree that, relative to our expectations, the city is getting worse, not better. An ambitious employment program in Detroit, for instance, did not significantly reduce the rate of unemployment in the city.[3] The almost endless supply of new housing in New York City has not alleviated that city's eternal housing crisis.[4]

4.1 Understanding the City as a System

There is not much use, and there may even be harm, in meeting these discouragements by redoubling our commitment to methods that have, on balance, failed. An increase in the efficiency of current programs is not enough. If we could achieve a vast improvement in the operation of current urban programs through the application of better tools, neither a better city nor the solution of current problems would be ensured. Merely raising the operational efficiency of the city is not sufficient because the urban structure we have developed does not necessarily satisfy the goals that went into its making.

Rather, we would do well to view the city as a complex social and economic system formed by the interactions of individual efforts to achieve personal goals. Unfortunately, in modern life such a system does not operate to further individual goals—or even, in some cases, human goals generally. Large corporations tend to ignore individual contentment; government agencies often seem to possess a will of their own; cities do not reflect the values of their residents. Complex systems such as these are not structured to pursue objectives defined in personal terms.

This point warrants heavy emphasis. Many individuals can take actions that appear to satisfy their own objectives; the aggregation of these efforts constitutes a complex social system. The characteristics of that system may cause it to behave in some very different ways from the expectations and the desires of its creators. The city is an excellent example of this perversity. Created so that efficiencies of scale could provide better physical, cultural, and economic opportunities for its inhabitants, the city has worked to trap many in poverty and to lower the physical and psychic health of those living in it.

We need a new theory that can effectively deal with urban behavior. That new theory must embrace a conceptual understanding of the city as a whole. It must facilitate analyzing the city's various activities as interrelated functions. Only when we are able to work within such a conceptual framework can we be certain that new urban programs will actually solve urban problems.

Since 1968, research by the System Dynamics Group at M.I.T. has been directed toward the development and application of a theory to explain urban behavior.[5] In that theory the key to understanding a city's total behavior is the concept of urban attractiveness. A definition of the concept follows in this article, together with a description of an urban model based upon it. Through simulation analyses of that model, it has been possible to study the effects of alternative programs and policies on the city as a whole. Analyses indicate that programs often have an effect exactly the opposite of that intended. On the basis of the research done at M.I.T., this article concludes by suggesting a new approach to the formulation of urban revival policies and a framework for the development of more effective future urban programs.

4.2 The Theory of Urban Attractiveness

The concept of urban attractiveness is familiar to everyone. We all make distinctions between urban areas that appeal to us and those that do not. The term "attractiveness" relates to our own preferences and biases in distinguishing among urban places. The sum total of all individual conceptions about the desirability of a given urban area constitutes the aggregate attractiveness of that area. Insofar as we have a choice, it is this combination of influences that determines where we choose to live and work. On a larger scale, it simply defines the ability of a city to draw and to hold people.

Attractiveness is related to the movement of people to and from places. In the United States, the population tends to be highly mobile. Almost 5 percent of the population decides each year to move from one city to another; three times that many move from one community to another within a single metropolitan area.[5]

The decision to settle in a specific area may depend on many factors. It can involve job opportunities, the availability of housing, nearness to friends and family, climate, economic costs, quality of schools, racial attitudes, and welfare benefits. Although attractiveness is a composite index and not a single objective measure, it has real meaning. People are quite consistent in their assessment of relative attractiveness.[6]

A city's attractiveness is closely related to its population growth or decline. When an area is perceived to be more attractive than its surrounding environment, its population will increase, as many people settle there in preference to other areas. Time lags are, of course, inherent in the perception of attractiveness. New job opportunities today will not mean new residents tomorrow. But over the long run, perhaps ten to twenty years, any perceived increase in attractiveness relative to other areas will result in net migration into that city. In-migration will continue so long as the area is thought to be relatively more attractive than the rest of the country. Only when this attraction fades will net growth resulting from migration cease. Migration will continue, but the number of new arrivals will tend to be offset by the number of those leaving the area.

If changes in the perceived attractiveness of a city always result in migration flows until the net attraction is rebalanced, from the viewpoint of the potential migrant, no city can remain more or less attractive than its surrounding environment. In the short term, delays in our perception of what a city is may produce uneven flows of people and the popular attitude that some city is "better" than another. In the long run, however, areas will tend to be equally attractive to the potential migrant.

Understanding how the attractiveness principle can be applied to urban analysis is the key to understanding a city as an urban system, the key to understanding why urban programs fail, and the key to structuring a new approach to the solution of our urban problems.

4.3 Growth and Feedback

California is a very large area that has been a powerful magnet for migration for over a century. Every year many thousands more people move to California than move away from that state. As the result of steady population growth in the last few years, one out of every ten people in this country today lives in California.[7] It is obvious that such a disparity of population flow cannot continue forever; long before California is completely filled (or the rest of the nation completely emptied), people will stop moving there. Why? The answer is quite simple: most elements of an area's attractiveness are decreased by an influx of people. Schools and other city services become overloaded, available job opportunities decrease, recreational facilities become crowded, travel becomes difficult, and natural beauty is continually despoiled by an expanding population.

All these symptoms are becoming increasingly evident in California, and they have called forth some strong language, as in the following quotation:

> So it is that in California one sees not only the consequence of unplanned, careless, or deliberately destructive past activity; one also gets the feeling that the worst is yet to come. There are times when the change without apparent

direction, and the growth without control, give the appearance of socially acceptable madness, of a human population irruption that may well end tragically both for the people and for the land.[8]

Increased perceived attractiveness leads to population increases. And more people eventually decrease the perceived attraction of any area! No city can escape this law. Unsettled areas may temporarily seem to be more attractive as initial population increases stimulate the creation of industry and urban amenities. Ultimately, however, the attraction of the area will be depressed by further population increases. Industrial expansion may enhance job opportunities in a city, but as these jobs are filled, the larger population drawn to the area will tend to depress other elements of the city's attractiveness. The opening of a new highway linking a city and a national seashore preserve will initially attract people who wish to take advantage of the new recreational opportunities. But migration levels off when the highway between the city and the seashore is finally packed with cars.

This feedback phenomenon that tends to create a constant relative attractiveness between cities is nothing extraordinary. The same dynamics are at work in the lines that form before the tellers' windows at a bank or in the lines of traffic in the lanes at a turnpike toll plaza. Each new arrival attempts to minimize his waiting time by joining the shortest line. On the average, all lines tend to be of equal length and therefore equally attractive to the next car entering the plaza.[9]

The concept of relative attractiveness implies that it is impossible to raise the aggregate attractiveness of any one city relative to its environment for any significant period of time. This conclusion has profound implications for urban programs. *Any* program that successfully improves a given city along some dimension will initiate a feedback response from the environment that worsens other aspects of the city.

The failure of many current programs suggests that the urban system is too complex to analyze intuitively; we cannot guess how the system will respond to the initiation of a new program. Individual parts of the system are sufficiently well known, however, to warrant the construction of a formal model to examine urban behavior. The model then allows us to analyze the system's response to programs and reach conclusions about policy decisions. Alternative policies that change the component indices of attractiveness will affect migration patterns in different ways. We wish to look for policies that will produce beneficial changes in the well-being of urban residents.

4.4 Modeling the System

A formal model that embodies the concept of attractiveness is necessarily complex, for the concept is a composite of many elements—each influenced by feedback relationships. As an illustration of the feedback loops involved, Figure 1 indicates some of the interconnections between housing and urban migration.

If enough new apartments are constructed in a particular city, occupancy levels will fall to the point where landlords tend to lower rents. As people are

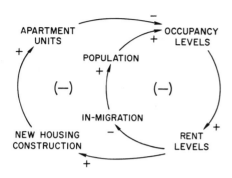

Figure 1 Interactions between housing availability and migration

attracted by lower rents, the housing again fills up. The cost of housing rises until people stop flowing into the area. More housing may be built in response to higher rent levels until no more land is available for building.

Another feedback relationship is illustrated in Figure 2, which shows some of the connections between population and industrial expansion in a given city. Local industrial expansion provides new jobs and thereby attracts people. In turn, increased population leads to the construction of additional housing units in the city, and the availability of a larger labor force attracts yet more industry. This growth cycle ends when the city's open land is almost exhausted, making it difficult for new industry to locate in the area.

A third relationship is shown in Figure 3. If more housing is constructed in a city, people are attracted to the area. A larger population places increased demands on urban services. Revenue requirements go up, followed by tax increases. New housing construction is slowed because of higher taxes, and fewer houses are built. The property base ceases to expand, and taxes must again be raised.

Delays are embodied in each of the preceding examples. The amount of time it takes for the effects of a change in one variable to be transmitted around any one of these loops is different in each case. New housing is generally sold during the year in which it is constructed. Filling up the land within a city, however, takes a much longer time, perhaps a century or more, while the interval between

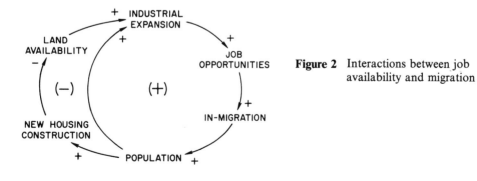

Figure 2 Interactions between job availability and migration

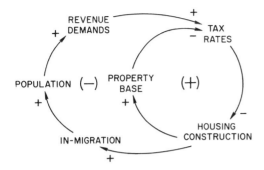

Figure 3 Interactions between revenue needs, population growth, and residential construction

the raising of taxes and the subsequent stagnation of the property base of any city varies greatly, according to the impact of higher taxes on local industrial expansion.

It is relatively easy to describe and discuss each loop independently. Sufficient information is available in the literature and from the experience of those involved in managing the urban system to form an accurate picture of each individual relationship. Together, however, these relationships form a complex system through which it is difficult, if not impossible, to trace the implications of a policy change by intuition. The construction of a formal model is imperative. Building a model upward from the many feedback loops characterizing an urban area permits us to piece the individual parts together into a coherent whole. When the model has been completed, it is relatively easy to simulate the effects of any suggested change upon the behavior of the total urban system.

Without a comprehensive model, we are limited to tackling one problem at a time. Thus we will fail to understand the influences that any solution will propagate throughout the system. For example, in recent years it has been learned the hard way not to assume that downtown traffic congestion can be alleviated by constructing off-street parking facilities for commuters' automobiles. The increased availability of parking in the downtown area encourages more commuters to drive to work, thereby raising the total number of cars in the city. As parking garages reach capacity, traffic congestion begins to rise again. Meanwhile, mass transit facilities deteriorate. Although this example may be hackneyed, the general point is valid. Long-term effects may be the opposite of short-term results. An ostensibly beneficial program may leave the city in a worse condition.

4.5 System Dynamics and Urban Dynamics

System dynamics is a philosophy of systems structure, a method of systems analysis, and a set of simulation tools for modeling a system's feedback-loop structure and its behavior over time. The system dynamics technique organizes the feedback processes of a system under study into a model and employs a digital computer to simulate the dynamic behavior of the system. The methodology has been applied to a wide range of industrial and social systems. A large portion of the work done by the M.I.T. System Dynamics Group, however, pertains specifically to urban dynamics.

The *Urban Dynamics* model centers upon the concept of an urban area as a system of interacting enterprises, housing, and people.[10] The model describes the development of a city over 250 years as it grows from a nearly empty land area into a large city. Normally, the internal dynamics of the sectors of a city cause it to develop, growing outward until the city's supply of vacant land is exhausted. Then the process of aging often causes blight. As the aging process unfolds, the population characteristics and the types of economic activity within the city change. Unless some force for renewal is present, high land occupancy turns the city from growth to stagnation. Once the city's land is densely occupied, new growth cannot occur as easily; the city shifts toward high concentrations of aged housing and industry.

The *Urban Dynamics* model depicts those forces that cause people to move to and from a city, and cause the city to grow and age over time. The internal system of the model is composed of three primary subsystems representing business activity, housing, and population. Each of these is in turn subdivided into three levels, in the following manner:

Business: new—mature—declining
Housing: premium—worker—slum
Population: managerial-professional—labor—underemployed

In this scheme, business is classified according to the age of the buildings that house business activity. The flow of business activity from one category to another depends upon both time and the condition of the entire urban system. Industry ages more quickly and employment levels decline as taxes increase or as the available labor supply drops.

The middle subsystem contains three categories of residential housing, corresponding to the cycle of construction, aging, and demolition. Dwellings enter the system as premium or worker housing and eventually exit through demolition.

The lower subsystem represents the distribution of population in three socioeconomic categories: managerial-professional, labor, and underemployed. These correspond roughly to income distinctions in today's society. Note that in addition to flows of people between categories, people in every category migrate in and out of the city. As internal conditions change, each of these three population categories will find the city either more or less attractive relative to its surrounding environment, and migration flows will occur as a result. Thus the composition of the population will respond to changing conditions within the urban area.

The categories just described are called system levels. These principal levels are affected by 22 rates of flow into and out of each of the levels. Each rate of flow is dependent at any moment upon the system levels. This network of levels and rates is connected by an information network. The model is too complex to show in its entirety, but a typical case is that of a single flow rate influenced by 35 discernible system interactions. The model flow rate in question represents the arrival of underemployed people coming to the city in response to their perceptions of changes in its aggregate relative attractiveness.

4.6 Solving Problems

We are all aware of a growing pressure within our central cities for increased quantities of low-income housing. Much of the housing stock in our central cities is rapidly deteriorating, while its cost is increasing.[11] Residents of the central city find themselves caught between an increase in price and a decrease in quality.

A common reaction to the problem is to construct low-cost housing. Such a program can be tested in the urban dynamics model. Consider, for example, a construction program that attempts to add 5 percent to the stock of low-income housing each year in a given city. Will this new housing alleviate the city's housing problem? In this instance, "success" in housing will mean that another problem within the system gets worse.

Figures 4 and 5 give the results of introducing a low-cost housing program in the city. The graphs show the outcome in rather vivid terms. Housing available to the underemployed begins to rise immediately as the program gets under way.

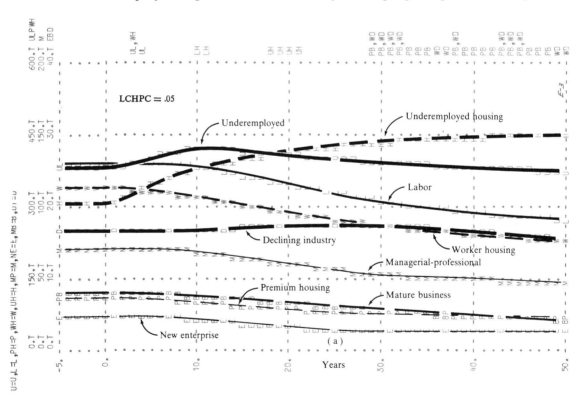

Figure 4 Low-cost housing program—changes in population, housing, and industry levels

Because of the increased availability of housing, more underemployed are attracted to the city, and the total underemployed population rises for the first 10 years. Filling the available land with low-cost housing also raises land prices, thereby depressing the construction of new industry. The combination of increased numbers of underemployed and fewer new job opportunities acts, over the long run, to increase local unemployment rates, thereby reducing the large in-migration of underemployed to the city. Also, after 50 years, housing conditions in the city have not materially improved as a consequence of increased local population densities. A new equilibrium has been reached, and it is probably worse than that which prevailed at the inauguration of the low-cost housing program.

American cities continue to form policies on the basis of short-term results. The vast majority of the programs that have been instituted to improve the city have had deleterious effects similar to those just illustrated. Is it any wonder, therefore, that urban problems are now reaching "crisis" proportions?

In the long run, most programs that strive to raise the city's attractiveness ultimately succeed in increasing in-migration and raising population, while keeping the system in the same relative position. This internal rebalancing of the system occurs automatically; as new pressures are introduced into the system,

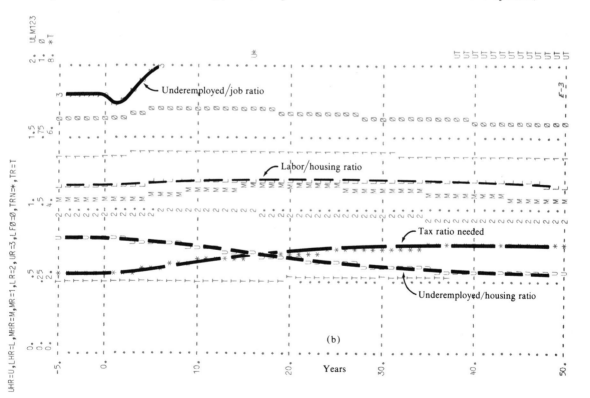

Figure 5 Low-cost housing program—changes in local tax rates, job availability, and housing availability

they are distributed within the system. When one component of relative attractiveness is raised, another component must suffer. When additional housing is created in a city, for example, economic standards fall. Alternatively, lowering one component of urban attractiveness must cause another to increase; for example, by restricting housing availability to control population, local unemployment may be reduced. Because urban resources are limited, it is impossible to increase the quantity and quality of everything for everyone. It is only through the deliberate manipulation of counterbalancing effects that we can gain a degree of control over the changing urban system.[12]

4.7 Negative Counterbalances

Efforts to raise relative attractiveness are defeated, we see, by negative counterbalances within the system. The inevitable negative counterbalance may even show up as a decrease in the component of attractiveness that was initially raised. A negative counterbalance can also appear elsewhere in the system to overshadow an attractive natural feature of an area. For example, in Los Angeles, the climate and the extensive beaches have not changed. However, the counterbalancing forces of smog, traffic, crowding, and urban sprawl have seriously detracted from that area's natural amenities. This sort of self-cancellation within the urban system occurs because large migration flows are directed toward urban areas that are perceived as being relatively attractive.

The principal lesson of *Urban Dynamics* is that such negative counterbalances need not be unexpected events forced blindly by the system and accepted indiscriminately. City administrations can decide which trade-offs they prefer and which amenities they wish to forego in gaining others. This decision will be politically difficult, but it cannot be avoided. If it is not made deliberately by citizens, it will through default be made implicitly by the system. When the system "decides," the outcome is rarely one that people would consciously choose. We must understand that when we decide to add housing to the city, we are also making a long-term choice to increase unemployment, or traffic congestion, or crime, or the cost of living. Cities must develop comprehensive strategies for dealing with their problems, strategies that will account for both the positive and the negative forces arising from any program.

4.8 Urban Trade-offs and Attractiveness

If the central city is to solve its urban problems, it must do so by explicit recognition of the impossibility of maintaining an overall attractiveness greater than that of the city's environment. To be effective, urban programs must involve trade-offs. Raising the total attractiveness of a city would entail raising the attractiveness of the environment—a task beyond local urban programs. Hence we must concentrate on shifts among the various components of urban attractiveness. We must identify the areas of city life that a city's residents deem most crucial. By deemphasizing the less important aspects that residents are willing to give up in return, the quality of urban life might be raised without raising the overall attractiveness of the city to potential migrants.

Since one of the basic urban problems is poverty and since efforts to raise the economic status of a city's residents are often given first priority, a discussion of trade-offs in the context of antipoverty programs well illustrates the principle involved. If programs designed to increase economic well-being take the form of welfare payments, low-cost housing, increased job training, or special employment programs, they will attract people from outside the particular city. Thus, if new programs are to succeed in providing jobs and income for city residents, the programs must take something away to keep newcomers from competing for those jobs.

What should a city do? Are there any high-leverage counterbalances that both make up a significant portion of the composite attractiveness of a city and are politically practical in the sense that the residents of a city might be willing to trade them for increased affluence?

Housing perhaps has the greatest leverage; a lack of housing or a tight housing market will act as a deterrent to in-migration. Scandinavian cities, for example, are known for their continuous housing shortage and lack of slums. A poor transportation system or a congested central city is another possibility, although perhaps less agreeable *and* less effective than tight housing. A third and

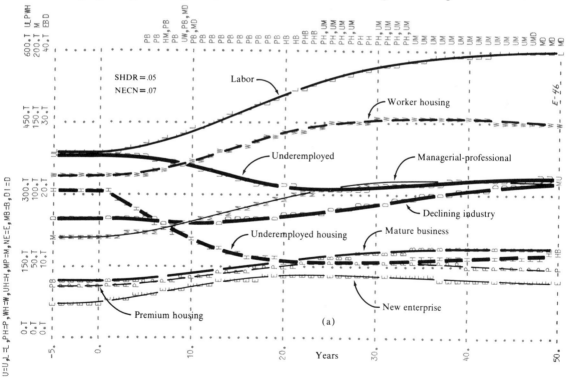

Figure 6 *Urban Dynamics* revival policies—changes in population, housing, and industry levels

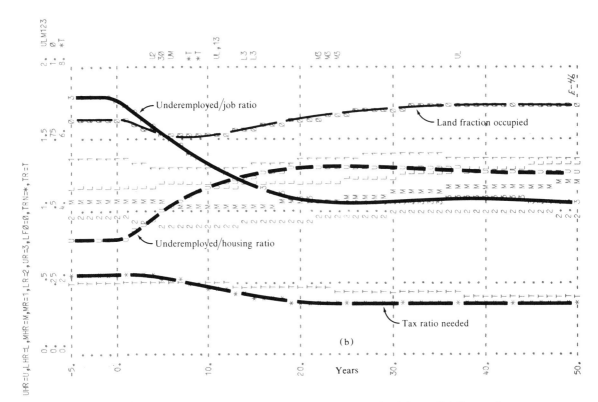

Figure 7 *Urban Dynamics* revival policies—changes in job availability and housing availability

as yet unexplored area of counterbalance might be to provide sizable tax incentives for employing local residents rather than commuters or newcomers. Such trade-offs, however, are difficult to discuss in the abstract. They must be tailored individually for each city. The important point is that if the economic well-being of a city's residents is to be improved, such trade-offs must be made.

Urban Dynamics describes many of these trade-offs in analyzing the effects of various hypothetical urban programs on the city. Model simulations show that programs for increasing housing, job training, financial aid, tax subsidies, and increased employment by themselves produce the type of urban failure illustrated earlier. These programs do not succeed in materially raising the quality of life in urban areas over the long run because migration and the consequent negative counterbalances offset any gains that are initially achieved.

Research indicates, however, that some programs do succeed in making gains in raising the economic standards of the residents of the city. Programs that encourage the construction of new enterprises in the city to provide jobs for residents and at the same time regulate in-migration by limiting the amount of housing available in the city tend to produce an increased upward mobility among residents. Because migration is controlled through a tight urban housing market, local economic conditions improve; as a result, the city is able to

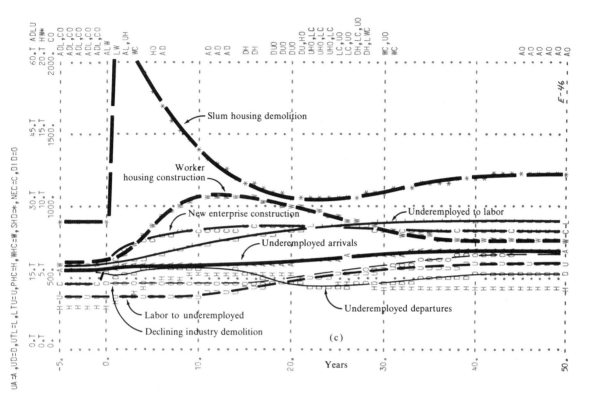

Figure 8 *Urban Dynamics* revival policies—changes in underemployed migration

accommodate an increased inflow of low-income families (Figure 8). Under this program, many of the poor acquire job skills and are upgraded both economically and socially.

Figures 6, 7, and 8 indicate the major changes that would result from this policy. Such a program involves a basic trade-off, of course: jobs for housing. It is a conscious choice, however, one that the residents of any city can make for themselves. The urban model permits us to project the results of similar policies and programs that can have a beneficial effect upon the city. Perhaps combinations of programs can be structured so as to boost the poor up the economic ladder rather than trap them in poverty through short-term policies.

4.9 Problems of Our Own Choosing

Urban programs designed to use negative counterbalances can succeed in reaching their goals because they are designed to operate within the system. They will take advantage of the system behavior to produce a new equilibrium point that is in harmony with the desires of its residents. Traditional urban programs have ignored the concept of negative counterbalances and, in attempting to raise the attractiveness of a city, have met with ultimate failure.

The adoption of policies such as those suggested by the *Urban Dynamics* analysis, along with the trade-offs that they require, should enable any city to become better off than it once was. Every city can improve the well-being of its own residents and regulate its attractiveness to outside migrants by selectively focusing upon the internal trade-offs that its residents prefer. Urban pressures will not disappear. But what we have failed to realize before is that we can choose which set of pressures we are willing to tolerate in our effort to achieve the broader goals of society.

Through enlightened urban policies, it is possible for the United States to move into an era of new urban prosperity that will be quite different from the era of urban problems that we face today. To do so requires a concentration of will, both on the part of the city residents in adopting trade-off policies and negative counterbalances and on the part of our national and state administrators and politicians in adopting policies that will further this process. At the center of such a process is the use of dynamic modeling techniques to evaluate new programs and suggest ways for improving old ones. The application of the systems approach to the city promises tremendous benefits. They far offset the price that we must pay to get them.

Notes

1. See *Statistical Abstract of the United States, 1969*; "Present Federal Programs," Laboratory for Environmental Studies, M.I.T., November 15, 1968; *Boston Globe*, October 18, 1970.

2. See "Crime Expense," *U.S. News and World Report*, October 26, 1970; "Welfare Dilemma," *Wall Street Journal*, September 17, 1970; "Rapid Transit," *New York Times*, June 1, 1970; "Slums," *Christian Science Monitor*, September 23, 1970; "Local Tax Rate," *Boston Globe*, September 6, 1970; "Smog," *Time*, August 10, 1970.

3. U. S. Department of Labor, Manpower Administration, "Area Trends in Employment and Unemployment," March 1967–June 1970.

4. "Decline of Bronx," *New York Times*, October 13, 1970.

5. U.S. Bureau of the Census, *Population Studies, 1960*.

6. See Ira S. Lowry, *Migration and Metropolitan Growth: Two Analytical Models* (San Francisco: Chandler, 1966), in which migrants' perception of employment opportunities as a factor in assessing attractiveness is shown to correlate quite well with actual unemployment data.

7. U. S. Bureau of the Census, *Population Changes, 1960–1970*.

8. Raymond F. Dasmann, *The Destruction of California* (New York: Macmillan Co., 1965), p. 21.

9. Several analogues to the attractiveness principle can be found in the economics literature. See, for example, Robert E. Hall, "Why Is the Unemployment Rate So High at Full Employment?" *Brookings Papers on Economic Activity* 3 (1970): 375–384.

10. Because of the crucial role played by the filling of land, it is most useful to study urban decay as the characteristic of a specific, constant area of land. Thus our focus throughout the remainder of this paper will be on the city as a specific area, not on the city as a legal entity whose legal borders are free to expand.

11. See "Low-Cost Housing Shortage," *Christian Science Monitor*, August 28, 1970.

12. It is essential, in this context, to differentiate between "relative attractiveness" and "quality of life." Relative attractiveness is an incremental concept, referring to the marginal drawing power of the city for a potential migrant. Quality of life is an average concept, measuring the average welfare of current city residents. See Jay W. Forrester, "Control of Urban Growth," Reading 19 in this volume.

Part Two
Conceptual Issues

Since its publication, *Urban Dynamics* has provoked discussion on a wide range of conceptual and methodological issues in urban modeling. Meetings of the M.I.T. project staff with urbanologists have helped to crystallize these issues, pointing to differing viewpoints among urban modelers on the procedures for constructing and testing quantitative urban models. Readings 5–11 examine some of the major assumptions and criticisms of the *Urban Dynamics* model; they deal with such issues as model conceptualization, city-suburb interactions, migration modeling, and policy evaluation. The analyses within this section and the next (dealing with model refinements) provide an avenue both for evaluating the urban dynamics theory and for determining future modeling and research priorities.

5

Aggregation and Definition: The Underemployed, a Case Study

Michael R. Goodman

Within any modeling methodology, one of the most critical stages of model construction is the determination of appropriate variables and classifications. In Urban Dynamics, *for example, Forrester sought to obtain a succinct and aggregate representation of the population composition of an urban area. Forrester divides the urban population into three groupings—managerial-professional, labor, and underemployed—according to differences in average job skills, potential for upward mobility, housing, tax needs, and migratory preferences. The following paper by Michael R. Goodman examines the scope and definition of the underemployed category in* Urban Dynamics. *Goodman contrasts Forrester's definition of the underemployed with available empirical categorizations of low-skilled urban residents; he then outlines several general principles that guide the process of aggregation in system dynamics models.*

5
Aggregation and Definition: The Underemployed, a Case Study

5.1 Introduction

An essential part of conceptualizing the structure of a dynamic system consists in defining a level of aggregation that can provide useful insights about the relationships and behavior of the system. The level of aggregation, once defined, provides a basis for establishing category definitions and groupings within the model.

Since many of the category definitions found in system dynamics models deviate from common usage and interpretation, it is important to delineate the general criteria by which such definitions are constructed. The intent of this paper is, first, to discuss how the system dynamics perspective leads to the formulation of aggregation criteria and, second, to illustrate how aggregation underlies category definitions within a model. The underemployed U classification defined in *Urban Dynamics* will serve as a case study. In particular, the definition of the underemployed will be contrasted with the definitions commonly found in the literature and examined to verify how its use in the model satisfies the aggregation criteria.

5.2 Conceptual View

The process of distilling the important feedback processes at work within the boundary of a dynamic system being modeled—the conceptualization of a system structure—dictates that the modeler not be constrained by existing conceptual viewpoints. Traditional viewpoints often manifest themselves in commonly employed classifications, categorizations, and definitions. The often subtle biases that such concepts embody can obstruct the modeler in his effort to achieve a better understanding of real-world behavior and relationships. Thomas Kuhn alludes to such conceptual hurdles when he discusses the "revolutionary impact of Einstein's theory as being a displacement of the conceptual network through which scientists view the world."[1] Further, he points out that the displacement was brought about primarily through changes in the "meaning of established and familiar concepts and not the introduction of additional objects or concepts."

The system dynamics approach to modeling focuses on identifying the causal feedback loops that give rise to system behavior. Hence the concepts and definitions employed within a dynamic model must be appropriate for representing feedback interactions.

5.3 Conventional Definitions

Standard definitions or categories typically exist because these concepts have been found useful for viewing a particular real-world system. A hazard in any type of modeling activity occurs, however, when one tries to adhere to definitions and classifications that may be incompatible with the purpose of a new model. This problem may frequently arise, for example, because the data and information available to the model builder reflect traditional or standard categorizations and viewpoints.

A striking illustration of the conceptual issues in model aggregation is Forrester's definition of the underemployed population class within the *Urban Dynamics* model. At the outset of a modeling effort, one might consider classifying the low-income, low-skill residents of an urban area along several feasible dimensions—for example, labor force participation, migratory characteristics, tax needs, and skill level. In *Urban Dynamics*, Forrester defines the underemployed as an aggregate of the "unemployed and unemployable, people in unskilled jobs, those in marginal economic activity, and those not seeking employment who might work in a period of intense activity" (p. 19).

Urban Dynamics examines the broad changes in population composition and job availability that occur in an urban area. Forrester's categorization of the underemployed establishes a focal point in this analysis. For the purpose of the *Urban Dynamics* model, the underemployed within an urban area form a relatively homogeneous grouping with regard to job skills, opportunities for upward economic mobility, and requirements for urban services. These relationships will be discussed further in the following sections of this paper.

Forrester's definition of the underemployed may be contrasted with other possible categorizations of low-skilled urban residents. For example, the "unemployed" category used by the United States Census Bureau is defined as follows:

> To be counted as unemployed a person must have had no employment during the survey week, must be available for work, must either have engaged in specific job seeking activity within the past four weeks, or be waiting to be called back to a job from which he had been laid off or be waiting to report to a new job, scheduled to start within the following 30 days.[2]

The Census Bureau's definition of unemployment on the basis of labor force participation obviously does not encompass all the possibilities of being out of work (for example, it does not include persons who are not available for work, such as old people, sick people, and transients or the "hidden unemployed"—those people who are not actively engaged in job seeking activities).[3] In addition, low-skilled workers in part-time or marginal activities are excluded from the Census Bureau's classification.

Alternative categorizations of low-income urban residents might be selected from the several definitions of the "underemployed" that can be found in the social science literature. For example, A. M. Ross defines underemployment as "employment which is relatively unproductive and unrewarding in comparison with normal levels of productivity in the economy and with the real capacities of the individuals involved."[4] Still, with regard to his definition of "underemployment," Ross admits that "so far no one has been successful in measuring the extent of the underemployment or the economic loss resulting therefrom ..." His "underemployed" definition is in many respects more consistent with Forrester's conceptual viewpoint than is the Census Bureau's "unemployed" definition because the former deals with the socioeconomic character of low-skilled workers. However, Ross's "underemployed" does not include the unemployed and unemployable population groups and those not currently in the labor force; because of these exclusions, his classification is somewhat limited from the standpoint of the *Urban Dynamics* model.

The preceding discussion raises the question of what are the attributes or qualities that guide the modeler in forming category definitions. To answer this question, it is necessary to review the principles of aggregation involved in system dynamics modeling.

5.4 Aggregation Criteria

In general, category definitions useful for dynamic models are dependent on dynamic considerations rather than on standard definitions. The modeler views the phenomena under study with the objective of identifying important feedback-loop interactions. With the model purpose precisely stated, the criteria for aggregation are used to determine appropriate groupings or partitions (levels). Two important criteria are:

1. Is the level of aggregation sufficient for answering the questions asked of the model?
2. Does the level of aggregation obscure important relationships that could significantly alter the overall behavior of the model?

The following discussion examines these criteria in the context of the *Urban Dynamics* treatment of the underemployed population class.[5]

The *Urban Dynamics* model illustrates how an urban area comes to be characterized by a large concentration of low-skilled, unemployed, and marginally employed persons. The model depicts the dynamic processes that attract underemployed migrants into the central city. The model also shows the impact of a growing underemployed population on residential and industrial construction within the city. For example, the presence of large pockets of underemployed within a central-city area may impede future local economic development. The underemployed tend to generate higher tax costs in a city and create demands for low-cost housing that competes with industry for central-city land.

The underemployed, as defined in *Urban Dynamics*, appear to resemble one another with respect to their average job skills, geographic mobility, housing needs, and demands on tax revenues. For instance, as a group the underemployed require more public services (such as welfare, unemployment compensation, and transportation) than the rest of the city's population. Also, as they come to dominate an area, the underemployed tend to gain political power, demanding further tax expenditures even though their tax contributions to the city are low because of their low personal income levels. For the purposes of the *Urban Dynamics* model, then, the underemployed form a logical grouping since their common economic and social attributes have an important impact on the development of an urban area.

As a rule, the level of aggregation within a model is appropriate when items or people grouped together share identical (or nearly identical) characteristics and behave in similar ways. For example, if the tax needs of the unemployable and the marginally employed differ appreciably in their relative magnitudes and in their impact on the urban area, then combining the two groups in a single class would be inaccurate. In *Urban Dynamics* the taxes needed by the underemployed represent an average value over the entire class. As discussed earlier, the underemployed have similar overall economic and sociological characteristics and thus form a reasonable aggregate.

It is important to recognize that, inherently, perfect population groupings can never be achieved in a model because real-world attributes (such as income or skill levels) tend to be distributed along a continuum. The choice of category definitions within a model is thus inevitably somewhat subjective. For this reason, model categorizations should be judged largely according to the insights they provide about real-world behavior. In general, the minimum amount of disaggregation is desirable in a model, for extensive disaggregation increases complexity at the expense of simplicity and understanding. As illustration, the broad aggregation within the *Urban Dynamics* model helps focus attention on the important demographic, economic, and social interactions within a city, while keeping the model relatively simple.

5.5 Conclusion

The level of aggregation appropriate to a particular model depends both on the similarity of individual behavior within aggregates and on the questions or problems to be addressed by the model. The approach to category definition in the *Urban Dynamics* model is appropriate for analyzing the long-term population composition of an urban area. Several behavioral attributes form the basis for the definition of the underemployed U population class used in *Urban Dynamics*. The underemployed category is an aggregate representation of low-skill urban residents having similar housing and tax needs, geographic mobility, and economic abilities. In *Urban Dynamics*, as in all dynamic models, category definitions depend on dynamic qualities—how people aggregated into a common group behave, given a similar array of conditions and information.

Notes

1. T. S. Kuhn, *The Structure of Scientific Revolutions* (Chicago; University of Chicago Press, 1970).

2. A. H. Scott, *Census, U.S.A.* (New York: Seabury Press, 1968), p. 104.

3. To give some indication of the magnitude of "hidden unemployment," Dernburg and Strand have estimated that the inclusion of hidden unemployment would have raised the nationwide unemployment rate in 1962 from 5.6 percent to 8.5 percent. See T. F. Dernburg and K. T. Strand, "Hidden Unemployment, 1953–1962: A Quantitative Analysis by Age and Sex," *American Economic Review* 56 (March 1966):94.

4. A. M. Ross, *Unemployment and the American Economy* (New York: John Wiley, 1964), p. 6.

5. A general discussion of aggregation principles is contained in Jay W. Forrester, *Industrial Dynamics* (Cambridge, Mass.: The M.I.T. Press, 1961), chap. 11.

6
Business Structures and Economic Activity in *Urban Dynamics*

Nathaniel J. Mass

The concepts employed in Urban Dynamics *to characterize urban activity frequently differ in emphasis or in scope from traditional viewpoints. One illustration of this concerns the representation of employment and economic activity within the urban model. Economic analyses of an urban area frequently focus on such quantities as value-added, wage and salary disbursements, or total employment. In contrast,* Urban Dynamics, *being primarily a land-use model, focuses on the level of business structures (industrial buildings) within an urban area and examines the changes in employment and assessed valuation that characterize business structures as they age.*

The succeeding paper analyzes the conceptual structure of the business sector in the Urban Dynamics *model. The primary objective of this examination is to interpret the industrial-aging hypotheses within the model in terms of the economic and technological processes which influence a city's internal level of business activity.*

6
Business Structures and
Economic Activity in *Urban Dynamics*

6.1 Introduction

The *Urban Dynamics* model consists of three parallel subsystems—housing, population, and industry—that interact to produce urban growth and decay. The business sector of the urban model differs particularly in its focus from most traditional analyses of urban industrial activity. The model depicts the economic changes in employment and assessed valuation that characterize industrial buildings (business structures) as they age. *Urban Dynamics* illustrates how a decaying city comes to be dominated by excessive concentrations of marginal and decaying industry.

A common misunderstanding, contained in several published reviews of *Urban Dynamics*, is that the industrial sector of the model portrays "business firms" rather than "business structures." This paper describes the representation of economic activity in the urban model and explains how the dynamics of aging are dependent upon technological and economic factors within the city. It further illustrates how the dynamics of the business sector influence the aggregate balance of labor and employment in an urban area.

6.2 An Overview of the Business Sector

The industrial sector of *Urban Dynamics* models the changes that accompany the aging of business structures. A business structure consists of a land and building area devoted to commercial use. More concretely, a business structure consists of a building along with the supporting infrastructure—access roads and sewage facilities, for example—necessary to initiate business activity.[1] All business structures are characterized by a few fundamental descriptors:[2]

1. Once they are formed, business structures have the potential for housing economic activity.
2. Business structures occupy urban land.
3. A business structure has an assessed value (which in a real city would be determined by the age of the structure, the value of improvements, and the value of capital equipment within it). The structure's occupants pay taxes to the city proportional to this assessed value.

Urban Dynamics further defines three classes of business structures: new enterprise NE, mature business MB, and declining Industry DI. Each new-enterprise structure ages into mature business and eventually deteriorates into declining industry before it is demolished. Figure 1 shows the flow rates connecting the three classifications of structures.

Within a city, new-enterprise buildings are constructed predominantly by established firms that are expanding their production capacity and employment levels. The construction of new-enterprise units thus proceeds vigorously during periods of high economic demand. In the urban model, the construction rate is heightened by the availability of skilled labor and supervisory personnel. New-enterprise construction may be further stimulated by low tax rates and by the availability of desirable construction sites. Finally, a speculative factor encour-

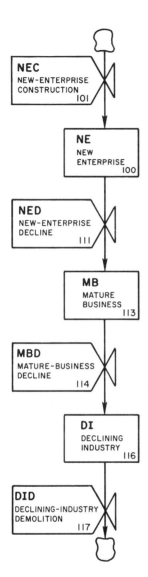

Figure 1 Flow pattern of aging industrial structures in *Urban Dynamics*

ages the construction of new enterprise when there has been a recent history of active construction and industrial growth.

New-enterprise structures shelter economic activity that is relatively land-intensive.[3] Employment densities in a new-enterprise building are comparatively high, and the building's tax contribution to the city is large because of its high assessed value.[4] Dynamically, a new-enterprise structure may be either newly constructed or newly renovated, as long as it possesses these two qualities. The model assumes that internal employment levels and assessed valuation decline as a building ages from new enterprise NE through mature business MB, and to declining industry DI; these occur as a consequence of changes in the buildings' tenancy and use. As will be explained later, while new-enterprise structures are occupied mostly by expanding firms, mature-business and declining-industry structures often house old business firms that have passed their peak levels of employment and economic activity. Alternatively, older industrial buildings may frequently house one or more incipient firms at low employment densities per unit of land area. In either instance, declining internal levels of employment tend to characterize aging industrial buildings.

The term "aging" has a special meaning in *Urban Dynamics*: aging, or obsolescence, is defined in terms of the economic changes that mark the life cycle of industrial buildings. Aging is largely a product of technological change; as a building grows older, its capital equipment and physical layout become relatively inefficient. For example, expanding technology creates changing requirements for work-flow patterns and for the circulation of people and materials within a business structure.[5] When an industrial building ages, its production efficiency is reduced, and rising production and maintenance costs gradually cause employment levels within the structure to diminish. Therefore, when a new enterprise obsolesces into mature business, the structure continues to occupy a fixed portion of urban land, but generates less in tax revenues and economic opportunities. With reduced competitiveness, the personnel mix of an aging structure may also shift toward a lower proportion of managerial-professionals compared with total jobs.

In *Urban Dynamics* the obsolescence rate of business structures depends on local economic conditions as well as on technological factors. Both new enterprise and mature business age more gradually in a period of high demand for new business than in a period of economic stagnation.[6] Thus, for example, aging will proceed slowly in a city where tax rates are low, local markets are expanding, and skilled labor is readily available. These influences are discussed further in the next section of this paper, which deals with the relationships among a city's internal conditions, business firms, and industrial structures.

6.3 Business Firms and Business Structures

The dynamics of the business sector in *Urban Dynamics* have often been misunderstood by readers of the book. In particular, many readers of *Urban Dynamics* have failed to perceive that the model depicts industrial buildings, believing instead that the model develops a life-cycle theory of business firms. For example, in his review of *Urban Dynamics*, Professor Jerome Rothenberg writes:

> The basic mechanisms present in the model are the life-cycle pattern for businesses and the migration processes for businesses and households. The life-cycle business hypothesis is highly vulnerable, both as to the dependability of an age-activity level relationship and to the attribution of relative magnitudes to different parameters. The first of these is more basic. There is just no evidence that business firms in the *aggregate* (i.e. across industrial categories) have either their size or their level of activity significantly predictable on the basis of age alone. The excluded explanatory variables explain most of what can be predicted. Moreover, identification of growth or size or level of activity

of a firm with age of the structure it occupies is misleading; a new firm can occupy old structures, old firms can occupy new structures; and size is certainly not predictable from age of building ...

Moreover, the model's attributions of relative magnitudes to parameters of the life-cycle relationship compounds the damage wrought. One example will suffice. New firms are cited as being larger than mature firms! Unless some time trend in enterprise size is being adduced—so that relative size does not refer to the same firm over time but simply to cross section comparisons of aggregates of firms of different age—the attribution is clearly wrong. New firms *grow* to *larger* mature size. Indeed, new firms have the highest failure rate of all; not only are they smaller, they are also, as a class, less secure, than mature firms. Moreover while the *successful* new firms may grow at a faster rate than mature firms as a whole, the *absolute amount* of growth may well be smaller.

If intended in a time-trend cross-section sense (which the text belies), this age-size relation does not appear to be supported by any known trend.[7]

How are business firms related to business structures, and how are these connected within the *Urban Dynamics* model? A city's internal conditions will normally influence the type of firm occupying a given building and will thereby influence the building's assessed value and internal employment. In *Urban Dynamics*, however, the city's internal conditions directly govern changes in a building's value and employment; the model's formulation treats the movements of individual firms implicitly rather than explicitly.

As stated previously, industrial buildings within urban areas undergo variations in employment and assessed valuation caused by changes in local business costs and business competitiveness. A given building transfers from one category to another for one of two reasons: either the occupying firm moves out and is replaced by another, less efficient, firm; or the occupying firm may discontinue expanding locally and undergo a reduction, through time, in its employment and the value of its capital equipment.

Firms vacate business structures for several reasons. A firm's facilities can become "land-locked" when its plant has no surrounding vacant land into which to expand. When a firm's business expands beyond the capacity of its present facilities, the firm may be forced to relocate. Alternatively, outdated facilities and high maintenance costs can make a move economical. Changing technology imposes changing requirements for headroom, floor weight capacity, power and lighting, and work-flow patterns. The turnover rate within a business structure also depends on the business climate within the community, in addition to the technological and physical considerations discussed earlier. Taxes, labor and manager availability, and the socioeconomic character of the urban area all influence a firm's decision to leave or stay. Certainly, a firm is less likely to move if it enjoys low taxes, has a skilled and abundant labor force, and is situated in a socially attractive neighborhood. Conversely, adverse business conditions—high local wage rates, for example—may induce a firm to vacate its present facilities. A city's internal conditions, then, can be expected to influence the turnover in industrial buildings.

High business turnover rates promote rapid obsolescence of industrial structures for several reasons. First, new tenants in an industrial building are rarely able to use it as efficiently as the original owner. Occupancy rates in old industrial structures are frequently low because of outmoded facilities, despite low rents. Moreover, former manufacturing space is quite frequently relegated to warehousing and storage operations, which are relatively land-extensive. All these factors will lower the number of employees in a building as it ages.

An industrial building can also decline in employment and assessed value under a single owner. With age, buildings tend to become technologically obsolescent and their physical layout to become increasingly inefficient. Over several decades the pattern of activity within an industrial building can change (for example, from machining to storage) even under the continuous ownership of a single firm. If a firm cannot expand, or if labor costs or taxes are high at its present location, there is considerable economic pressure to change the building's use toward less productive activity. Even if the facility is not vacated, then overall employment within the structure will be gradually contracted.

The preceding discussion has focused on the changes in usage of industrial buildings. *Urban Dynamics* describes these changes, especially changes in employment and assessed value, as transitions from new-enterprise, through mature-business, to declining-industry buildings. It is important to realize that a growing business firm's movements through the three categories of buildings is generally opposite from the time path of a business structure. Few young companies can afford a new industrial building. A young firm is far more likely to be found among the several tenants of a declining-industry building. As the firm grows, it can move into larger quarters more suitable to its operations—probably a mature-business structure. At some point during a company's growth, it will have amassed enough capital to build its own facility, or the first sections of one. If a company ceases to grow (or actually declines) it will follow somewhat the reverse path, steadily losing economic vitality and efficiency as it progresses from new-enterprise buildings, to mature-business, to declining-industry buildings. Depending on the characteristics of the particular firm, this process may extend over long periods of time. The general relation between the movement of business firms and business structures is shown in Figure 2.

On the basis of the analysis just presented, several essential elements of the business sector in *Urban Dynamics* may be summarized. First, new-enterprise structures in a city are generally occupied by established and growing firms that are able to afford the costs of constructing new facilities. On the other hand, declining-industry structures are occupied either by young firms that are as yet unable to construct a new plant or by older firms that are presently contracting their employment levels. In *Urban Dynamics*, industrial structures typically decline in assessed value and employment because of technological obsolescence and loss of competitiveness. Industrial obsolescence rates are thus determined both by technological change and by changes in the local business climate.

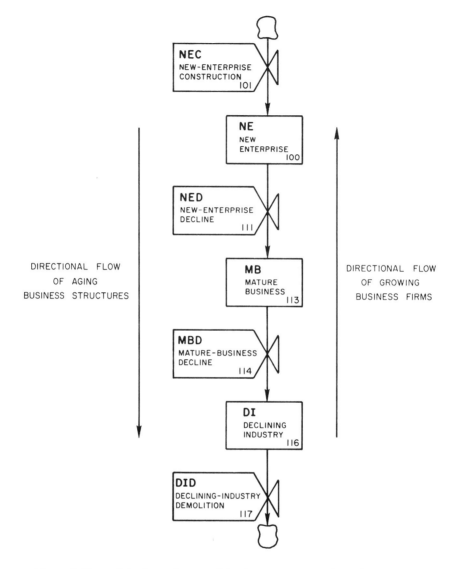

Figure 2 Flow of business firms and business structures through new enterprise, mature business and declining industry

6.4 Urban Decay and the Composition of Economic Activity

Over its lifetime the hypothetical *Urban Dynamics* city undergoes a significant shift in its internal proportions of new-enterprise, mature-business, and
declining-industry structures. In particular, as the city moves from growth into a
stagnant equilibrium, the proportion of marginal industries within the city rises
substantially, with associated losses of job opportunities and tax revenues. These
changes are summarized in Figure 3.

The transition in a city's industrial base toward declining industry is caused
by several factors. First, as land occupancy rises within the urban area, land

Years	0	50	100	150	250
New enterprise NE	200	1,860	10,860	3,550	4,880
Mature business MB	1,000	1,770	10,520	5,380	7,800
Declining industry DI	100	1,120	5,660	19,270	16,470
Fraction of business stuctures in declining industry category	0.07	0.24	0.21	0.70	0.57
Underemployed/job ratio UR	0.07	0.78	1.07	1.70	1.81

Figure 3 Industrial composition of new enterprise, mature business, and declining industry in *Urban Dynamics*

prices tend to increase and firms currently within the area find it difficult to construct new business structures in proximity to their existing facilities. These influences tend to curtail new industrial construction, heighten the rates of obsolescence of new enterprise and mature business, and lead to an excess of declining industry. Concomitantly, as local employment opportunities decline, high land occupancy impedes housing construction, causing the city to shift toward increased concentrations of underemployed housing and increased residential densities.[8] In the stagnant urban area, high tax rates caused by a declining tax base and rising needs for tax revenues cause new industrial and residential construction to be diverted from the central city to the suburbs and other outlying areas. Figure 4 shows the equilibrium proportions of business structures and housing units within the stagnant urban area.

The *Urban Dynamics* model provides an integrated framework for analyzing the impact of taxes, labor availability, population composition, and land prices on economic activity within a city. The model shows how the aging of industrial structures leads to an eroded industrial base and a decaying city in which upward

Residential Structures Category	Number	Percentage of Total Structures
Premium housing PH	111,000	15
Worker housing WH	335,800	44
Underemployed housing UH	309,900	41

Business Structures Category	Number	Percentage of Total Structures
New enterprise NE	4,900	17
Mature business MB	7,800	26
Declining industry DI	16,500	57

Figure 4 Equilibrium proportions of residential and industrial structures in the decaying city

economic mobility is restricted by inadequate employment opportunities and "job-ladders." It further demonstrates how well-designed policies can promote economic development and materially reduce the concentrations of decaying industry within a city.[9] With improved understanding of the dynamics of industrial growth and obsolescence, we may be able to devise better policies to enhance upward economic mobility and to create economic opportunities for central-city residents.

Notes

1. In this paper, for purposes of exposition, we will refer primarily to "industrial buildings" rather than to "business structures."

2. Pp. 19–20 in *Urban Dynamics* discuss the industrial sector in relation to the whole model.

3. "Land-intensiveness" refers to high employment densities per acre of industrial land.

4. In Forrester's terminology, a new-enterprise structure contains an *average* of one "productive unit", which is a measure of the intensity of business activity. Each new-enterprise productive unit normally consists of 4 managerial-professionals, 20 labor, and 10 underemployed. In the model the actual number of jobs in any structure open to the underemployed depends on the labor/job ratio. When skilled labor is in oversupply, a portion of the jobs normally allotted to underemployed will be filled by labor persons. When labor is in undersupply, more underemployed will be hired in response.

5. Evidence for the increasing technological inefficiency of aging industrial structures is given in a study of the old textile mills in Lowell, Massachusetts: "Community Renewal Program—Mill Rehabilitation Study," prepared by the Lowell City Development Authority, January 1972. See also John Strongman, "The Lowell Model: A Comparison of Model Behavior and the City of Lowell, Massachusetts," System Dynamics Group Working Paper D-1681-9 (Cambridge, Mass.: Massachusetts Institute of Technology, July 1973).

6. The average age of declining industry, however, shortens in periods of high economic demand. "This presumes that much of the new enterprise that is constructed will be on the geographical site of old enterprise that has reached the end of its effective life" (*Urban Dynamics*, p. 200).

7. Jerome Rothenberg, "Problems in the Modeling of Urban Development: A Review Article on *Urban Dynamics* by Jay W. Forrester," Department of Economics Working Paper no. 81 (Cambridge, Mass.: Massachusetts Institute of Technology, October 1971), pp. 16–17.

8. See *Urban Dynamics*, pp. 38–50, for a discussion of the effects of aging on the equilibrium proportions of residential structures within a city.

9. See Section 5.7 of *Urban Dynamics*.

7
Dynamic Migration Models

Michael W. Laird

Migration flows in the Urban Dynamics *model respond to the relative attractiveness of the city compared with its external environment. As migration occurs, changing population in the city alters local job availability, housing and revenue needs, market size, and product demand. These changes, in turn, influence the composite attractiveness of the urban area for further migration. Attractiveness and migration are thus related in a circular chain of cause and effect.*

To illustrate the importance of feedback in explaining long-term migration patterns, Michael Laird has contrasted the migration formulation in Urban Dynamics *with the classical gravity model frequently employed in demography and economics. Although the gravity model depicts migration occurring in response to differentials in attractiveness, it does not also measure the subsequent feedback of population on attractiveness. For this reason, gravity models may explain adequately only short-run migration flows. Laird's analysis of the gravity model provides a cogent illustration of several differences in methodology and purpose between* Urban Dynamics *and traditional urban economic models.*

7
Dynamic Migration Models

In 1969, Professor Jay W. Forrester of M.I.T. presented in his book *Urban Dynamics* a feedback simulation model that examines the interrelations of people, housing and economic activity within an urban boundary. Unlike much university research, the book attracted attention in several disciplines at once and some popular interest as well. A note of controversy is evident in numerous reviews.[1]

This examination from many angles and in a contentious spirit has been a useful exercise to the extent that it has informed people of a new methodology and new theories of dynamic behavior. However, many of the reviewers have skimmed over the methodology, over the behavioral theories embodied in the model equations, and over the theory of causality implied by the model's structure. Instead they tend to become embroiled in controversy about specific policy implications. Policy questions are important, but they will not be settled until considerably more research has been done to verify the conceptualization used in formulating the model and each individual equation contained within it. Few of the early critics offered concrete suggestions along those lines. Unfortunately, issues of validity tended to be supplanted by declarations "for" or "against."

Recently, however, the System Dynamics Group at M.I.T. has received a few detailed alternative formulations through informal channels. In particular, it has been suggested that the migration behavior of people could just as well have been described by using traditional gravity models of migration and that equation (2), developed below, should be substituted in the urban dynamics model to describe the arrival of each class of people in a city. The present paper is a discussion of the problems that arise from applying gravity concepts to the *Urban Dynamics* model or to *any* long-range model involving internal migration. These problems arise because the assumptions used in constructing a gravity model, although often fully adequate for short-term predictive studies, are inadequate for long-term explanatory studies. A critical problem is the fact that the relation borrowed from a description of gravity does not in any manner represent the social processes of feedback that occur in and dominate long-run migration behavior.

7.1 Gravity Models

A gravity model of migration assumes that the flow of migrants between two locations is proportional to the product of the number of people at one location and the number of people at the other location and is inversely proportional to the distance between these locations raised to the s power.[2] Mathematically, the relation is analogous to the law of gravity:

$$F_{xy} \propto \frac{P_x P_y}{D_{xy}^s},$$

(1)

where

F_{xy} –	flow from y to x
P_x –	number of people at location X
P_y –	number of people at location Y
D_{xy} –	distance between X and Y
s –	an empirically observed parameter.

If this formulation is applied to migration between a city and its surrounding environment, then the city represents location X and the surroundings, as a collection, are location Y. Now the distance D_{xy} between X and Y is not a single value, because Y, the surrounding environment, is no longer a single point. Consequently, a summation over rings of constant distance must be performed to find total migration to the city. Also, a more accurate representation of migration behavior can be obtained if net migration is disaggregated into socioeconomic classes. Disaggregation by socioeconomic class makes it possible to represent the different choice criteria each class uses in a decision to migrate. Disaggregating in- and out-migration allows for the fact that people may come to a city in response to a particular attractive feature but may later leave for other reasons, even though the original attraction remains.

These relations can be incorporated into equations describing the inflow and outflow of a particular class. For example, equations representing labor-class migration are:

$$\text{Inflow of labor} = I = gP_x \sum_{\text{all } y} \frac{L_y}{D_{xy}^s}, \tag{2}$$

where

D_{xy} –	distance between X and Y
P_x –	number of people in city X
L_y –	number of laborers in environment Y
g –	constant of proportionality for labor in-migration
s –	an empirically observed parameter.

$$\text{Outflow of labor} = OF = hL_x \sum_{\text{all } y} \frac{P_y}{D_{xy}^s}, \tag{3}$$

where

D_{xy} –	distance between X and Y
L_x –	number of laborers in city X
P_y –	number of people in environment Y
h –	constant of proportionality for labor out-migration
s –	an empirically observed parameter.

These equations indicate that the in-migration of labor to city X will increase when the city's population increases. Presumably, more laborers are required to support the activities of the growing city and are attracted by the opportunities there. An alternative reading would be that in-migration to the city increases when the number of laborers in the surroundings increases. This assumes that people migrate in a manner that tends to create an equilibrium in the population size at the two locations. Similar relations are expressed by the outflow equations. In both cases, the driving force for migration is the number of people at the two locations—city and surroundings. The intervening distance represents the resistance to migration flow.

Migration models using this general gravity formulation have been quite successful in explaining statistically the historical movement of people between locations over rather short periods of time. G. K. Zipf showed that the gravity formulation adequately reproduces data from a variety of intercity movements.[3] His data were derived from monthly travel statistics during the years 1933 and 1934. D. J. Bogue and W. S. Thompson showed that the inverse-distance rule adequately reproduces the 1935–1940 census data on migration among regions and subregions of the United States.[4] They note in particular that the exponent on the distance factor appears to be a function of parameters that describe the economic conditions of the two end locations and the socioeconomic class of the migrants. In a summary of migration models, T. R. Andersen maintains that greater accuracy would result if exponents were added to all terms in the equations.[5] These exponents should be functions of the characteristics of the migration. In a more recent and highly influential study, I. S. Lowry modified the basic gravity formula and incorporated a dimensionless attractiveness factor that depends on relative wages and relative unemployment.[6] Lowry's modification constitutes a significant improvement because it moves toward a description in which an attractiveness term provides the driving potential for migration in the model, and the population term provides a scaling factor or reference rather than the driving force.

7.2 Drawbacks and Limitations

In all these applications the time span covered is rather short. In other words, assuming migrations occur because of the greater attractiveness of the end location over the starting point, these short-term studies postulate a roughly constant magnitude of relative attractiveness between the two locations and then find relations that describe the flow of people in response to this differential. Most migration studies are confined to cross-section analysis because the gravity formulation does not include variables that are internal to the model *and* change the attractiveness differential between starting and ending points. Bogue and Thompson confronted this fact when they noted that describing migration to the West Coast required significantly different exponent parameters than those used for migration in the rest of the United States. They attributed this to the high expectations of economic growth in the West and the favorable climate. In light of current economic and environmental conditions on the West Coast, an entirely different set of parameters would be produced by a similar study done today. Yet the change is largely a direct, but delayed, result of the accumulation of past migrants. It is evidence of the feedback nature of migration.

Lowry notes the feedback nature of migration: "If the condition of labor markets at origin and destination 'causes' the flow of migration, migration in turn alters the labor market condition." He admits that his "model is in this sense incompletely specified ... " But he argues that "the unspecified feedback relationships should not be of great importance since we are dealing with relatively small flows of migration between pairs of relatively large labor markets."

Contrary to Lowry, however, it should be made clear that an economically rational decision to migrate does not depend solely on the existence of large numbers of people who already hold jobs. Rather, it depends on the belief there are *additional* jobs that are currently vacant. A similar argument applies to the incremental effect of other urban assets above the amount of those assets already in use. The size of the incremental vacant jobs is comparable to the flow of migration; consequently, significant feedback control effects on migration can occur, even though the size of the *total* job stock is much larger than the annual migration flows. Second, the fact that migration is often small in comparison to the total population of a city is not grounds for ignoring feedback effects. Migration is a rate of change that is summed or integrated over time. Rather modest rates of change, continuously summed, lead to significant changes in total population. A 2 percent annual rate doubles the population in 35 years. Add to this the fact that migrants are usually young families during their fertile years, and the doubling time can be much shorter. These population pressures affect the quality of schools, city services, taxes, and future job opportunities. These factors, generated by migration and natural increase, "feed back" to affect future migration. Given the need to represent migration as a feedback process, it is apparent that there is a fundamental problem in the form of the gravity equation when used in long-term studies.

Refer again to equations (2) and (3), expressing the migration of laborers to and from a city. The inflow equation states that as the city's population P_x increases, so the inflow of laborers I increases, which of course increases the population of the city. This further increases the labor inflow, which further increases the city's population, ad infinitum. Thus an implicit but very powerful positive-feedback loop is taken for granted, one that by itself creates exponential growth limited only by the total population of the nation (or possibly an even larger area if people are free to cross national boundaries when they are attracted by this exploding city). The effect is much like the accumulation of interest in a bank account. In the short run, the accumulation is negligible, but in the long run the effect is quite substantial. Since most migration studies deal with short-run behavior, the gravity equation "fits." But in the long run is such a loop believable? Growth processes (though not unlimited exponential ones) do occur in cities, but they should not be attributed solely to numbers of residents. Even Lowry's equation will not suffice, because the wage and unemployment figures are not readjusted by the model to reflect unfavorable job conditions brought on by the surfeit of people. A more serious fault is the fact that this effect is an implicit creation—a by-product of a gravity formulation. Feedback loops have powerful consequences on the behavior of a system, and they should be included in a model in an explicit fashion. A system or process should be modeled by explicitly determining the important feedback relations and including only these relations—not the implicit creations of borrowed formulations.

The out-migration equation indicates that an increase in a city's labor class L_x will increase labor out-migration OF. Similar criticisms apply. The out-migration of laborers may not in fact increase if their services are in demand in the city. The equation implicitly creates a negative feedback loop; that is, an increase in a city's laborers increases their departure rate, which tends to decrease the number of laborers. This relation tends to counteract the previous exponential growth relation, but its implicit inclusion is as adventitious as the growth assumption. The question of whether in-migration or out-migration dominates is completely controlled by the relative values of *g* and *h*. If *g* is large, exponential growth occurs. If *h* is large, a contraction of population results. If the two functions strike a balance, inflow and outflow are equal and population size is constant. Thus the behavior of this migration model is completely controlled by the relative values of *g* and *h*. Once they are set, the behavior of the population size can assume only one of three possible modes.

Consequently, the gravity formulation is appropriate only for analyzing short-term migration behavior or nearly static situations in which migration occurs in response to an atractiveness differential that remains roughly constant in nature and magnitude.[7] Long-term or dynamic situations require an entirely different formulation that will represent the sources of many possible modes of behavior.

7.3 Reformulation

Despite the need for a new formulation, much of the old one can be salvaged, so long as the relationships are clearly defined and we are willing to add new refinements to describe accurately the processes at work. Labor in-migration provides a concrete example to explain the derivation. The inflow of labor arrivals is a function of the population size of the city. Large, healthy cities tend to attract a larger stream of migrants than smaller cities because larger cities require more services and offer more opportunities. This portion of the process may be more accurately described. Labor arrivals are a function of the size of the labor population. The size of a city's labor population is not the criteria laborers use in choosing to migrate, but for modeling purposes it serves as a reference or scaling factor that combines with the fractional increase to generate the size of the flow. This reformulation also aids application because normal arrival rates expressed as a percentage change per year can be calculated from migration statistics.[8] This much is similar to the previously criticized gravity formulation. However, labor arrivals are also a function of many dimensions of attractiveness. These factors include economic opportunities, housing, public services, tax levels, and schools; and this attractiveness is in part a function of the number of laborers because there are consumable, limited resources that must be allocated among the population. The attractiveness function should be included explicitly in the reformulation to represent the effects of changing the many dimensions of attractiveness. In the sample labor migration model, this attractiveness function is the labor-attractiveness multiplier perceived at point Y, $LAMP_y$. It is included explicitly like Lowry's treatment, but it is defined in a different way. The attractiveness multiplier modifies the normal arrival rate in response to changed perceptions of jobs, housing, services, and other factors. It differs from Lowry's methods in that changes in the city's internal conditions feed back to affect the attractiveness term, and thus migration, in future periods. It also differs from Lowry in that the normal rate constant is a figure with dimension, percent per year, that represents a normal or standardized percentage change in population due to migration. This differs from Lowry's and other econometric studies in which a "normal rate" refers to all terms in the equation except the dimensionless attractiveness term.

Migration is usually inversely related to distance, but this is not a true causal relation. In causal terms, migration is inversely related to costs. These costs include monetary costs and the inconvenience of long moves, plus uncertainties and inaccuracies in the perception of a distant city. Frequently, distance is closely correlated to total costs, but a model should measure cost as the relevant determinant of migration flows. The only reason for using distance would be a need to have a surrogate to represent the costs of migration—quite different from ascribing causal significance to distance. A cost surrogate is not necessary to the development of this model; hence the total costs of migration from y to x, C_{xy}, will be used as a reminder that there are many human and social costs to be included with the monetary cost of a move.

$$\text{Inflow} = \text{labor arrivals} = \text{LA}_{xy} = (\text{LAN})(L_x)\frac{(\text{LAMP}_y)}{C_{xy}^s}, \qquad (4)$$

where

LA_{xy} –	labor arrivals at X from point Y
L_x –	number of laborers in city X
LAMP_y –	labor-attractiveness multiplier perceived at point Y
C_{xy} –	total cost of migration from y to x
s –	empirical constant
LAN –	proportionality constant, labor arrivals normal.

Equation (4) describes the migration rate of labor from Y to X. To find the total labor arrivals at X, a summation over all Y is necessary. This summation is difficult to obtain in actual application because it requires knowledge of attitudes at all points Y and the arrival rate from all points Y. However, it is the total labor arrival rate at city X that has an important effect on X; so the point of origin Y and the cost of each individual trip is not of interest. Likewise, the city's reputation at all points Y is not important—only the effective net attractive pull that a city exerts on potential migrants is important.

Consequently, in the formulation, we can use an average cost of migration to X and an average measure of attractiveness. Hence

$$\text{Inflow} = \text{labor arrivals} = \text{LA} = (\text{LAN})\,(L_x)\frac{\text{LAMP}_{\text{average}}}{C_{xy_{\text{average}}}}. \qquad (5)$$

This equation can be simplified further by assuming that the average cost of travel is not determined by the conditions in a city. Under this assumption, the cost becomes a constant relative to a given city. Even if the magnitude of the total cost changes with improved transportation and communication, this change affects migration to and from all cities equally. Thus the relative cost is likely to remain constant over very long periods of time. It is a comforting simplification to know this term is constant; however, measuring it would be difficult because it is composed of a variety of tangible and intangible costs. But the two terms $LAMP_{average}$ and $C_{xy_{average}}$ suggest a benefit-cost ratio that motivates migration. The two terms can be combined to form a labor-attractiveness multiplier perceived LAMP. This variable describes a net attractiveness to labor relative to costs. It changes primarily in response to changes in urban attractiveness because absolute changes in the magnitudes of cost affect all areas equally so that the relative costs remain constant. The remaining equation is:

$$\text{Inflow} = \text{labor arrivals} = LA = (LAN)(L)(LAMP), \qquad (6)$$

where

LA –	labor arrivals at city X
L –	labor population of the city
LAMP –	labor-attractiveness multiplier perceived
LAN –	proportionality constant (= labor arrivals under normal or standardized conditions)

Our reformulation is in fact the general formulation used to describe the migrations of all socioeconomic classes in Forrester's *Urban Dynamics*. These equations can exhibit many modes of behavior because the attractiveness multipliers are functions, in part, of the size of the labor population. A diagram of the network of relations implied by the labor equations is given in Figure 1. When the labor-arrivals rate increases, the labor population increases, which tends to increase the arrival rate. However, as the labor population increases, it consumes the available jobs, housing, and services. This decreases the city's attractiveness, which tends to decrease the arrival rate. Also, the lowered attractiveness of the area increases the departure rate, which decreases the labor population. This, in turn, increases attractiveness as the local population is reduced. That a verbal description sounds circular emphasizes the presence of feedback. Migration and feedback processes all occur continuously within an urban area, and, depending upon the parameter values and delays, the system will grow steadily, decay, oscillate around a growth trend or a decay trend or, after initial exclusions, stabilize at an equilibrium level.

This theory of migration behavior can be developed into mathematical models that describe concrete situations. Because of the differences as compared with gravity models, new research techniques and data sources must be used for applications. Data on the labor population of cities are readily available. The arrival and departure rates are also easily obtained, providing the labor popula-

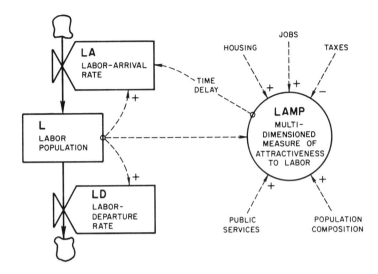

Figure 1 Simple diagram of factors affecting migration

tion term L and a proportionality constant LAN. The arrivals multiplier requires survey data. One would want to measure attractiveness, considering benefits relative to costs—a concept that is probably close to the complex mental decision calculus performed by a person contemplating migration. This similarity should enhance a respondent's understanding of the survey questions and lead to more reliable responses. Attitudes concerning the perceived attractiveness for migration to a city can be plotted on a Guttman scale against actual measures of attractive features in a city. These attitudes should be divided into various dimensions (such as attractiveness because of jobs and attractiveness because of housing) and plotted against appropriate measurements of actual urban conditions. Data from cities in a variety of attractive (or unattractive) situations can be used to construct most of the scale, and the remaining portions can be hypothesized. The curves should then be normalized so that the city's actual job and housing conditions yield a multiplier value of unity. Thus the migration rates will be the values specified by actual data at a given point in time. What has been developed is a larger framework to view long-term migration behavior as a system of interrelated variables, a system in which feedback interdependencies explicitly represent, as much as possible, the actual behavior occurring in migration. Once the theory is converted to equation form, it can be analyzed extensively within the *Urban Dynamics* model structure.

If the purpose of dynamic study is to investigate the causal relations that affect movement to a city and to project probable future migration patterns, then the results of such a study must be interpreted properly and the conclusions tempered in light of modeling limitations. The attitudinal variables will be approximate relations, particularly if they turn out to be nonlinear functions, and the data appropriate to this type of investigation may be scarce. Consequently, the results will probably not reach the point-reproducing accuracy of historical studies. However, a careful dynamic investigation should indicate the direction of migration trends. More important, it should also indicate, with greater reliability than current gravity models, the nature of the policies that could affect this migration behavior and the impact of a given policy relative to other alternatives. Sensitivity analysis will indicate probable ranges of variation about a trend.

Migration studies such as those discussed previously are well within the current capabilities of social science, although they promise to be time consuming and expensive. In the final analysis, purpose is the chief criterion for the choice of models. So long as a study is concerned with reproducing migration data over short-run, nearly static time periods (static in terms of the type and magnitude of attractive forces), a gravity formulation will often replicate the data. However, if a study is concerned with long-run behavior during which attractive forces change noticeably or if it is focused upon the underlying real processes that are at work, then a feedback analysis of the causal network is a necessity.

Notes

1. See, for example, the reviews by G. K. Ingram, *Journal of the American Institute of Planners* 36 (May 1970); H. Weinblatt, *Policy Sciences* 1 (1970): 377–383; and H. T. Moody, *Economic Geography* 46 (October 1970):620–622.

2. G. K. Zipf, "The $P_1 P_2/D$ Hypothesis: On the Intercity Movement of Persons," *American Sociological Review* 11 (1946):677–686.

3. Ibid.

4. D. J. Bogue and W. S. Thompson, "Migration and Distance," *American Sociological Review* 14 (1946): 236–244.

5. T. R. Andersen, "Intermetropolitan Migration: A Comparison of the Hypotheses of Zipf and Stouffer," *American Sociological Review* 20 (1955): 287–291.

6. Ira S. Lowry, *Migration and Metropolitan Growth: Two Analytical Models* (San Francisco: Chandler, 1966).

7. That result holds true for all variants on this form of the equation. For example, if population is weighted by per capita income, the equation becomes:

$$\text{Inflow} = q' I_x \sum_{\text{all } y} \frac{I_{\text{labor}, y}}{D_{xy}^s}.$$

If per capita income at city X is high, the equation requires a large flow of laborers such as to deplete surrounding Y of migrants in the long run. At the same time the equation indicates nothing about the effect of the large inflow on per capita income in city X. Similar results are obtained, for the same reasons, if population is weighted by employment opportunities.

8. This normal arrival rate is considerably different from the normal rate in econometric parlance. Econometricians often call all independent variables except the dimensionless attractiveness term a "normal rate" because the combination of these variables has the dimension of a rate—people per year. However, the normal arrival rate discussed here expresses a percentage change in population due to migration during a standardized or normalized reference period. It has units of inverse time.

8
Issues of Empirical Support for the Migration Formulations in *Urban Dynamics*

Michael R. Goodman and Peter M. Senge

From the published reviews of Urban Dynamics, *it is possible to discern several fundamental differences in philosophy and approach between system dynamics and other modeling methodologies. One important set of issues concerns the applicability of statistical methods to social science models. The following paper by Michael R. Goodman and Peter M. Senge delineates several difficulties in using statistical inference techniques to derive parameters for the migration equations in* Urban Dynamics. *The migration equations, because they are highly nonlinear and involve long delays in the perception and averaging of information, pose several estimation problems that have not previously been encountered widely in linear statistical model building. The analysis by Goodman and Senge suggests that current estimation techniques may frequently be inadequate for reliably testing hypotheses within continuous state–variable feedback models such as* Urban Dynamics.*

The elaboration of the issues examined in this paper represents an important focus for methodological research in the social sciences. The insights gained from such an analysis should prove valuable in evaluating procedures for model testing and in assessing reasonable standards of model validity.

8
Issues of Empirical Support
for the Migration Formulations
in *Urban Dynamics*

8.1 Introduction

This paper raises several issues associated with estimating parameters and functional relationships in a multivariate feedback model. The analysis describes four difficulties in bringing empirical evidence to bear on the migration equations in *Urban Dynamics*. The migration formulations were chosen as a concrete focus in discussing these issues because considerable empirical research has been done into the causes of urban migration.[1] An important question, therefore, is: can one apply either the results or the methods of this research to the *Urban Dynamics* model? The issues to be discussed are:

1. Limitations on inferences which can be drawn from statistical techniques in the face of the restricted time span and range of existing migration data;
2. Problems in interpreting parameter estimates derived from cross-sectional data analysis;
3. Difficulties in estimating nonlinear relationships containing significant time delays; and
4. Problems in drawing statistical inferences regarding the error process of a continuous dynamic system.

It is important that these issues be examined in the context of the purpose and use of the *Urban Dynamics* model. That model was developed to simulate the long-term life cycle of a city and to explore the future impacts of various urban policies. Its conceptual framework is therefore both closed loop and extensively nonlinear. Whether or not statistical methods can be profitably applied to such a model remains an open question. Statistical model building in the social sciences has largely centered on the development of linear models designed for short-term prediction or policy testing. As a result, the applicability of statistical methods to nonlinear feedback systems has not been widely examined. The issues raised herein, while hardly exhaustive of the potentially major questions in this area, should be viewed as an aid in focusing future investigation.

8.2 Limited Time Span and Range of Existing Migration Data

The *Urban Dynamics* model generates behavior covering the entire life cycle of the central city from its growth through its stagnation stages (a period of roughly 250 years). In addition, the model is designed for experimentation with various urban policies that can cause the city's internal conditions to shift over a wide range of values. Because the urban model was designed to operate over a wide range and mix of urban conditions, functional relationships within the model must be drawn to encompass the full range traversed by each independent variable. The wide operating range of the model variables, in turn, makes it important to incorporate nonlinearities within most causal relationships. However, data limitations may frequently restrict the modeler's ability to draw statistical inferences about the form of these nonlinear relationships.

As an example of such limitations, consider the problems entailed in estimating the relationship between migration and job availability hypothesized

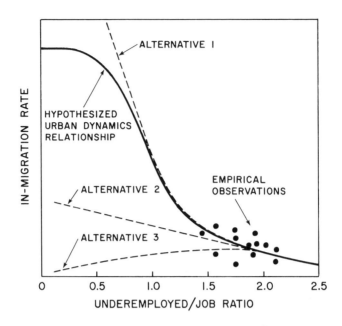

Figure 1 Influence of job availability on underemployed migration

in *Urban Dynamics*. The relationship is shown in Figure 1. The function assumes that high job availability within an area (relative to its environment) will encourage a high rate of in-migration. However, progressive increases in job availability are assumed to exert a diminishing influence on in-migration. Similarly, unfavorable job opportunities (represented by population/job ratios greater than one) are assumed to discourage in-migration but with diminishing influence.

Suppose, for simplicity, that job availability is the exclusive determinant of migration into and out of the city, and that time-series data are available for both the migration rate and the job availability. For any given area, available data might cover at most a 20- or 30-year period since, for example, census data on migration have only been published since 1940. Within a data sample covering roughly 20 years, observations are likely to be taken during a single phase of the city's life cycle. Many older American cities, for instance, have passed through their growth and transition stages and are now nearing population equilibrium.[2] For this reason, available time-series data for each of these cities would reflect only a narrow operating region compared to the full range of the migration function. An example of such clustered time-series data is pictured in Figure 1. Given these data alone, one would be unable to draw reliable statistical inferences about the slope and convexity of the full nonlinear relationship shown in the figure.[3] The analyst could not, for example, distinguish among the alternative shapes shown in Figure 1 on the basis of statistical tests alone. The choice between the alternatives would then have to be made principally on the basis of a priori knowledge or theoretical reasoning.[4]

8.3 Interpretation of Parameters Derived from Cross-sectional Data Analysis

To circumvent the limitations arising from the restricted range of independent variables, cross-sectional data for a number of urban areas are often employed in empirical work; cross-sectional data frequently yield a wider and more varied range of observations than would be obtainable from time-series data for a single urban area.[5] This section examines the issues related to estimating parameters for an individual city using cross-sectional data.[6]

Before estimating the parameters in the migration equations in *Urban Dynamics* using cross-sectional data, the real-world counterparts of each parameter must be considered. To take a concrete example, consider the problems involved in estimating the underemployed arrivals normal UAN in the model equation for underemployed migration (*Urban Dynamics*, equation 1, p. 135):

$$UA.KL=(U.K+L.K)(UAN)(AMMP.K) \qquad\qquad 1,R$$

$$UAN=.05 \qquad\qquad 1.1,C$$

UA	– UNDEREMPLØYED ARRIVALS (MEN/YEAR)
U	– UNDEREMPLØYED (MEN)
L	– LABØR (MEN)
UAN	– UNDEREMPLØYED ARRIVALS NØRMAL (FRACTIØN/ YEAR)
AMMP	– ATTRACTIVENESS-FØR-MIGRATIØN MULTIPLIER PERCEIVED (DIMENSIØNLESS)

In this equation the rate of underemployed arrivals UA depends on three factors:

> The first is the sum of underemployed and labor populations, which is here taken to represent the size and activity of the urban area which attract people from the outside. The second term UAN is a "normal" multiplier which represents the fraction of existing inhabitants U + L that would come to the area each year. With a UAN value of .05 in Equation 1.1, the statement is made that under normal circumstances the inflow to the area would represent 5% of the underemployed plus labor inhabitants . . . [AMMP] . . . is a modulating term representing the attractiveness of the area compared to normal. The normal value of AMMP is 1. A more attractive area will have a multiplier lower than 1. As the area becomes more or less attractive relative to its surrounding environment, the multiplier value changes. [*Urban Dynamics*, pp. 135–136]

In equation 1, the underemployed arrivals normal UAN embodies the intrinsic qualities of an urban area such as geographic location, climatic conditions, and historical background. Such attributes are not likely to change significantly over time in their influence on migration. In general, each urban area should have a UAN characterizing its unique qualities. An important point, then, is that no single value of UAN would be necessarily representative of all urban areas. For example, San Francisco, because of its favorable location and climate, might have a 5 percent per year normal population influx while Alamogordo,

New Mexico, having a less attractive climate and location, might have a lower than 1 percent normal in-migration rate.[7]

If one should attempt to derive a parameter such as UAN from data over a cross-section of twenty cities, the results would be inapplicable to any particular city.[8] The parameter estimate from cross-sectional analysis might represent an *average* value of UAN over several cities rather than a unique estimate for any single urban area. Furthermore, each set of cities forming a cross-section would, in general, produce a different estimate of UAN. From the standpoint of the *Urban Dynamics* model, the adequacy of any parameter estimate derived from cross-sectional data must be assessed relative to the model's purpose and use. A cross-sectional estimate cannot be used with confidence, for example, when attempting to adapt the *Urban Dynamics* model to a particular city. However, if the parameter were to be used in the generic *Urban Dynamics* model, then the estimate obtained from cross-sectional data might be generally adequate. Even in the latter case, however, it should be recalled that parameter estimates derived through cross-sectional analysis may vary widely according to the grouping of cities comprising the cross-section. For a generic model, therefore, cross-sectional estimates may often be no more appropriate than heuristic estimates of the parameters of an "average" city.

The value of cross-sectional data in urban modeling needs to be examined more closely in the future. For example, experiments using data from a dynamic model with known structure might be conducted to assess the reliability of cross-sectional estimates. Procedures of synthetic data analysis are often used in empirical research, but they have rarely been utilized to address basic methodological questions.

8.4 Difficulties Involved in Estimating Nonlinear Relationships Containing Significant Time Delays

The statistical estimation of long delays in the perception of information, formation of expectations, and flow of materials has been recognized as an important focus for econometric research for a considerable period.[9] Nevertheless, the challenges for estimation posed by the extensive use of information delays within highly nonlinear formulations in the *Urban Dynamics* model appear to equal or exceed available estimation techniques; this section describes one such difficulty, taking as an example the influence of perceived economic mobility on migration as hypothesized in *Urban Dynamics*.

To deal with information delays, the statistical model builder must employ a distributed-lag formulation, which is simply a scheme for applying varying weights to past values of data. For a data distribution covering a long period of time, use of the distributed lag requires the estimation of a large number of parameters (corresponding to each weight). For example, a distributed-lag formulation for the potential migrant's perception of economic mobility would require lagged values stretching at least 20 years into the past if the actual delay time constant were on the order of 10 years. A frequently employed technique to reduce the number of parameters to be estimated assumes that adjacent weights form a geometrically declining series (which corresponds exactly to a first-order exponential delay). The use of this weighting scheme permits a simple algebraic transformation (known as the Koyck transformation) on the equation.[10] Unfortunately, the Koyck transformation is inapplicable to nonlinear formulations such as occur frequently in the *Urban Dynamics* model. These formulations are characterized by the occurrence of a lag distribution divided or multiplied by another variable, which generally renders the Koyck transformation inapplicable.

The difficulty of estimating delays within the urban model is well illustrated by the presence of underemployed mobility UM in the model equation for underemployed arrivals UA (*Urban Dynamics*, equation 4, p. 138). Forrester hypothesizes that the potential migrant's perception of upward economic mobility plays a role in his migration decision. In the model, the impact of the mobility of the underemployed on migration depends upon the average percentage rate of upward mobility. This average mobility rate (called underemployed mobility UM) is computed as the perceived flow of underemployed to labor UTLP divided by the level of underemployed U. Underemployed to labor perceived UTLP represents a 10-year averaging of the actual flow of underemployed to labor UTL. Migration is assumed to depend on the average mobility rate since the actual rate is an instantaneous quantity that can be perceived only through an information-smoothing process.

How can one estimate the influence of mobility on underemployed in-migration? An analytic representation for underemployed mobility UM is given in equation (1). As stated previously, UM is defined as the ratio of UTLP to U, where UTLP is a distributed-lag function of UTL:

$$\mathrm{UM}(t) = \sum_{\tau=0}^{\infty} \frac{\beta \lambda^\tau \,\mathrm{UTL}(t - \tau)}{\mathrm{U}(t)}, \tag{1}$$

where

$$\beta = 1/\mathrm{UTLPT}$$

$$\lambda = 1 - \beta$$

To apply the Koyck transformation to equation (1) involves subtracting $\lambda[\mathrm{UM}(t\text{-}1)]$ from both sides of the equation. This transformation would succeed in truncating the lag distribution on UTL if $\mathrm{U}(t)$ were not in the denominator of equation (1). However, with $\mathrm{U}(t)$ present, the Koyck transformation results in the following equation:

$$\mathrm{UM}(t) - \lambda[\mathrm{UM}(t - 1)] = \sum_{\tau=0}^{\infty} \frac{\beta \lambda^\tau \,\mathrm{UTL}(t - \tau)}{\mathrm{U}(t)} \tag{2}$$

$$- \sum_{\tau=0}^{\infty} \frac{\beta \lambda^{\tau+1} \,\mathrm{UTL}(t - \tau - 1)}{\mathrm{U}(t - 1)}$$

It can be seen that no cancellation of terms occurs in equation (2) unless U(t) = U(*t* − 1); the transformation is unsuccessful in reducing the number of parameters to be estimated.[11]

The estimation of delay-time constants in the context of highly nonlinear formulations of the sort discussed here represents an important area for future econometric research. It appears, at present, that the extensive attention devoted to distributed-lag estimation has failed to address this issue adequately.

8.5 Problems in Drawing Statistical Inferences Regarding the Error Process of a Continuous Dynamic System

In applying statistical estimation techniques to system dynamics models it is essential that the modeler be able to draw reliable inferences regarding the time structure of noise present in the system. It is well known, for example, that the ordinary least squares estimator will not, even with unlimited data, yield accurate parameter estimates for a dynamic model if the noise present in the real system is "autocorrelated," that is, if the current value of the noise is correlated with its previous value.[12] The statistical model builder can often compensate for the presence of autocorrelated noise through the use of more sophisticated estimation techniques; however, the ability of these techniques to correct for autocorrelated noise rests on the conditions (1) that autocorrelation be detectable in the first place; (2) that the model builder be able to gauge the structure of the autocorrelated noise; and (3) that the model builder be able to measure the degree of his success in correcting for autocorrelation. Typically, all three of these inferences are drawn from an analysis of the residuals of an estimation—the discrepancies between historical data and model behavior obtained using estimated parameter values. Therefore, the entire process of detecting and correcting for autocorrelated noise can be said to rest on the presence within the residuals of the significant characteristics of the actual process noise. This section explains why, in working with continuous dynamic systems such as the *Urban Dynamics* model, the model builder may be unable to correct for autocorrelated noise.

In contrast to the estimation of time delays, the basic issue raised in this section has been all but totally ignored in the econometrics literature. This is not surprising, because recognition of the issue comes from the assumption made in system dynamics modeling that social systems belong to the class of continuous-time state-variable feedback systems. This class of systems can be represented by the first-order feedback system in equation (3):

$$\dot{L}(t) = f(L(t)) + \epsilon(t) \tag{3}$$

In the above equation, L is a level variable that changes as a result of a continuous process of integration; ϵ is a zero-mean noise input. A simple (linear) example of such a system is shown in Figure 2. In Figure 2, the deterministic component of the rate of increase in the level L depends upon L multiplied by a constant α. This basic structure resembles several formulations within the *Urban Dynamics* model; for example, in the model the rate of underemployed in-

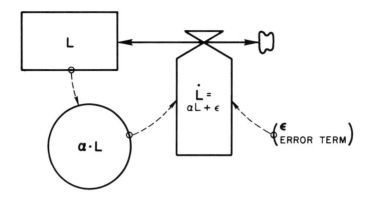

Figure 2 A first-order feedback system with noise

migration depends on the level of underemployed, as a measure of both job availability and the size and drawing power of the city (*Urban Dynamics* pp. 20–30).

To estimate the parameter α, the system in Figure 2 must be represented as discrete:

$$\Delta L(t) = \text{SI}[\alpha L(t - \text{SI}) + \epsilon(t - \text{SI})], \tag{4}$$

where

$$\Delta L(t) = L(t) - L(t - \text{SI}).$$

SI represents the sampling interval of available data—the period of one month, one quarter, or one year separating the available observations of the system. For simplicity, it will be assumed that $\text{SI}=1$ month in the following illustration, that is, the available data are monthly.

As noted, a critical condition for obtaining an accurate ordinary least squares estimate of α in equation (4) is that the error term $\epsilon(t)$ not be autocorrelated. If $\epsilon(t - 2)$ is correlated with $\epsilon(t - 1)$, then $\epsilon(t - 1)$ and $L(t - 1)$ will also be correlated. This occurs because $\epsilon(t - 2)$ is a cause of change in $L(t - 1)$. Thus autocorrelation in ϵ produces correlation in $L(t - 1)$ and $\epsilon(t - 1)$, thereby violating a general condition for obtaining accurate (unbiased and consistent) estimates of α. Now, to detect the presence of autocorrelation in ϵ, the residuals of the estimation are formed as follows:

$$u(t) \equiv \Delta L(t) - \hat{\alpha} L(t - 1), \tag{5}$$

where $\hat{\alpha}$ is the estimated value of α. Forming the product of the first and second residual terms results in:

$$u(1) \equiv \Delta L(1) - \hat{\alpha} L(0) = \epsilon(0) + L(0)[\alpha - \hat{\alpha}] \tag{6}$$

$$u(2) \equiv \Delta L(2) - \hat{\alpha} L(1) = \epsilon(1) + L(1)[\alpha - \hat{\alpha}] \tag{7}$$

$$u(1) \cdot u(2) = \epsilon(0) \cdot \epsilon(1) + \epsilon(0) \cdot L(1) \cdot (\alpha - \hat{\alpha}) + \tag{8}$$

$$\epsilon(1) \cdot L(0) \cdot (\alpha - \hat{\alpha}) + L(0) \cdot L(1) \cdot (\alpha - \hat{\alpha})^2$$

The product expressed in equation (8) is a measure of autocorrelation in the input of equation (4). In general, if the expected value of $\epsilon(t) \cdot \epsilon(t - 1)$ is zero, then the noise is "white" or completely free of autocorrelation. Conversely, if the expected value of $\epsilon(t) \cdot \epsilon(t - 1)$ is nonzero, then the error term has some (positive or negative) autocorrelation. As can be seen from equation (8) the measured autocorrelation in the residuals $u(t)$ will approach the product $\epsilon(0) \cdot \epsilon(1)$ as $\hat{\alpha}$ approaches α. That is, the measured autocorrelation in the residuals becomes completely attributable to the autocorrelation in $\epsilon(t)$ as the parameter estimate $\hat{\alpha}$ approaches the true value of α.

However, equation (4) is only an approximation to the correct system—equation (3)—which is identical to that of equation (4), except that it is continuous; the true system operates over an infinitesimally small discrete interval rather than over the interval SI. That is, the true system can be represented as:

$$L(t) = \lim_{\delta \to 0}[L(t - \delta) + \delta(L(t - \delta) + \epsilon(t - \delta))] \tag{9}$$

How does the fact that the true system is continuous affect the residuals? This effect can be illustrated by setting the interval δ in equation (9) to one-half and forming the product of $u(1) \cdot u(2)$ once again; reducing δ in this way more nearly approximates the continuous system described by equation (9) with δ close to zero.[13] The results for the residuals $u(t)$ are given in equation (10), (11), and (12):

$$u(1) \equiv \Delta L(1) - \hat{\alpha} L(0) \tag{10}$$

$$= .5[\alpha L(.5) + \epsilon(.5)] - \hat{\alpha} L(0)$$

$$= .5\{\alpha[L(0)(1 + .5\alpha) + .5\epsilon(0)] + \epsilon(.5)\} - \hat{\alpha} L(0)$$

$$= [.25\alpha\epsilon(0) + .5\epsilon(.5)] + L(0)[.5\alpha(1 + .5\alpha) - \hat{\alpha}]$$

$$u(2) \equiv \Delta L(2) - \hat{\alpha} L(1) \tag{11}$$

$$= [.25\alpha\epsilon(1) + .5\epsilon(1.5)] + L(1)[.5\alpha(1 + .5\alpha) - \hat{\alpha}]$$

$$u(1) \cdot u(2) = [.25\alpha\epsilon(0) + .5\epsilon(.5)][.25\alpha\epsilon(1) + .5\epsilon(1.5)] \tag{12}$$

$$+ [.25\alpha\epsilon(0) + .5\epsilon(.5)] \cdot L(1) \cdot [.5\alpha(1 + .5\alpha) - \hat{\alpha}]$$

$$+ [.25\alpha\epsilon(1) + .5\epsilon(1.5)] \cdot L(0) \cdot [.5\alpha(1 + .5\alpha) - \hat{\alpha}]$$

$$+ L(0) \cdot L(1) \cdot [.5\alpha(1 + \alpha) - \hat{\alpha}]^2$$

The residuals $u(1)$ and $u(2)$ are still defined as in equations (6) and (7); but now the fact that $L(1)$, for example, depends on $L(.5)$ rather than on $L(0)$ alters the product $u(1) \cdot u(2)$. Equation (12) should be compared with equation (8) to gauge the implications of changing the interval δ for inferences drawn from the time structure of the residuals. It can be seen that, even if $\hat{\alpha} = \alpha$, the product $u(1) \cdot u(2)$ in equation (12) does not accurately reflect the autocorrelation of ϵ in that system. For example, if there is no autocorrelation in the real noise inputs (that is, $E[\epsilon(t) \cdot \epsilon(t - .5)] = 0$ for all t), the residuals of equation (12) will show a strong autocorrelation arising from the $\epsilon(.5) \cdot L(1)$ and the $L(0) \cdot L(1)$ products in the second and third terms, respectively, on the right-hand side of that equation. Both products involve variables that are highly correlated; $\epsilon(.5)$ and $L(1)$ are correlated as a consequence of the causality of the system, while $L(0)$ and $L(1)$ are correlated because of the feedback structure of the system. More fundamentally, it can be shown that autocorrelation arises in this example as a result of the general property of continuous dynamic systems to integrate white noise inputs and thereby transform them into autocorrelated noise. This property generally implies that the statistical analyst may not be able to discern whether or not the system he is studying has an uncorrelated noise input and may not, therefore, obtain accurate parameter estimates.

The problems raised in this section are of a fairly fundamental nature and go beyond questions of particular estimators or estimation techniques. If one cannot draw reliable inferences from the residuals of an estimation regarding the characteristics of the error process, then any method of estimation whose application depends upon knowledge of those characteristics (which includes all methods known to the authors) rests on tenuous ground. Research needs to be done to assess the sensitivity of standard autocorrelation estimators (for example, the Durbin-Watson statistic for first-order autocorrelation) to this type of difficulty.[14] It is possible that new estimators can be developed that will overcome this problem; but insofar as the real problem lies with the assumed continuous nature of social systems and the properties of feedback systems to transform white noise inputs into autocorrelated outputs, the challenge seems formidable.

8.6 Conclusion

There is little dispute regarding the desirability of utilizing statistical methods to derive parameters and functional relationships within the *Urban Dynamics* model. However, the characteristics of the migration equations in *Urban Dynamics* require that one exercise considerable caution in applying current estimation techniques to them. First, to draw useful statistical inferences of the overall shape of the relationship, a fairly wide range of values of the independent variable relative to the degree of nonlinearity in a functional relationship is required. Unfortunately, wide data dispersion for a single city may be difficult to amass. For instance, older cities that have passed their growth phase are not likely to display wide variations in most endogenous variables.

Second, analysts must be aware of the assumptions underlying the use of cross-sectional estimations. Any parameter derived from cross-sectional data must realistically be interpreted as an average for the collection of cities within the sample; the derived parameter cannot be applied directly to any one urban area.

Third, estimated equations should include the time lags and information delays that influence behavior within a social system. Conventional estimation techniques, however, cannot handle certain cases of delays embedded within nonlinear relationships. Further work must be done before this problem can be easily overcome.

Finally, the estimation of parameters within a continuous dynamic system poses several formal statistical problems. For example, because the analyst may not, in general, be able to discern the time character of noise within a dynamic system, he may be unable to derive accurate estimates of the parameters of that system.

The important question to ask is, "How significant are these sources of error and difficulty in deriving parameters in the *Urban Dynamics* model?" The model's purpose offers some insight into this question. The *Urban Dynamics* model is a policy model designed to describe the direction in which various policies are likely to move the urban system. Because the overall qualitative behavior of the generic urban model tends to be insensitive to most parameter values over a wide range, the effort exerted generating exact parameter estimates may be marginally productive relative to the model's use. However, as the *Urban Dynamics* model is adapted to describe specific cities or extended to analyze shorter-term policy outcomes, statistical techniques may prove useful in formalizing levels of confidence in the predictive capabilities of the model.

At the present time, the applicability of statistical techniques to nonlinear state-variable models has only been preliminarily assessed. The coupling of statistical estimation with feedback modeling techniques may yet provide a cogent tool for analyzing social behavior and policy. But progress in this area will require more thorough consideration of the properties of feedback systems and isolation of the unique challenges they present for estimation methods than has been seen to date.

Appendix

An outgrowth of much of the empirical research into the phenomenon of population movement has been the creation of a number of analytical models of migration. These models have assumed that migration can be explained in terms of origin-destination differentials in employment and wages, as well as demographic variables such as age and education.[15] Existing migration data have lent considerable support to these models.

At present, the two models most similar to Forrester's migration formulation are those of Lowry and Pack. Both the Lowry and the Pack models are single-destination (origin) models as distinguished from place-to-place models. The latter considers total flows regardless of origin (destination). Single-destination models most nearly approximate the conceptual structure of Forrester's model.

Variable Type	Lowry Model	Pack Model	Forrester Model
Dependent	dM_i*—net change in population 15–64 attributable to migration-rate per 1000, 1950–1960 in SMSA (i)	W—white migrants to central city, 1955–1960 as a % of central city population[1]	UA—underemployed arrivals rate
Population size	dP_i—net change in number of residents 15–64 years of age in absence of migration	P—population	L—labor population U—underemployed population
Employment	dQ_i—net change in civilian non-agricultural employment	UN—unemployment rate in metropolitan area, 1960	UR—underemployed/ job ratio
Education	dE_i—net change in number of school enrollees 14–29 years old	ME—median years of education, population 25 years or older	UM—underemployed mobility
Income	dI_i—change in median income for families and un-related individuals (% 1950 median income)	Y—median family income y*—% change in median family income, 1950–1960	
Miscellaneous	dA_i—net change in number of Armed Forces personnel		
Housing		HO—percentage of housing stock owner occupied HU—percentage of housing stock unsound	UHR underemployed/ housing ratio UHPR—underemployed- housing program rate
Tax		T—per capita taxes EX—educational expenditure per capita ADC—average monthly ADC payment per recipient	TPCR—tax per capita ratio

[1] Only the version concerned with white migrants is described here.

[2] The variables used here are the basis for the multipliers found in *Urban Dynamics*, Figure 2–6, p. 22. For simplicity, the perception time delay AMMPT is omitted. Precise definitions of each of the variables would require too much space to reproduce here, so only variable names are used.

Figure 3 Migration variables

Figure 3 contains the variables used in the migration models of Lowry, Pack, and Forrester. With the exception of Lowry's net change in median income variable (dI) and Pack's percentage change in median family income variable (y^*), none of the models share variables having identical definitions. The Lowry and Pack models are based on different sources of migration data: Lowry uses the 52 largest SMSAs in the United States, while Pack uses data for 20 central cities. Their equations are as follows:

$$dM^*_i = a_0 + a_1\, dp_i + a_2\, dQ_i + a_3\, dA_i + a_4\, dE_i + a_5\, dI_i + u \qquad \text{(Lowry)}$$

$$W = a + b \cdot Y + c \cdot Y^* + d \cdot UN + e \cdot ME + f \cdot HO + g \cdot HU + h \cdot EX$$
$$+ i \cdot T + j \cdot ADC + k \cdot P \qquad\qquad\qquad \text{(Pack)}$$

Notes

1. The appendix to this paper contains a brief description of two econometric models to familiarize the reader with examples of empirical migration research.

2. Examples of cities that have neared population equilibrium can be found in Walter W. Schroeder III and John E. Strongman, "Adapting *Urban Dynamics* to Lowell," Reading 16 in this volume, Figure 2.

3. For substantially "noisy" data over a narrow range, even the slope of the relationship over the observed range might be indeterminate. The model builder, however, would be alerted to the impossibility of drawing reliable inferences from the data by the high variances of individual coefficient estimates.

4. It might be argued that any significant variation present in the data taken from cities in their equilibrium stage originates mainly from exogenous (environmental) forces. Exogenous factors such as national economic conditions, or random events such as war, affect the area but are not generated within it. Since the model measures relative attractiveness, any exogenous factors impinging equally on the area and on its environment would not affect the area's relative attractiveness. To be applicable to the urban model, historical data for the city would need to be normalized (relative to regional or national values) in order to measure the relative attractiveness of the city compared with its surroundings.

5. The use of cross-sectional data per se does not guarantee that a wider dispersion of observations will be obtained. If, for example, data were to be collected for several cities, each within roughly the same phase of its life cycle, then the narrow dispersion of available data would still persist. Some evidence of this narrow dispersion is available in cross-sectional census data on occupancy distributions within urban areas. Data from the 1960 Bureau of the Census is reproduced below. The numbers in the table give the percentage of the total housing stock falling within different occupancy ranges for ten American Standard Metropolitan Statistical Areas (SMSAs).

SMSA	Persons per Room		
	0.50 or less	0.51 to 0.75	0.76 to 1
Boston	46	25	22
Los Angeles	45	23	22
New York	36	28	24
Dallas	40	26	22
Chicago	41	24	25
Seattle	45	24	23
Philadelphia	50	25	17
Detroit	42	23	26
Baltimore	46	24	20
Buffalo	47	24	21

6. The economics literature contains some discussion of problems in the interchangeable use of cross-sectional and time-series data; see, for example, Edwin Kuh, "The Validity of Cross-Sectionally Estimated Behavior Equations in Time Series Applications," *Econometrica* 27 (1959): pp. 197–214. Kuh cautions against the use of cross-sectional data unless time series are also available.

7. A statistical comparison of the UAN values for different cities would require suitable "normalization" of all the explicit migration factors hypothesized in *Urban Dynamics*. For example, the normal migration rates of two areas might be compared only when conditions of job availability, housing availability, upward mobility, and tax assessments were identical between the two areas, so that differences in attractive qualities must reside in inherent physical or geographical factors.

8. If, additionally, large areas such as SMSAs (Standard Metropolitan Statistical Areas) were used in the cross-sectional analysis, then an aggregated variable representing an average of central-city and suburban conditions would not adequately reflect or measure central-city attributes. Moreover, there is no reason to believe that the determinants of migration to a region or a large metropolitan area are precisely the same as those governing migration to a central city.

9. An examination of much of the current migration literature reveals that little attention has been given to either the specification or the estimation of temporal lags. See, for example, Ira S. Lowry, *Migration and Metropolitan Growth: Two Analytical Models* (San Francisco: Chandler, 1966); V. Renshaw, "The Role of Migration in Labor Market Adjustment," Ph.D. thesis, M.I.T. Department of Economics, 1970; and J. R. Pack, "Models of Population Movement and Urban Policy," *IEEE Transactions on Systems, Man, and Cybernetics* 2, no. 2 (April 1972): 191–195. The Lowry and Pack models, for instance, assume that there is no significant displacement in time between a change in internal conditions and their subsequent impact on migration into or out of the urban area. For a short study interval (representative of most migration studies) ignoring temporal lags could cause significant misspecification of real-world processes—changes in job conditions during the study interval may not properly explain migration flows within the same period of time. Alternatively, significant changes in migration during the study interval may be attributable largely to conditions existing prior to the study.

10. See J. Johnston, *Econometric Methods* (New York: McGraw-Hill, 1972), pp. 298–300; also Zvi Griliches, "Distributed Lags: A Survey," *Econometrica* 35 (1967): pp. 6–49.

11. Similar estimation problems arise, for example, because of the nonlinear (multiplicative) formulations in the model equations for the attractiveness for migration multiplier perceived AMMP (*Urban Dynamics*, pp. 20–30) and underemployed to labor UTL (*Urban Dynamics*, pp. 147–152).

12. In this section, the term autocorrelated will be used to refer to first-order autocorrelation, i.e., the correlation of successive values of a discrete random process. The presence of higher-order autocorrelation structures in the noise inputs to a system will complicate the effects caused by first-order autocorrelation but in no way alters the basic problems discussed here.

13. The reduction of δ in equation (9) to approximate a continuous process is the basis for the computer simulation of system dynamics models. The interval δ corresponds to the "solution interval" DT as explained in Jay W. Forrester, *Principles of Systems* (Cambridge, Mass.: Wright-Allen Press, 1968), chap. 5.

14. The applicability of statistical estimation techniques to system dynamics models is currently the focus of a series of experiments being conducted by Peter M. Senge under the sponsorship of the Rockefeller Brothers Fund. The objective of these experiments is to take a comparatively simple dynamic model with known structure, and use synthetic (model-generated) data to examine the effects of measurement noise, sampling phenomena, specification error, and other conditions of imperfect information on the capability of statistical procedures to recover the parameters of that system.

15. This type of model can be described as a place-to-place migration model. Examples are seen in Lowry, *Migration and Metropolitan Growth*, chap. 2, p. 7.

9
Metropolitan Population Growth, Land Area, and *Urban Dynamics* Model

Wilbert Wils

One of the key assumptions of the Urban Dynamics *model is that population growth within any urban area is ultimately limited by the availability of land. Reflecting this assumption, the model examines the processes of urban growth within a fixed land area that is independent of the political boundary of the city. Although the primary focus of the model is on a central-city land area,* Urban Dynamics *illustrates how the onset of urban decay gives rise to suburban growth and outward metropolitan expansion.*

To analyze the influence of land availability on metropolitan development, Dr. Wilbert Wils has examined population statistics for a sequence of concentric areas around central Boston. He found that population growth patterns in Metropolitan Boston were consistent with the Urban Dynamics *theory, as growth continued longer in each progressively larger segment of land. This paper provides a beginning framework for a future system dynamics study of metropolitan development.*

9
Metropolitan Population Growth, Land Area, and the *Urban Dynamics* Model

9.1 Introduction

Urban Dynamics describes the principal interactions between housing, population, and industry within a geographically fixed sector of an urban area and portrays the city's interaction with its external environment. In simulations of the urban model, as the city's land area becomes filled, population and industrial growth are curtailed, leading to a period of urban decline and eventual stabilization. Over the course of time, when low land availability inhibits the city's development, the aging of industrial and residential structures leads to an unfavorable balance between population and employment; housing "filter-down" leads to increased residential densities concurrently as the city's job base deteriorates.

A major assumption in the *Urban Dynamics* model is that the major forces restricting continued growth of a city can be subsumed in a tightening of the availability of urban land. Not explicitly treated in the model, for example, are transportation difficulties, shortages of resources or energy, insufficient diversity in local industry, or inadequate consumption demand.

The purpose of this paper is not primarily to demonstrate the appropriateness of the causal structure in the *Urban Dynamics* model but, rather, to show the consistency of the assumptions in *Urban Dynamics* with the observed urban growth patterns in a concrete case. In particular, time-series data for population of the Greater Boston area are examined for increasingly large concentric areas around the old central city.

It will be shown that the assumptions underlying the *Urban Dynamics* model lead consistently to a theory of metropolitan growth whereby vigorous expansion initially occurs in the central city, but growth later moves outward to the periphery of the city where population densities are lower. In this way a "tidal wave of metropolitan expansion"[1] is generated.

The analysis reported in this paper shows that a wave of outward movement indeed characterizes the Greater Boston area. Similar examinations for other areas have been documented in the urban literature,[2] where time-series data for population density as a function of the distance to the central city have been examined. The conclusions stemming from these observations are well reflected in the following quotation of Colin Clark:

> The preparation and detailed study of dozens of density maps is an overwhelming task unless we can begin with some hypothesis which will enable us to organize and simplify the data. We can begin with two generalizations the validity of which is now universally recognized:
>
> 1. In every large city, excluding the central business zone, which has few resident inhabitants, we have districts of dense population in the interior, with density falling off progressively as we proceed to the outer suburbs.
>
> 2. In most (but not all) cities, as time goes on, density tends to fall in the most populous inner suburbs, and to rise in the outer suburbs, and the whole city tends to "spread itself out."[3]

The present study is complementary to the work of W. W. Schroeder and J. Strongman who report on patterns of population change in 18 American central cities.[4]

9.2 Patterns of Metropolitan Population Growth

Theoretical Considerations.   Large cities tend to be characterized by a geographic distribution of people, houses, and enterprises over a wide metropolitan area. Vigorous growth occurs in the central city until the available land area is almost fully occupied. Once this occurs, new industrial and residential development is directed outside the central city, frequently to proximate suburban towns. As far as new industry is established in the central city, it is largely of a different type than before, with service industries replacing the former manufacturing industries. These service industries frequently do not provide many jobs for the unskilled in the city, as they tend to maintain high proportions of white-collar employment. Also, within the central city, housing ages and filters down to generate an increased stock of low-cost housing that competes with industry for the city's remaining land. As a direct result of these influences, the central urban area eventually stagnates and its population diminishes. Regional growth continues, however, as larger and larger areas within the metropolitan region become populated.

Urban Dynamics examines the processes of growth and decay within a fixed urban land area:

> The area could be the political boundary of a city but usually will differ. The area treated here would be only a part of our larger cities. The appropriate area is small enough so that cultural, economic, and educational interchange is possible between its component populations. It could be a suburban area or the core area of a city but probably not an area containing both. [p. 2]

As stated above, the *Urban Dynamics* model does not apply to a whole metropolitan area but rather to a part of the metropolitan region. Therefore, it is not directly possible to show that the urban model implies a tidal wave of metropolitan expansion. But a system dynamics model should not be separated from the basic assumptions underlying it, and a theory of shifting growth rings at the periphery of the city is well compatible with the hypotheses on which the *Urban Dynamics* model is based.

Simulations of the *Urban Dynamics* model for a fixed land area exhibit a population that at first increases and eventually decreases and stabilizes. If the land area within the model were increased, the expansion of the population, given the same initial conditions, would continue somewhat longer but undergo a similar long-run trend. If one thinks of this experiment as representing two subregions of a metropolitan area, that is, a central city and a somewhat larger area, and if we also assume that originally the central area has the relatively larger population, the following picture emerges. The population in both areas increases at first. But when at some point the inner area is filled up and stagnates, growth shifts toward outlying suburban areas. Much the same reasoning can be applied to a set of nested areas around the central city, and the analysis leads quite logically to a theory of shifting growth rings.

The interesting point in the preceding demonstration is that metropolitan growth can be described conceptually by the superposition of a series of nested urban dynamics models that all interact only within themselves, and in which growth is hampered only by a lack of land. Growth shifts progressively outward from the central city to the inner suburbs, to the outer suburbs, and to the greater metropolitan area. Without exploring this approach in great detail, we shall proceed to show how the available empirical evidence supports the outlined theory.

Techniques of Measurement and Data. With Boston proper taken as center, a system of 8 concentric rings was drawn with an approximate width of 2.5 miles

Figure 1 Boston and outlying concentric rings

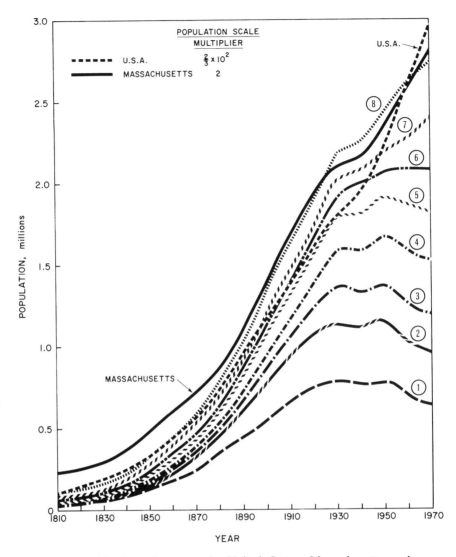

Figure 2 Number of persons in United States, Massachusetts, and areas around Boston

each. The rings were formed as conglomerates of towns, and the towns residing in each ring were identified. The smallest ring, numbered 0, is not a ring proper but consists only of the city of Boston. The last ring extends well beyond Route 128, which is a major beltway and industrial area surrounding Boston. The rings are numbered 0 through 7, with the index increasing as the rings become farther from the central city. In addition, 8 regions are formed, numbered 1 through 8. Each region consists of the union of all rings having a lower index than the index of the region (see Figure 1).

The aggregate number of inhabitants of each ring and region was calculated from the decennial U.S. census data from 1800 through 1970. In addition, the relative (percentage) growth of each area was computed.

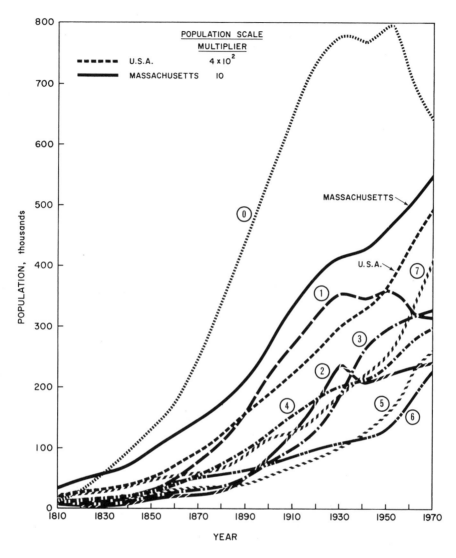

Figure 3 Number of persons in United States, Massachusetts, and rings around Boston

The results are represented graphically in Figures 2–5. For reference purposes, additional population data for the United States and Massachusetts were added to the figures. Figures 2 and 3 show the number of inhabitants in each of the regions around Boston.

Figure 2 shows that growth in the geographic areas around the central city has tended to continue longer within each progressively larger land area. Boston proper reached its peak population in 1930. Regions 2–5 all peaked in 1950. Growth in region 6 is leveling off in the early 1970s , while regions 7 and 8 continue to expand. The resulting pattern is that growth shifts over time from the center to the periphery of the metropolitan area. This pattern of shifting growth

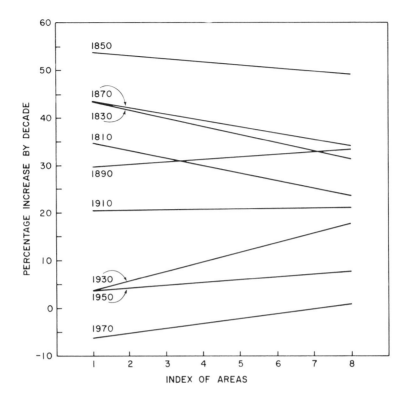

Figure 4 Regression lines giving percentage of population growth by decade
for areas as a function of the index of the areas

is also illustrated in Figure 3. Ring 1 is currently no longer experiencing population growth. Population in ring 2 has begun to level off, and it appears that rings 3 and 4 are undergoing a similar transition. Growth in ring 5 also is slowing down, but rings 6 and 7 still exhibit a rapidly expanding population.

Much the same conclusions follow from Figures 4 and 5, which exhibit regression lines indicating the percentage of population increase by decade for the regions and the rings, respectively.

In the beginning of the twentieth century, metropolitan growth shifted significantly from the inner rings around Boston to the outer rings. In addition, the absolute rate of growth has since decreased in all except the most outward rings. Since 1950 the inner rings have been losing inhabitants, while growth continues in the outer rings and in the larger metropolitan areas.

In Figure 6 some older population time series are given for Boston and for the various towns that have historically been annexed by the city. The data show that the observed phenomenon of shifting growth began very early within the Boston metropolitan area. Boston proper, East Boston, South Boston, and Charlestown all reached their maximum population in the early nineteen hundreds.[5]

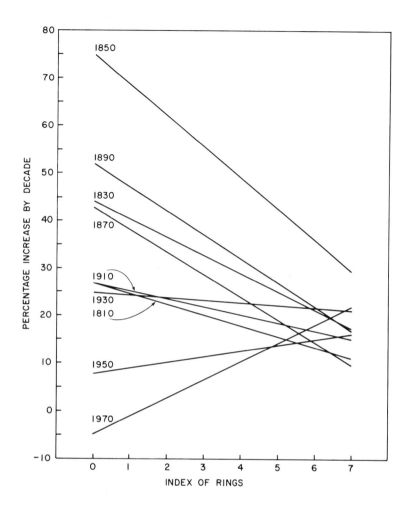

Figure 5   Regression lines giving percentage of population growth by decade for rings as a function of the index of the rings

The "tidal wave of metropolitan expansion" observed here for the Greater Boston region has been carefully documented for many other metropolitan areas in this country, as is clear from the quotation by Colin Clark in the introduction to this paper.

9.3 Conclusions

First, the data exhibited in this paper show that growth patterns within the Greater Boston area are generally consistent with the outcomes of the *Urban Dynamics* model. The influence of land availability appears to be a major factor in regulating population expansion within fixed geographic areas. Moreover, the population of the larger areas surrounding Boston exhibits the characteristic population overshoot shown in the *Urban Dynamics* model.

| | | | | | Annexations | | | | | | | | | |
Census Years	Census taken by—	Boston Including Annexations	Boston Proper Settled, 1630; Made a City, 1822	Annexed Territory	East Boston Proper (Excluding the Islands) (1637)	The Islands.	South Boston (1804)	Washington Village (1855)	Roxbury (1867)	Dorchester (1869)	West Roxbury (1873)	Brighton (1873)	Charlestown (1873)	Hyde Park (1912)
1790	U.S.	18,320	18,038	282	—	282	—	—	2,226	1,722	—	—	1,583	—
1800	U.S.	24,937	24,655	282	—	282	—	—	2,765	2,347	—	—	2,751	—
1810	U.S.	33,787	32,896	891	18	519	354	—	3,669	2,930	—	608	4,959	—
1820	U.S.	43,298	—	—	24	264	—	—	4,135	3,684	—	702	6,591	—
1825	City	58,277	56,003	2,274	—	—	1,986	—	—	—	—	—	—	—
1830	U.S.	61,392	—	—	—	344	—	—	5,247	4,074	—	972	8,783	—
1835	City	78,603	72,057	6,546	607	277	5,595	—	—	—	—	—	—	—
1840	U.S.	93,383	85,475	7,908	1,455	292	6,176	—	9,089	4,875	—	1,425	11,484	—
1845	City	114,366	99,036	15,330	5,018	325	10,020	—	—	—	—	—	—	—
1850	U.S.	136,881	113,421	23,460	9,526	530	13,309	—	18,361	7,969	—	2,356	17,216	—
1855	State	160,490	126,296	34,194	15,433	1,000	16,912	1,319	18,469	8,340	4,812	2,895	21,700	—
1860	U.S.	177,840	133,563	44,277	18,356	1,300	24,921	—	25,137	9,769	6,310	3,375	25,065	—
1865	State	192,318	141,083	51,235	20,572	1,700	29,363	—	28,426	10,717	6,912	3,854	26,399	—
1870	U.S.	250,526	138,781	111,745	23,816	1,927	39,215	—	34,753	12,261	8,686	4,967	28,323	4,136
1875	State	341,919	140,669	201,250	27,420	1,545	54,147	—	50,429	15,788	11,783	6,200	33,556	6,316
1880	U.S.	362,839	147,075	215,764	28,381	2,139	56,369	—	57,123	17,890	14,032	6,693	33,734	7,088
1885	State	390,393	147,138	243,255	29,280	—	61,534	—	65,965	20,717	17,424	8,523	37,673	8,376
1890	U.S.	448,477	161,330	287,147	36,930	—	66,791	—	78,411	29,638	24,997	12,032	38,348	10,193
1895	State	595,380	172,473	422,907	48,229	3,105	67,436	—	111,261	90,011	41,076	21,806	39,983	11,510
1900	U.S.	560,892	167,257	393,635	43,478	2,278	67,809	—	105,393	77,483	37,263	19,279	40,652	13,244
1905	State	595,380	172,473	422,907	48,229	3,105	67,436	—	111,261	90,011	41,076	21,806	39,983	14,510
1910	U.S.	670,585	193,274	477,311	55,085	3,403	71,703	—	117,727	115,780	45,594	26,575	41,444	15,507
1915	State	745,439	196,300	549,139	62,377	3,303	69,745	—	127,683	138,119	56,071	34,782	39,601	17,458
1920	U.S.	748,060	181,193	566,867	60,778	2,273	63,815	—	126,525	156,006	63,067	42,102	34,272	18,029
1925	State	779,620	172,101	607,519	64,069	2,465	64,803	—	129,883	167,015	73,621	47,900	37,918	19,845
1930	U.S.	781,188	151,818	629,370	59,242	2,212	58,039	—	122,509	187,103	88,327	56,362	31,663	23,913
1935	State	817,713	152,003	665,710	61,642	2,663	56,610	—	131,192	197,257	94,442	66,995	29,610	25,299

Figure 6 Population of Boston by geographical subdivisions, 1790–1935

Source: J. S. Davoren, "Cities and Towns," in *The Story of Massachusetts*, ed. D. L. Marsh and W. M. Clark, vol.3, chap. 72 (New York: American Heritage Society, 1938).

In several of the older metropolitan areas in the United States, stagnation and lack of land are extending beyond the core city into the nearest suburbs and creating the first signs of what has been called "the spreading great central crud." The situation is well sketched in the following quotations from Jack Rosenthal and Linda Greenhouse, respectively:

> In the distant exurban greenery, planners worry about how to channel new growth. In closer suburbs, officials struggle to show that age need not bring decay. In the closest, decay has already begun.[6]

> Thirty years ago, only 2 out of every 10 Americans lived in the suburbs. Now the suburbs claim 4 of every 10. Only recently have these people come to realize that the city they now live in—the new Outer City—is becoming the city they thought they had left behind, with many of the same problems and responsibilities.[7]

Second, some critics of the *Urban Dynamics* model have pointed to the shifting growth pattern within a metropolitan area as one of the major causes of the decline and stagnation in the central city. According to this viewpoint, the outward movement of the crest of the growth wave would originate in exogenous factors such as the introduction of the automobile.

> It has previously been observed that Forrester's city has no suburbs. Despite this lack, the city does show some behavior similar to that exhibited during recent years in many central cities as a result of the expansion of the suburbs. However, the processes causing this behavior are substantially different in the two cases. In real cities the increased availability of the private automobile has made possible a movement of both people and industry to the suburbs, thus tending to discourage further expansion of the total amount of housing and industry in many central cities.[8]

In *Urban Dynamics* the argument that metropolitan expansion generates urban decay is reversed; shifting metropolitan growth patterns are seen as a consequence of the filling up of increasingly large central areas and the concomitant spread of urban decay. It might, of course, be that improved transportation, along with other factors, tips the balance earlier in favor of suburban expansion than would otherwise occur. Once growth has shifted, however, the central city loses its original function, as shopping and industrial center, to the emerging outer city situated along the golden beltways. As urban blight becomes severe, the attractiveness of the inner city relative to the surrounding suburbs tends to decrease. The resulting outward flows of business and the city's high-income population may erode the position of the central city still further and guarantee the stagnation of the hub.

In a survey of five large cities concerning the reasons why businesses are leaving the inner city Richard Reeves found that "The need for land to expand is a primary factor that drives corporate offices, manufacturing and assembly plants, and even athletic teams, out of central cities."[9] Other factors such as high tax rates, crime, and urban congestion are also cited as reasons for companies to move outward: "Though companies are always reluctant to move, the frustrations pile up to a point that overcomes the traditional advantage of operating in the heart of the metropolis: quick access to other people and specialized services."[10]

One of the major points of *Urban Dynamics* is that outward metropolitan expansion is largely internally generated within the central area through a lack of land, an abundance of low-quality housing, and a dearth of employment opportunities for low-skilled workers; it follows that solutions to urban blight can be found only in policies that aim at creating a new and healthier internal balance between housing, population, and employment within the inner cities. This one premise has extensive ramifications, that cannot be fully dealt with within the scope of this paper.

Finally, the analysis presented in this paper shows the limitations of the applicability of the *Urban Dynamics* model to a metropolitan area. A future metropolitan dynamics model should include a geographical disaggregation based, for example, on distance from a central city. Individual subareas of the metropolitan region—for example, inner suburbs and outer suburbs—would be in differing stages of their development. The resulting flows of population and enterprises within the region should explain the historically observed "tidal wave of metropolitan expansion."

In addition to these refinements, a metropolitan model might deal effectively with the diverse forces that may arise to limit regional growth. Transportation difficulties, congestion, and problems of obtaining water and other necessary resources all tend to increase with expanding urbanization. Investigation of these interactions within a metropolitan context promises to shed new light on national urban and regional policy alternatives and on the dynamics of metropolitan growth.

Notes

1. H. Blumenfeld, "The Tidal Wave of Metropolitan Expansion," *Journal of the American Institute of Planners* 20 (1954), no. 1:3–14.

2. See ibid.; C. Clark, "Urban Population Densities," *Journal of the Royal Statistical Society*, ser. A, vol. 114, pt. 4 (1951). pp. 490–496; B. E. Newling, "Urban Growth and Spatial Structure," *Geographical Review* 56 (1966), no. 2: 213–225; R. S. Yuill, *A General Model for Urban Growth: A Spatial Simulation*, Michigan Geography Publications, no. 2 (Ann Arbor: University of Michigan, Department of Geography, 1970); and Urban Survey Corporation, *An Urban Survey Chartbook: The Relative Growth of Cities in Metropolitan Areas since 1920* (Cambridge, Mass., 1968).

3. Clark, "Urban Population Densities."

4. See W. W. Schroeder and J. E. Strongman, "Adapting *Urban Dynamics* to Lowell," Reading 15 in this volume.

5. J. S. Davoren, "Cities and Towns," in *The Story of Massachusetts*, ed. D. L. Marsh and W. M. Clark, vol. 3, chap. 72 (New York: American Heritage Society, 1938).

6. J. Rosenthal, "The Outer City: U.S. in Suburban Turmoil," *New York Times*, May 30, 1971.

7. L. Greenhouse, "The Outer City: Growth Crying Out for Guidance," ibid., June 3, 1971.

8. H. Weinblatt, *Policy Sciences* 1 (1970): 382. For a more extensive treatment of city-suburb interactions from the point of view of *Urban Dynamics* see L. E. Alfeld; "A Preliminary Discussion of Urban Dynamics and the Suburbs," System Dynamics Group working paper, (Cambridge, Mass.: M.I.T., Alfred P. Sloan School of Management, 1973).

9. R. Reeves, "Concerns in Many Cities Leaving for the Suburbs," *New York Times*, April 28, 1971.

10. "Why Companies Are Fleeing the Cities," *Time*, April 26, 1971, p. 86.

10
Urban Dynamics and Its Critics

Louis Edward Alfeld

Because system dynamics is a comparatively new approach to analyzing social behavior, many of the principles underlying the methodology have not been adequately conveyed to the larger academic and scientific community. Still, convergence between system dynamics and classical methods of social systems modeling (such as econometrics) has been slow in developing because of the disparate views held by professionals within each field on issues of model validity, model structure, and model purpose.

The following paper by Louis Edward Alfeld attempts to analyze the viewpoints and backgrounds reflected in many published criticisms of Urban Dynamics. *Alfeld makes several general points, in addition, concerning the conflicts inherent between new science and traditional science. By illuminating several points of contention or disagreement between the various modeling methodologies, this examination may help to focus future debate on those obstacles impeding significant progress in urban and social research.*

Continually since its publication, Jay W. Forrester's book *Urban Dynamics* has generated controversy to an unusual degree. Three separate reviews have appeared in the *Journal of the American Institute of Planners* alone.[1] The spectrum of attention from popular to technical has been wide, and notice has been taken in a surprising variety of professional fields.[2] Opinion seems to be divided over whether to castigate the book or to praise it. It is not unknown for a reviewer to straddle the issue by criticizing Forrester's dynamic modeling technique and the conclusions that follow from it while hailing the work as a significant step forward for the urban sciences.

In disputing policy, many reviewers are content to object to Forrester's conclusions without attempting to refute them or to propose alternatives. Forrester holds, for example, that people move to places they perceive to be more desirable. Programs designed to make a city more desirable will draw people in. The arrival of ever more people, if unchecked, compounds the problems the programs were meant to solve, driving the attractiveness of an area down to equilibrium with its environment. Potentially successful programs are swamped before they can benefit those for whom they were designed. In brief, a feedback process is at work, which has not been examined before; yet the reviewers do not seem to be aware of the relatively little research done on the determinants of internal migration and the impact of migration on urban areas.[3] Similarly, although Forrester's assertion of a close relationship between housing and migration draws objections, the critics adduce no empirical evidence to the contrary.[4] Nor do they suggest alternative counterbalances to migration.

Besides objections in a vacuum, *Urban Dynamics* has been subject to egregious misrepresentation on the question of economic benefits. The whole purpose of trying to control migration is to induce economic revival in stagnating central cities. The revival of the traditional function of the city as a place of economic opportunity for those who seek it is what *Urban Dynamics* is all about. The first to benefit would be the urban poor. It is therefore painful to see a critic imply that the underemployed will somehow be driven *out* of the city by heartless taxpayer associations if the recommendations in the book are followed.[5] Exactly the opposite is true. In fact, Forrester's policy recommendations to encourage new-enterprise construction by 40 percent and to attempt to reduce slum housing by 5 percent every year were chosen precisely because they bring significant economic gains to the underemployed in the hypothetical model city. Higher demolition rates might well have forced some underemployed out of the city. But, with the policy shown in *Urban Dynamics*, at no time during the implementation period does the model show out-migration of the underemployed to exceed in-migration of the underemployed. Instead, poor people are being drawn *into* the city at a controlled rate. They come because the opportunities for economic advancement have multiplied. Still, there are *fewer* underemployed in the city after the revival policy because more poor are flowing through the system, upgraded every year into self-supporting citizens.

Given a dispute heated enough to engender misreadings, it is remarkable how little has been said about the premise that orthodox diagnosis of the urban crisis may actually be harmful. One of the main contentions of *Urban Dynamics* is that current urban programs, based on faulty understanding, would, if applied on a wide scale, make things worse. Reviewers tend to slide over this contention in silence and take up methodological issues, which suggests that "urbanology," young as it is, already suffers from inertia.

If one is to believe Forrester's critics, apparently the greatest sin in the urban sciences is to formulate a dynamic model without recording empirical data. The problem, of course, is one of degree.

The *Urban Dynamics* model was designed to examine the common processes underlying urban growth and decline. Consistent with this purpose, the model portrays the time lags, perception delays, and nonlinear relationships that influence a city's long-term balance of housing, population, and industry. Although statistical methods have often been successfully applied to linear systems, the application of these same techniques to highly nonlinear systems poses several pitfalls. Many of these difficulties are well known; for example, the estimation of time delays may frequently yield biased results even within a linear system.[6]

The application of statistical techniques to a long-term generic model such as *Urban Dynamics* poses several unique difficulties as well. For example, the model omits many internal processes that operate within urban areas but are not essential to creating the 250-year life cycle of urban development. Also, the model omits exogenous forces that may affect absolute population levels within a city or a city's absolute growth rate over time but are not basic to the city's long-term development. For the purposes of the original urban model these simplifications are reasonable. However, those internal and external forces omitted from the model are manifest in data collected from any city and would need to be accounted for in any statistical estimation procedure. Attempts to estimate the parameters of the general urban model using data for a particular city would confront diverse statistical problems occasioned by specification error and serially correlated noise.[7]

In general, the reviews of *Urban Dynamics* have shown scant recognition of the problem entailed in estimating parameters within nonlinear feedback systems. This lack of attention is consistent with the predominant emphasis in the urban science literature on linear, short-term predictive models. However, in the future, significant progress in social systems modeling will require much greater cognizance of the problems involved in bringing statistical techniques and empirical data to bear on a nonlinear, long-term model such as *Urban Dynamics*.

Of course, some types of empirical data can readily be incorporated into *Urban Dynamics*. Such items as normal birth rates, average family size, and average housing densities might be changed. The critic who considers these adjustments important, however, ought to be forewarned that they will not appreciably affect the behavior of the model.[8]

Data have other uses, however. They can be used to help define terms, for instance. But data recorded with traditional meanings may not be appropriate if those meanings fail to capture the essential dynamic behavior that is being studied. The term "underemployed," for example, when used in the book, refers not to a group defined by the Department of Labor but to a group who share common dynamic qualities consistent with the purpose of the model.[9] Because the need to define urban concepts in terms of dynamic behavior never arose before, traditional definitions and the definitions employed in *Urban Dynamics* obviously do not correspond. It follows that census data or any other empirical groupings compiled on different principles cannot be imposed upon the model. No thoughtful critic would insist that the book cite inappropriate data.

It could be argued from the dubious critical performance recounted here that urban scientists are susceptible to the frequent disability of established professionals in a field to recognize new theories that radically conflict with the conventional wisdom. Urban scientists have judged *Urban Dynamics* by conventional standards and found it wanting; they have praised its innovations but are nonplused by the consequences; they have, in short, reacted as an "establishment" is supposed to react when confronted with a fundamentally new perspective.

Thomas S. Kuhn, in *The Structure of Scientific Revolutions*, has called attention to the process of "paradigm building" that goes on among scientists.[10] He maintains that all scientific communities tend to establish a central pattern of accepted truths and approved methods, for the acceptance of a unifying paradigm is essential to the advancement of research. The practitioner trained within such a framework finds it extremely difficult to perceive, much less to operate within, a new paradigm when one arises.

It is unnecessary as well as uncharitable, however, to press the point home against the critics of *Urban Dynamics*. System dynamics need not threaten the established order. Dynamic modeling has its limitations, just as other methodological approaches have theirs. It is not clear that the scope of dynamic modeling overlaps into traditional fields so as to create any areas of disputed territory. The conceptual questions to which *Urban Dynamics* and its successors are addressed are not the same as those largely pragmatic questions to which traditional urban science has addressed itself. The development of a general theory of urban behavior requires a broad-brush technique. Those same broad strokes cannot fill in the detail; case studies, data analysis, and policy judgments are required for that.

Dynamic modeling techniques make possible the kind of evaluation of the overall urban system that can tell us where to concentrate our best research efforts for maximum results. The issue of the importance of migration is an example of this question-identification ability. We now have an extraordinary tool that can tell us *where* to look for answers; the importance of this achievement to the field of urban research can only be guessed at—but hardly overestimated.

When viewed in perspective, it seems obvious why attempts to judge *Urban Dynamics* by traditional standards have failed. Its traditions do not lie in the field of urban science but emerge from the field of control theory. Moreover, the model cuts across the boundaries of formal academic disciplines to show how the many parts of a city interact through time.

Measured against these strengths, the failures of *Urban Dynamics* are small. No one doubts that much work is still needed. Forrester's major failing, perhaps, was in not making clear that the book was an example to be followed and not a set of final conclusions to be implemented. Surely no one should object if the basic tenets of urban research can be improved.

Notes

1. The three reviewers for the *Journal of the American Institute of Planners* were Donald A. Krueckeberg (September 1969); Gregory K. Ingram (May 1970); and Aaron Fleisher (January 1971).

2. For a representative sample of opinion, see the following reviews: Thomas A. Barber, *Datamation*, November 1969; David L. Birch, *Industrial Management Review*, Spring 1970; Herman L. Danforth, *Public Management*, January 1971; Allan G. Feldt, *American Sociological Review*, April 1970; Walter Helly, *Operations Research*, July–August 1970; James A. Hester, *Science*, May 8, 1970; John F. Kain, *Fortune*, November 1969; William K. Stevens, *New York Times*, October 31, 1969; and Herbert Weinblatt, *Policy Sciences*, Fall 1970.

3. Indications that internal migration rates are still very large come from comparing 1960 and 1970 census data. The migration of southern blacks to northern cities has not diminished in the past decade (*New York Times*, March 4, 1971). For a startling visual summary of recent migration patterns, see *Fortune*, February 1971, p. 83.

Among recent studies bearing on migration, the following may be mentioned: D. J. Bogue, *Principles of Demography* (New York: John Wiley, 1969); Samuel Bowles, "Migration as Investment: Empirical Tests of the Human Investment Approach to Geographical Mobility," *Review of Economics and Statistics*, November 1970; Everett S. Lee, "A Theory of Migration," *Demography*, 3 (1966); and Ira S. Lowry, *Migration and Metropolitan Growth*: *Two Analytical Models* (San Francisco: Chandler, 1966).

Recognition of the importance of migration as a component of population composition is growing. See, for example, "Needs for National Studies of Population Dynamics," in *Vital and Health Statistics*, ser. 4, no. 12, a publication of the National Center for Health Statistics of the U.S. Department of Health, Education, and Welfare.

4. Some support for correlating housing and migration can be found in studies based upon interviews; respondents usually regard housing *quality* as a reason for moving. See, for example, Peter H. Rossi, *Why Families Move* (Glencoe, Ill.: Free Press, 1955). The impact of housing on urban migration is analyzed by Alexander G. Makowski in an unpublished System Dynamics Group Working Paper, "Urban Dynamics: Housing and Migration."

5. One example of this is found in Gregory K. Ingram's review in the *Journal of the American Institute of Planners*, May 1970, where he states: "Programs that move the problem out of the city tend to get higher marks than those attempting to solve it" (p. 206).

6. See, for example, Zvi Griliches, "Distributed Lags: A Survey," *Econometrica* 35 (1967): 16–49.

7. Several difficulties in applying statistical methods to the *Urban Dynamics* model are described in Michael R. Goodman and Peter M. Senge, "Issues of Empirical Support for the Migration Formulations in *Urban Dynamics*, Reading 8 in this volume.

8. A new set of demographic coefficients and residential densities used to describe the city of Lowell, Massachusetts, is given in Walter W. Schroeder III and John E. Strongman, "Adapting *Urban Dynamics* to Lowell," Reading 11 in this volume.

9. See Michael R. Goodman, "Aggregation and Definition: The Underemployed, a Case Study," Reading 5 in this volume.

10. Thomas S. Kuhn, *The Structure of Scientific Revolutions* (Chicago: University of Chicago Press, 1970).

11
Understanding *Urban Dynamics:* An Analysis of Garn's Interpretation

Alan K. Graham

The publication of Urban Dynamics *has stimulated many reviews of the book—both favorable and unfavorable—written by individuals from a wide array of professional fields. While the substance of each review varies with the interests and background of the individual author, many critics touch on similar points in their reviews.*

One of the most extensive analyses of the Urban Dynamics *model was undertaken by Harvey Garn of the Urban Institute. Garn's review is of considerable interest because it contains many of the frequently raised criticisms of* Urban Dynamics, *and because Garn proposes several explicit and testable alterations to the urban model. The following paper by Alan K. Graham is a detailed analysis of Garn's criticism of* Urban Dynamics. *Graham's paper provides a fairly comprehensive examination of both the local and the national impact of Forrester's proposed revival policies and of the representation of city-suburb interactions within the* Urban Dynamics *model. In addition, many of the issues raised in the sections of the paper dealing with the "Frame of Reference" and "The Utility of Simulation" carry over broadly to illuminate the value and scope of formal dynamic modeling procedures.*

11
Understanding *Urban Dynamics*:
An Analysis of Garn's Interpretation

Urban Dynamics by Jay W. Forrester has evoked wide response from within the field of urban studies. The book is unique. It answers a broad range of theoretical questions concerning the forces that make cities grow and stagnate, and it points a way to urban revival. The book clearly demonstrates the importance of the feedback structure of social systems in producing the interactions between urban population, housing, and employment. Feedback concepts were used to forge a new theory of urban behavior, which is expressed in the form of a computer simulation model. The simulation model is designed not merely to "fit data," as are most urban models, but to answer policy questions—to test in advance the consequences of possible alternative actions. The results of the study are startling, for many current programs meant to ease the plight of the city actually prove to make it worse.

The novelty of Forrester's approach and the surprising nature of his results have confused many readers. Most reviews of *Urban Dynamics* seem only to have added to that confusion. Although a reviewer's customary task is to assess a work, most writers have done little more with regard to Forrester's book than communicate their own perplexity. Their misgivings arise because the book does not fit the patterns to which they have become accustomed.

A critique of *Urban Dynamics* written by Harvey A. Garn for the Urban Institute perhaps typifies the confusion.[1] Although Garn is skeptical of numerous aspects of *Urban Dynamics*, he is not incisive in his objections. The circulation of his original critique and of a revised version has propagated unease about Forrester's approach to urban problems, but it has not similarly contributed to a deeper understanding of that approach.

The questions raised in Garn's critique, and indeed in most other critiques, stem from a small number of fundamental misconceptions. These mistaken ideas merit careful examination and correction, for they can frustrate any attempt to understand *Urban Dynamics*.

11.1 The Impact of Model Policies on the Underemployed

From the concerned reader's viewpoint, the most serious doubt Garn raises about the book pertains to the revival policy that Forrester recommends and its effect on the city's underemployed—that is, loosely speaking, a city's lower-income residents. Chapter 5 of *Urban Dynamics*, through simulation experiments, analyzes various policies for reviving a city's economic health. "Health" in this case means returning population and jobs to a balance with one another, increasing the upward economic mobility of the underemployed, and expanding the capacity of the city to assimilate incoming underemployed people. Only after testing and dismissing several policies does Forrester find a combination of policies that are both humane and effective. The policy recommended in Section 5.7 of *Urban Dynamics* combines the yearly removal of a fraction of slum housing (much of it presumably already abandoned) and the encouragement of construction for new enterprise (to provide jobs and opportunities for individual economic advancement).

In his examination of the policy, Garn questions "whether or not an individual city would remain an island of wealth with the poor outside."[2] He failed to note that Forrester considerably extended his policy search specifically to find an effective combination that would eliminate any such exclusion.[3]

Policies tested in the beginning of the chapter on "Urban Revival" have undesirable traits that are not present in the combination policy. Doing nothing more than removing a fraction of slum housing each year (Section 5.5 of *Urban Dynamics*), a policy that Forrester does *not* recommend, reduces the underemployed arrival UA rate below the underemployed departure UD rate for the first 18 years of that policy; eventually, however, arrivals become higher and departures become lower than they would have been without the policy. Inversely, the construction of new enterprise NE (Section 5.3) immediately raises the arrivals of the underemployed and reduces their departures, but—after 22 years—departures climb to a higher rate than they would have without the policy. For obvious reasons, therefore, Forrester does not recommend this policy by itself. It is no accident that the combination of these policies both permits inflow and encourages urban revival, which is acceptable to Forrester.

The combination policy, finally arrived at in Section 5.7, produces conditions markedly different from those to which Garn refers; the underemployed are *not* excluded from the new economic vitality of the city. Rather, their arrival rate into the city eventually increases 20 percent, from 17,283 underemployed per year to 20,884 per year after 50 years. Thus the economic improvement in the city adequately compensates for the restricted housing availability, for the poor are drawn in and assimilated faster than before. In addition, the underemployed depart from the city at a lower rate under the combination policy; underemployed departures UD drop 4.8 percent, from 17,275 to 16,431. In brief, the effects of Forrester's economic revival policy are directly opposite to those of a simple pressure tactic that reduces the number of poor in the city by forcing them out and keeping them out; at no point in time under the combination policy are more underemployed leaving the city than are entering it.[4]

It is important to distinguish what prompted Garn's assumption about the poor from the assumption itself. With the model operating in the revival mode, the size of the underemployed population does drop. As a result, Garn hypothesizes that the underemployed population is reduced by making the city less attractive for them:

> [Forrester] is prepared to significantly reduce the attractiveness of the city to the underemployed in order to increase the attractiveness of the city to managers, labor, and new enterprise. In his two most preferred policies, the underemployed have been reduced by 23 percent and 11 percent, managers have increased by 52 percent and 53 percent, laborers 48 percent and 53 percent; and new enterprises 65 percent and 63 percent, respectively. He prefers to accomplish this in both cases by a program which eliminates substantial amounts of low-cost housing. In short, a richer city can be obtained by having fewer poor people in it.[5]

It is obvious from what has been said before, however, that attractiveness has not been "significantly reduced"; more underemployed migrate into the city after revival than before, and fewer leave. Together with the decrease in the underemployed population, there is a rise in the number of jobs for the underemployed. The result is a dramatic drop in the ratio of underemployed to jobs, from 1.81 to 1.07—employment opportunities are greatly improved. The attractiveness for migration due to jobs rises to compensate for the lessened attractiveness due to the reduction of available housing.[6]

If the combination policy causes more underemployed to arrive per year and fewer to leave, how does the size of the underemployed population eventually drop from 377,000 to 335,000? Garn suspected simple pressure tactics because a drop does occur. Yet the real cause is the movement of the underemployed into higher socioeconomic brackets. Favorable economic conditions stimulate this upward flow of the underemployed into the labor class. Combining the encouragement of new-enterprise construction NEC with the removal of slum housing increases the net conversion rate of underemployed to labor UTL by 67 percent, from 5,500 upward transfers per year to 9,200 per year. People formerly underemployed become skilled workers.

The conversion rate, however, is only a partial indicator of the true gains in economic opportunity that the combination policy produces. As the underemployed population is reduced, smaller and smaller numbers of people remain to compete for promotion into the labor class. A fuller measure of economic opportunity is the average time it takes for a newly arrived underemployed person to progress into the labor class.

In the stagnant city, as described in Chapter 3 of *Urban Dynamics*, there are a large number of underemployed residents, relatively few of whom will ever escape from their class. Out of 377,000 underemployed people in the stagnant city, only a net total of 5,500 per year join the labor category. To be in such a pool is to have little hope for advancement. The average time for advancement is 377,000 underemployed/5,500 underemployed per year, or 69 years—several generations. In such a situation, the children of the poor will rarely escape from poverty. It would require an extraordinary effort (or extraordinary luck) on the part of an underemployed person to break this "poverty cycle" by advancing into the labor category.

In sharp contrast to conditions in the stagnant city, the combination policy from Section 5.7 of *Urban Dynamics* boosts the net conversion rate to 9,200 people per year, reducing the underemployed population to 335,900. Not only are more and better jobs continuing to open up, but fewer people are competing for them. Economic opportunity rises more than the greater conversion rate would indicate; the advancement time drops to 335,900 underemployed/9,200 underemployed per year, or 36 years. The combination of new-enterprise construction NEC and slum-housing demolition SHD does not produce a perfect city, but it breaks down the generations-long "poverty cycle" by reducing the average advancement time by almost a factor of two.

In short, a richer city can indeed be obtained by having fewer poor people in it, but not necessarily with the drawbacks that Garn fears. The city in revival is a "richer" city for the poor as well as the rich. The combination policy of new-enterprise construction and slum-housing demolition so enhances the conversion of underemployed to skilled labor that more underemployed can enter the city per year and fewer need to leave. Employment opportunities for the underemployed increase remarkably. As beneficial to the city as these changes are, they may be more important to the country as a whole because the city ceases to burden the nation with its needs, instead contributing toward raising the national standard of living. The increased inflow rate of underemployed is matched in equilibrium by an increased outflow of labor and managerial-professionals; the skill level of the country's population can be raised by economically effective urban areas.

11.2 The National Impact of Model Policies

So far, the effects of new-enterprise construction and slum-housing demolition have been examined in terms of the individual city, the primary focus of *Urban Dynamics*. Garn asserts that by adopting such a viewpoint Forrester precludes himself from considering the impact of revival policies outside the city:

> [Forrester] chose to develop a closed boundary model of a fixed land area communicating with but not affecting the external environment. He explicitly ruled out, by his particular boundary choice, consideration of problems of ... possible effects of actions taken to improve the situation in the city on the larger society.[7]

Such an assertion misses the mark, however, and actually clashes with what Forrester has written:

> [*Urban Dynamics*] focuses on an urban area and its improvement. But no conflict need exist between the well-being of that area and the health of the surrounding urban and rural areas. A healthy city is a more effective economic converter for upgrading the underemployed than is a decayed city. A healthy city generates new industry, managers, and skilled labor beyond those who can remain employed within the city area. These men and enterprises leave to start nuclei of rising economic activity at other places.
>
> The policies for controlling population balance that the city must establish are not antisocial. No purpose is served by operating a city so that it is a drain on the economy of the country and a disappointment and frustration to its occupants. An urban area that maintains effective internal balance can absorb poor people from other areas at a faster rate than can one that is operating in deep stagnation. The healthy area does not act as a drag on the other parts of the country by requiring assistance from the outside. Furthermore, the well-balanced urban area can contribute to raising the standard of living of the entire country.[8]

In truth, the effects of policies on the larger society do appear in the *Urban Dynamics* model, both explicitly and implicitly. As was clear in the previous section, information directly available from the model indicates the impact of policies on movements of various socioeconomic classes to the city from its environment and vice versa. Similarly, changes in the composition of the work force, jobs, and enterprises implicitly show how the policy affects economic flows between the city and its environment. The revival policy augments these flows through increased business activity.

Economic upgrading can draw people out of the underemployed category and raise them into the labor class. This upward flow, when coupled with the resulting in- and out-migrations, can help shift the composition of the population outside the city in the same way. The city, under policies that stimulate revival, functions as an economic converter, taking in unskilled people from the environment and returning skilled labor and managers. When Forrester's hypothetical city is in stagnation under the policies being followed today (discussed in *Urban Dynamics*, pp. 38–50), underemployed arrivals and departures are virtually equal. But under the suggested revival policies based on new-enterprise construction and slum-housing demolition, the net underemployed arrival rate rises to over 4,000 per year—the city becomes a net importer of the poor. During the same time, the net out-migration rate of laborers and managers rises from 10,000 to 15,500 per year.

Just as economic opportunity within the revived city draws its residents from the underemployed category into the labor category, so the economic vitality of the revived city draws in underemployed people from the environment and correspondingly returns labor and managers. The area interacts with its surrounding environment through migrations. Through these flows, the same mechanism that benefits the city—economic advancement—benefits the larger national society.

11.3 City-Suburb Interaction

As the two previous sections have shown, migration is an important interaction between an area and its environment, and migration patterns can be altered by choice of policies. The city's environment of course includes its suburbs, just as it includes other cities and their suburbs and rural areas. Garn, elaborating his objections about boundary choice, believes that Forrester's simulation model excludes city-suburb interaction and therefore fails to address a major problem of the cities:

> . . . The particular boundary choice made by Professor Forrester rules out central city-suburb problems and effects on the larger society. In particular, many have noticed that one of the major problems for central city mayors has been to develop a means of coping with the out-migration of many of the higher-income groups to the suburbs and the concomitant loss of tax revenues which this move entails. Many of these people continue to hold jobs in the central city—their exodus for residential purposes has not opened up anything like the same number of jobs in the central city . . . In Professor Forrester's model there is no commuting across the boundary—people who work in his city reside there. One of the most interesting and difficult problems, therefore, is lost in this formulation.[9]

Implicitly, Garn seems to suggest here that commuting causes urban blight. While this hypothesis has some merit, it begs more questions than it answers. Why should "higher-income groups" so selectively leave the city in the first place? Higher-income people have entered and left the cities throughout history—the commuting theory alone does not explain why contemporary cities should be so vulnerable to out-migration. In addition, city governments derive the bulk of their income from property taxes, and when residents depart, taxable property remains within the city. Although the commuting theory contains elements of truth, a fuller explanation is necessary for understanding urban growth and decay.

Urban Dynamics outlines a theory of urban evolution that constitutes such an explanation. Chapter 3 describes the forces that cause a city to grow, stop growing, decay, and possibly renew itself. The hypothetical area Forrester portrays enjoys a period of rapid growth and prosperity in the earlier part of its history. While the area grows in population, two things happen. First, as the area fills with buildings, land becomes much less available for new construction. Economic and geographical limitations stemming from the lack of desirable building sites eventually terminate the era of growth because housing and enterprise can no longer be as readily constructed. Second, the buildings in the area age, and their occupancy changes correspondingly. As housing ages, luxury housing becomes middle-income housing, and middle-income housing becomes lower-income housing. More people crowd into the same housing stock.

When the area is still growing, most of the housing stock is new, and relatively little lower-income housing exists. This shortage restrains the rate at which the underemployed arrive from the environment, since housing for them is comparatively more abundant in older cities and rural areas. Because of high employment opportunities during the growth phase, the underemployed who do arrive are converted to the labor class more rapidly than they will be when the area is decaying. When growth stops, aged low-cost housing becomes more available, enabling more underemployed to migrate into the area from the environment. The underemployed become an increased fraction of the city's population P.

As land becomes fully occupied and the underemployed begin to constitute a sufficiently large segment of the population, the area becomes less desirable for enterprise. Much of the area's land is occupied by run-down or abandoned housing, which makes new economic expansion difficult. The occupants of the older housing require more social services than they pay for in taxes. Taxes rise and the symptoms of urban blight appear.

In the eyes of the affluent, the crowding, high taxes, social conflict, and lack of amenities in the inner city all make newer areas, such as the outlying suburbs, more desirable places to reside. Relatively fewer managerial-professionals arrive during the stagnation phase than during the growth phase, and more depart. *Urban Dynamics* deals explicitly with the very phenomena underlying Garn's concern that "one of the major problems for central city mayors has been to develop a means for coping with the out-migration of many of the higher-income groups to the suburbs and the concomitant loss of tax revenues which this move entails".[10] Equations 55 through 63 in the urban model detail the causes of managerial-professional departures MD. The premium-housing sector, equations 64 through 80, shows how decreased demand for premium housing hastens its conversion to worker housing, which eventually lowers the tax base indirectly. In addition, the enterprise sector, in equations 100 through 120, portrays the forces that cause a reduction in the relative number of jobs as the city settles into stagnant equilibrium.

Urban Dynamics describes the processes that eventually result in a high rate of managerial-professional departures. The undesirable conditions in the central city naturally give rise to residential construction around the city. In this country those who do not wish to live in the city and who have the means to build homes outside the city do so, and the suburbs are born. Given the large cost of constructing a new home, the growth of the suburbs in postwar years is a rather graphic commentary on life in the cities. The development of suburbs surrounding the cities stems not from independent causes but from simple growth, coupled with the decay of economic vitality and quality of life in the city.

Commuting accompanies the early phases of suburbanization, when places of work are still inside the city. In terms of problem solving, commuting is better viewed as a symptom of suburbanization rather than as a cause of urban blight. Commuting is the inevitable consequence of whatever mechanisms cause places of residence to be separated from places of work in the central city. Similarly suburbanization is better viewed as a necessary consequence of urban blight, not as its cause. Suburbs are the inevitable habitat of people with means who wish to live neither in the central cities nor in inaccessible rural areas. Solutions to problems of urban blight must focus upon causes and not upon related manifestations of that blight.

Urban Dynamics, as described here, accounts for urban decay in terms of land occupancy, aging, and migration to and from the environment. Contrary to Garn's claims, Forrester's model contains the essence of city-suburb interactions. The upper-income groups will move out if conditions in the city become sufficiently undesirable. The primary determinant of upper-income departures is the economic health and desirability of the central city. Forrester's model represents this interaction by rates of population flow, modulated by comparisons of conditions within the city with those in the outside environment.

It is ironic that commuting suffers widespread popularity as a scapegoat for urban ills, for an equally one-sided case could be made for commuters as the benefactors of the city. Large office buildings, for example, occupied by commuting suburbanites represent desirable additions to the city's taxable property base. The city taxes those buildings without incurring obligations to provide full services to the occupants of the buildings or to school their children. Of course, commuters use transportation facilities, and commercial buildings require some city services, but these demands are not the ones that drain a city's treasury.[11]

Garn, along with many others, therefore errs in several ways when he asserts that commuting, which is "one of the most interesting and difficult problems, therefore, is lost in [Forrester's] formulation."[12] First, the study of commuting, no matter how "interesting" it may be, is not basic to the problem of urban stagnation. The theory that offers commuting and suburbanization as the causes of urban blight obscures more than it can explain. The true causes lie within the city. Second, the urban model correctly depicts those causes by showing how migration out of the city responds to conditions within the city. Third, it is not at all clear that commuting as such is a harmful process. A city, despite possible indirect and delayed costs to it, certainly benefits from the ability to tax a building without incurring significant obligations to the occupants. These issues are far more subtle, and demand more careful study, than implied by Garn.

11.4 Frame of Reference as a Basis for Model Formulation

Urban Dynamics offers a theory of urban behavior that interrelates many facts about the real world. To model the large number of causal relationships involved, it is necessary to adopt a point of view that imposes organization upon them. Forrester views these relationships in terms of three subsystems:

> business, housing, and population. These three subsystems are chosen because they appear to be the dynamic framework of urban structure. The changes in housing, population, and industry are the central processes involved in growth and stagnation. They are more fundamental than city government, social culture, or fiscal policy. Observation of the city suggests that the important changes involve shifting populations as housing structures age and industry falls behind the outside economy.[13]

Garn misperceives this organization as a specification of facts to be included and excluded from the model rather than as a way of structuring a subject:

> It is not, I think, a mere quibble to ask how one is to know whether or not [the statement quoted above] is true. Professor Forrester's model has an aging process for housing and industry built in and the model does produce periods of growth, decline, and stagnation ... It is not clear that this should be taken as proof that housing is more fundamental than social culture, for example, in explaining what happens in cities or what is important for us to understand about cities in devising social policies.[14]

Garn assumes that Forrester chose to exclude "city government, social culture, and fiscal policy" from his model; that assumption is false. In fact, Forrester chose to view the city—including its subcultures and its government—in terms of population, housing, and business. These three subsystems describe the city simply yet comprehensively.

Forrester incorporates the effects of city government into the framework provided by the three subsystems. For example, the political forces involved in setting the tax rate appear explicitly in equation 127 of *Urban Dynamics*, as do assessment (equations 128–130) and tax collection (equation 121). Urban services (for example, fire, police, maintenance, and recreation) appear as tax needs TN (equation 126). Educational expenditures, which constitute a large part of tax needs, influence rates of economic advancement (equations 27, 40). Finally, many of the programs Forrester examines (equations 140–150) reflect actions by the city government.

The same model organization just as readily incorporates sociological knowledge. The underemployed differ sharply from managerial-professionals in their attitudes toward work; the migration equations and the job sector reflect the consequent behavioral differences (equations 10, 44, 56, 131–139). The migration equations also reflect the importance people of each category attach to living near members of their own class (equations 1, 45, 57). The birth rate equations (15, 28, 51) reflect the transmission of general cultural values from parents to children. The transmission of skills and attitudes between adults of different classes influences economic advancement (equations 26, 39).

Forrester's organization, then, can incorporate many phenomena that are not usually expressed in terms of population, housing, and business. The relevant phenomena could have been organized according to academic disciplines (into sociological, economic, demographic, and political sectors) or according to any arbitrary scheme. However, Forrester's frame of reference most easily incorporates diverse phenomena into a uniform structure. The dynamic consequences of those phenomena are most explicable in that frame of reference—it provides a fundamental description of the city.

Garn's error here is conceptual: choice of organization is a choice of viewpoint, not a choice of what a model will include. As such, Forrester's frame of reference can be judged only by its effectiveness.

11.5 The Utility of Simulation

The approach followed in *Urban Dynamics* can render policy making less equivocal, less captious, and far more objective. Simulation experiments can test many different policies, revealing their impact on each of the hundreds of interrelated elements of the urban system. They can eliminate the need for hazy, uncertain speculation about the impact of policies.

Conventional policy analysis relies upon discussion and debate to arrive at conclusions. Such verbal techniques in turn rest upon intuition to predict dynamic response in the social system. Intuition, however, is usually ineffective in dealing with systems as complex as a city. Even when intuition has been sharpened by years of exposure to the urban system, the mind is usually incapable of dealing simultaneously with the myriad factors necessary to anticipate correctly the effects of a policy.

The wide gap between intuition and policy simulation is revealed at those points where Garn discusses Forrester's equations in detail and draws conclusions about the behavior that the model would exhibit if some of those equations were changed. Simulation experiments can support or refute intuitive judgments. That such experiments were run and they gave results contrary to Garn's expectations demonstrates the need to supplant present verbal policy analysis with the more powerful approach of *Urban Dynamics*.

One such experiment pertained to the combination policy recommended in Section 5.7 of *Urban Dynamics*. As originally presented, that policy moves a portion of the underemployed population in the hypothetical city into the labor and manager population. Garn erroneously attributes the cause of this shift to differences in the way the population categories respond to job and housing availability:

> Again, managers, laborers, and the underemployed receive differential treatment from Professor Forrester. In this case, however, managers and laborers are more responsive to job opportunities than the underemployed ... This assumption is intuitively more appealing than the one made with respect to housing. Given this set of assumptions, however, it is easy to see why creation of new enterprises (which create more managerial and labor jobs than underemployed jobs by assumption) should cause a population shift in favor of the wealthier groups in Professor Forrester's model ... Again, it is possible to wonder what policy conclusions would be derived from changing simultaneously all the assumed functional multiplier relationships which make the laborers and managers relatively more responsive to job opportunities and the underemployed to housing opportunities.[15]

If Garn's perceptions are correct, changing the model so that all classes would be equally responsive to jobs and housing availability should prevent the combination policy from shifting the population "toward the wealthier groups." But Garn overlooked the dominant causal mechanisms. After the proposed changes have been made in the model, the combination policy recommended in Section 5.7 of *Urban Dynamics* still shifts the population and also remains an effective revival policy; the net flow of underemployed to labor UTLN increases by 75 percent.[16] As noted earlier, the true cause of the population shift is upward economic mobility.

Intuition again serves Garn poorly when he attributes the failure of a training program to the form in which Forrester wrote an equation:

> It is interesting to note that this equation (1,R) could produce an increase in the number of underemployed as a result of any increase in the number of laborers without any change in attractiveness. The equivalent equations for laborers and managers (41,R and 53,R respectively) require changes in attractiveness to produce such changes. This is one of several cases where the underemployed sector is treated differently from the other population sectors for no apparent reason in the Forrester model ... This is one reason why a training program for the underemployed does not turn out very well in the policy simulation reported on pp. 57–61.[17]

Two simulation experiments show Garn's reasoning to be incomplete. An extreme job shortage persists despite changes made in conformity with Garn's remarks.[18] This result illustrates how intuition may be an inadequate guide for predicting the consequences of urban policies; often, cities, and adequate models of cities, have behavior very different from normal expectations. Intuition and judgment developed from a lifetime's experience with simpler systems are nearly valueless in analyzing complex systems.[19]

Behavioral analysis is not the only aspect of policy evaluation; in addition to knowing how policies can change the behavior of the urban system, it is necessary to know the approximate magnitude of the changes. The policy maker, who is expected to decide among policy alternatives, must have the information necessary to decide which policy can produce the most desirable changes.

The intuitive estimation of the relative magnitudes of changes is even more difficult than the intuitive prediction of behavior. Many factors are in opposition to one another, and all the factors are interrelated. For example, consider the premium-housing-construction program that is simulated in Section 5.2 of *Urban Dynamics*. It is impossible to judge accurately whether additional premium housing PH will stimulate new-enterprise construction NEC by attracting more managerial-professionals or whether the extra housing will inhibit new-enterprise construction NEC by making land scarcer and therefore more expensive. Long-term effects are more elusive. In the short run, premium housing may lower tax rates by increasing the tax base. In the long run, however, premium housing ages and is converted into housing for labor and the underemployed, which may eventually increase tax rates through the residents' increased tax needs. Will the tax rate be higher or lower than before? A dynamic simulation model is required to resolve such questions.

In the following statement, Garn suggests two parameter changes that he predicts will make a low-cost housing program less harmful and the combination policy less beneficial:

> Professor Forrester does not show in his sensitivity analysis the effect of a shallower function for the underemployed housing program multiplier coupled with a reduction in sensitivity of the underemployed housing multiplier. Given what he has said, however, one can conclude that such a change in the assumption would further improve the performance of a low-cost housing program and possibly reduce the attractiveness of the revival policies proposed. It is conceivable that it might do better, even on Professor Forrester's definitions of better or worse, than the revival policies he has supported in his book.[20]

View these statements in terms of policy decisions: what does Garn's analysis say about which policy is more desirable? If altering the assumption about the sensitivity of the underemployed housing multiplier UHM results only in small changes, then the combination policy remains superior to the low-cost housing program. But if the proposed alteration renders the combination policy so much less effective and the housing program so much more effective that the relative desirability of the two policies is reversed, then the basic assumption concerning the underemployed/housing multiplier UHM should be reexamined. However, when Garn's suggested modifications are actually simulated, only small changes occur, so the combination policy in fact remains a sound policy choice.[21] By analyzing the model's dynamic response without simulation testing, Garn merely confuses the issue. This type of analysis by intuition is inadequate to make policy decisions within complex systems. Solutions to today's problems demand the far more rigorous simulation approach of *Urban Dynamics*.

11.6 Summary

Urban Dynamics describes a computer simulation model that can become a powerful decision-making tool when used to analyze the effects of urban policies.

The method of analysis is comprehensive and unambiguous.

After testing many possible alternatives, Forrester proposes a policy based upon new-enterprise construction and slum-housing demolition. This policy produces large social and economic gains within the city, for both job availability and upward economic mobility show dramatic improvement. Despite a reduced availability of housing under this policy, the arrival rate of underemployed people significantly increases. Moreover, the city's underemployed population actually decreases because of enhanced upward economic mobility. Garn incorrectly attributes this drop in the underemployed population to a reduction in the attractiveness of the city for the underemployed. The truth is that the city in revival functions as a socioeconomic converter, continuously accepting an incoming stream of underemployed who are then converted into the labor class and eventually returned to the outside environment as skilled workers and managers. Contrary to Garn's doubts, Forrester's policy recommendation benefits the larger national society as well as the individual city.

Urban Dynamics describes the forces that cause the growth and stagnation of cities. Interaction with the city's environment is represented in the model through migration flows. Migration patterns change as the growth of the city stops. During the city's transition from growth into stagnation, manager departures rise suddenly. These departures, caused by central-city stagnation, set in motion the expansion of the suburbs and the rise of commuting.

The *Urban Dynamics* model constitutes a logically complete theory of urban behavior. That theory is expressed in terms of population, housing, and business. Contrary to Garn's fears, that viewpoint does not restrict the diversity of phenomena that the theory is able to embrace; the present model incorporates many political, demographic, sociological, and economic relationships into the same uniform framework.

Although the structure of the *Urban Dynamics* model is straightforward, intuitive reasoning, even when based upon that model, cannot match the surety and comprehensiveness of simulation analysis. Garn's difficulties in predicting the dynamic consequences of simple changes in the model underscore the need to replace inadequate intuitive policy analysis with the clarity and precision of simulation models.

Notes

1. Garn's most comprehensive critique is "An Urban System Model: A Critique of *Urban Dynamics*," Urban Institute, Working Paper 113–125 (Washington, D.C., 1969). Garn coauthored an abbreviated version of this paper, augmented by the results of two computer simulation experiments, with Robert H. Wilson, which appears as "A Look at *Urban Dynamics*: The Forrester Model and Public Policy" in the *Proceedings of the Second Annual Pittsburgh Conference on Modeling and Simulation* (Pittsburgh: University of Pittsburgh, 1971). A version of these proceedings was published as the April 19, 1972, issue of the *IEEE Transactions on Systems, Man, and Cybernetics*. The original critique published by the Urban Institute has been more widely circulated than the Pittsburgh paper and is the primary focus of this analysis. All quotations and page numbers cited hereafter as Garn refer to the Urban Institute working paper; the paper presented at the Pittsburgh conference is cited as Garn and Wilson.

2. Garn, p. 24. Although this phrase does not appear in the 1971 version, no correction of this misinterpretation appears either.

3. Chapter 5 in *Urban Dynamics* follows a progression of testing individual policies, noting their effectiveness, and combining the most promising. All the policies tried in Sections 5.1–5.5 contain flaws that Forrester concludes make them unacceptable as policy recommendations. All quotations and section and page numbers cited hereafter as Forrester refer to Jay W. Forrester, *Urban Dynamics* (Cambridge, Mass.: The M.I.T. Press, 1969).

4. Reference to the computer printout reproduced on p. 100 of *Urban Dynamics* will allow the reader to verify these figures. The graphs on pp. 98–99 plot several of the more important variables and provide a convenient comparison between the underemployed arrival rate and the departure rate.

5. Garn, p. 24; see also Garn and Wilson, p. 164.

6. In any region where free population interchange occurs, attractiveness will tend to equalize. If people perceive an advantage at one location, they will migrate to that location until the pressures of added population drive the favored area down to equilibrium with the areas from which the migration originated. It appears impossible to permanently alter an area's composite relative attractiveness, although different elements of attractiveness may be traded off.

In equilibrium, changes in population movements and rates of internal mobility are consequences of policy changes. The system readjusts to produce a new set of pressures but remains in equilibrium. The city's composite attractiveness relative to the limitless environment remains unchanged. Forrester discusses the attractiveness concept on pp. 117–118.

7. Garn, p. 5; Garn and Wilson, p. 160.

8. Forrester, pp. 115–116.

9. Garn, pp. 6–7; Garn and Wilson, pp. 160–161.

10. Ibid.

11. People rather than buildings account for the major part of a city's expenditures. According to *City Government Finances in 1964–1965*, issued by the Census Bureau, population services (e.g., education, hospitals, welfare, parks, and recreation, housing and urban development, health, and libraries) accounted for 52 percent of expenditures in cities of over 1 million in 1964/65. In contrast, services for buildings (police, fire, sewage, sanitation, and utilities) accounted for 30 percent of the expenditures. Commercial concerns staffed by commuters pay for these costs through property taxes, which also partly pay for population services for city residents. Expenditures for highways were only 6.2 percent of the total expenditures—less than for "financial administration, general control, and interest on general debt."

12. Garn, pp. 6–7; Garn and Wilson, pp. 160–161.

13. Forrester, pp. 15–17.

14. Garn, p. 7; see also Garn and Wilson, p. 161.

15. Garn, pp. 14–16; see also Garn and Wilson, p. 162.

16. The model changes that test Garn's speculations are
$$\text{T UHMT} = 1.3/1.25/1.2/1.1/.75/.5/.35/.2$$
$$\text{T MAHMT} = 1.75/1.5/1/.35/.1/.05/.02$$
$$\text{T LAHMT} = 1.75/1.5/1/.35/.1/.05/.02$$
$$\text{T LAJMT} = 2/2/1.9/1.6/1/.6/4/.3/.2$$
$$\text{T MAJMT} = 2/2/1.9/1.6/1/.6/.4/.3/.2$$

These changed functions assert that underemployed in-migration is less responsive to housing availability than are either labor or managerial-professional migrations, reversing the assumptions made in *Urban Dynamics*. The changes also make the arrival rates of all classes equally responsive to job availability.

Forrester's combination policy proves to induce the same behavioral response in the changed model. The population shifts and increases in job opportunities still result as in *Urban Dynamics*.

To test the policy, the changed model must be allowed to reach a new equilibrium (not numerically identical to that in *Urban Dynamics* although the two are qualitatively alike). The underemployed population in the new equilibrium constitutes 41.4 percent of the total work force (underemployed + labor + managerial-professionals). The combination policy reduces this fraction to 35.5 percent.

Even under these extreme parameter changes, the policy proposed in Section 5.7 of *Urban Dynamics* still produces sizable improvements. The underemployed/job ratio UR drops 25 percent, while the tax ratio needed TRN drops 18.5 percent. The net flow of underemployed to labor UTLN increases 75 percent.

These figures, however, are only indicative of the potential improvement available from the combination policy. Forrester's prescription of 40 percent more new-enterprise construction and 5 percent slum-housing demolition, discussed in Section 5.7, is not appropriate for a city in which the underemployed are less sensitive to housing. If the underemployed are less responsive to reductions in housing availability, then more slum-housing removal is necessary to obtain a revival of the magnitude shown in *Urban Dynamics*. For instance, under the parameter changes listed previously, the policy recommended in Section 5.7 of *Urban Dynamics* reduced the underemployed/job ratio UR from 1.611 to 1.206. If slum-housing demolition is increased from 5 percent to 7 percent per year, the underemployed/job ratio UR drops to 1.086; nearly as many underemployed jobs are available as there are underemployed workers to fill them. The relation between parameter specification and policy testing is further discussed in Nathaniel J. Mass, "Self-Learning Revival Policies in *Urban Dynamics*," Reading 17 in this volume.

17. Garn, p. 11. This conjecture does not appear in the abbreviated 1971 version.

18. Garn suggested that the training program is ineffective because of the form Forrester assumed for the equation defining underemployed arrivals UA (equation 1,R). The first experiment removes this assumption and again simulates the training program, to test Garn's suggestion. For the experiment, UA is made a function of only the underemployed population, and the underemployed arrivals normal UAN is also raised to retain the same equilibrium arrival rate:

$$1,R \quad UA.KL = (UAN)(U.K)(AMMP.K)$$
$$1.1,C \quad UAN = .103$$

Thus the assumption that underemployed migration responds to total city size is removed in accordance with Garn's objection. The underemployed are now assumed to prefer to migrate to cities that have the largest pools of poor, regardless of the size of the city. Section 4.2 in *Urban Dynamics* describes the impact of the job training program under the original assumptions: the net rate of conversion of underemployed to labor UTLN more than doubled but was not accompanied by a noticeable economic revival. The underemployed/job ratio UR declined from 1.81 to 1.78. An extreme job shortage still existed. When the model is changed, the training program reduces the underemployed/job ratio slightly, from 1.81 to 1.74. The tax ratio needed TRN also declines slightly in the changed model, from 2.25 to 2.018, as opposed to 2.06 in the original. The job training program, although it considerably enhances upward economic mobility, still does not cure the undesirable conditions within the city. Contrary to Garn's suggestion, the form of equation 1,R is not the cause of the training program's ineffectiveness.

The second experiment changes only the equation for underemployed arrivals UA (1,R), while retaining the underemployed arrivals normal UAN at its original value; under these assumptions, there are significantly fewer underemployed arrivals UA per year. This experiment produced an equilibrium that seems "healthier" than the city described in *Urban Dynamics*, and the training program was slightly more effective. The underemployed/job ratio UR dropped from an equilibrium value of 1.593 to 1.463, and the tax ratio needed TRN dropped from 1.974 in equilibrium to 1.689. Thus, although the training program is somewhat more effective when the assumption about underemployed migration is changed, the problems of high unemployment and high taxes are not solved.

The apparent economic improvement in the second experiment, however, is mostly illusory, for the changes involved have two ramifications that are not immediately apparent.

The equation for underemployed arrivals UA was modified so that, under the same conditions within the city, arrivals are much lower than in the original urban model. This modification not only alters the response of underemployed arrivals UA to changes in population levels but also alters the definition of the underemployed population class: the modified equation in effect classifies a smaller fraction of the total arrivals into the city as underemployed. Definitional changes of this nature must be carefully avoided in a model of an urban area; the quality of life within a city is not altered by calling some people labor rather than underemployed.

The second difficulty follows directly from the first. In the *Urban Dynamics* model, many equations describe the characteristics of the underemployed class, as described earlier (Section 11.4). Changing just one of these equations, the arrival equation (1,R), is ambiguous. The people who were classified as underemployed in the original model and were classified as labor by the altered arrival equation have tax needs, employment characteristics, and migration priorities that are dissimilar to those of both labor and the remaining underemployed. The tax, employment, and migration equations should all reflect the definition of underemployed in the second experiment, and they do not. These same problems with redefinition occur in Garn and Wilson's second experiment (p. 166).

Garn and Wilson also combined an underemployed training program with new-enterprise construction (p. 165). Although this policy creates favorable changes in the original *Urban Dynamics* model, massive training programs should in general be suspect. Training programs have so far proven to be ineffective in upgrading large numbers of poor. If a 10 percent "success" rate is achievable for underemployed enrolled in a training program, then fully one-half of the underemployed must always be enrolled to achieve the desired underemployed training rate UTR of 5 percent per year.

19. See Forrester, pp. 9–11, 107–14.

20. Garn, p. 14; see also Garn and Wilson, p. 162.

21. The changes implementing Garn's suggestions are:
$$\text{T UHMT} = 1.3/1.25/1.2/1.1/1/.75/.5/.35/.2$$
$$\text{T MAHMT} = 1.75/1.5/1/.35/.1/.05/.02$$
$$\text{T LAHMT} = 1.75/1.5/1/.35/.1/.05/.02$$
$$\text{T UHPMT} = 1/1.066/1.166/1.3/1.366/1.66$$
By making underemployed arrivals UA much less responsive to housing programs and housing availability, these model alterations made the low-cost-housing program less detrimental; the area no longer receives such a massive influx of underemployed drawn in by increased housing opportunities. In *Urban Dynamics*, Section 4.4, the low-cost-housing program attracted enough underemployed to boost the underemployed/job ratio UR by 30 percent; in the changed model this ratio rises 12 percent. Tax ratio needed TRN rose 36 percent in *Urban Dynamics* and only 6.9 percent with the alterations. The harmful impact of a low-cost-housing program, although diminished, is still clear in the changed model.

In *Urban Dynamics* the combination of new-enterprise construction with slum-housing demolition reduced the underemployed/job ratio by 41 percent. This combination policy when implemented in the altered model reduced the underemployed/job ratio by 32 percent. The overall impact of the combination policy as formulated in Section 5.7 of *Urban Dynamics* is diminished when the model is changed. However, as pointed out in note 16, the amount of slum housing removed per year can be increased to compensate for the lowered responsiveness of the underemployed to housing availability. This change will produce results as favorable as those produced by the policy simulation in Section 5.7 of *Urban Dynamics*.

Part Three
Model Alterations

Extensions of the *Urban Dynamics* model serve several important purposes. They provide a means of testing individual assumptions and relationships within the model. For example, an important criticism concerns the exclusion of suburban areas from the model's boundary. To help determine the impact of this assumption and the potential benefits of building a detailed city-suburb model, Reading 13 appends a small suburban sector to the urban model for purposes of policy testing.

Model refinements may also serve to elaborate individual sectors of the *Urban Dynamics* model in order to explore specific policy areas in greater detail. Reading 15 in this section on land pricing and land zoning provides one illustration of this function.

The five papers in Part Three cover a range of practical and theoretical questions, and represent preliminary efforts to expand the *Urban Dynamics* model structure.

12
Structural Changes in *Urban Dynamics:* Housing Obsolescence and Housing Demand

Nathaniel J. Mass

Within urban neighborhoods, aging residential structures tend to become inhabited by progressively lower income groups over time, until the buildings are finally rehabilitated or demolished. Local rates of housing obsolescence (or "filter-down") influence the age mix of housing within an urban area and thereby affect the demographic and social composition of the area.

To examine the pressures leading up to the conversion of premium housing into worker housing and the conversion of worker housing into underemployed housing, Reading 12 analyzes the influence of housing demand on housing obsolescence rates. It focuses in particular on the effects of housing competition between the different income groups of an urban area on residential filter-down rates. Several modifications to the obsolescence equations in the Urban Dynamics *model are developed; in addition, the effects of these changes are simulated to test the sensitivity of the model to varying assumptions about the relative housing demands exerted by a city's managerial-professional, labor, and underemployed populations.*

12
Structural Changes in *Urban Dynamics*: Housing Obsolescence and Housing Demand

12.1 The Question of Housing Obsolescence

The housing sector of *Urban Dynamics* depicts the economic and social forces governing the "filter-down" rate of a city's premium-housing PH stock into worker housing WH and eventually into underemployed housing UH. Within the urban model, for example, the average lifetime of premium housing is determined by the premium-housing-obsolescence multiplier PHOM, which measures the demand exerted by managerial-professionals for retention of the area's premium-housing stock.[1] Premium-housing obsolescence is increased when the housing stock is in excess, and it is reduced in periods of high demand for premium housing.

In his doctoral thesis, "Analysis and Improvement of a Dynamic Urban Model,"[2] Daniel Babcock has criticized the formulation employed in *Urban Dynamics* to compute housing-obsolescence rates. Babcock argues that the obsolescence rate of premium housing or worker housing ought to depend on the extant market demand for housing in the next lower category. According to this view, when worker housing is in excess supply, for example, the filter rate of premium housing into worker housing should be reduced. Conversely, a shortage of worker housing should stimulate increased premium housing filter-down.

Forrester's model does not include any influence of "demand from below" on housing lifetimes. Does *Urban Dynamics*, then, validly portray the dynamics of housing obsolescence? A more detailed representation of real-world behavior would probably entail explicitly noting the influence of worker competition for premium housing and of underemployed competition for worker housing on housing lifetimes. But are these details significant?

12.2 Changes in the Model

To answer this question, a structural change will be made to incorporate the effects of intergroup housing competition on housing obsolescence.[3] Forrester models premium-housing obsolescence PHO as

```
PHO.KL=(PHON)(PH.K)(PHOM.K)                              1, R
PHON=.03                                                 1.1, C
     PHO    - PREMIUM-HOUSING OBSOLESCENCE  (HOUSING
                UNITS/YEAR)
     PHON   - PREMIUM-HOUSING OBSOLESCENCE NORMAL
                (FRACTION/YEAR)
     PH     - PREMIUM HOUSING  (HOUSING UNITS)
     PHOM   - PREMIUM-HOUSING-OBSOLESCENCE MULTIPLIER
                (DIMENSIONLESS)
```

This formulation assumes that in periods of high managerial demand for premium housing PH, the premium-housing-obsolescence multiplier PHOM will be low, and premium dwellings will be maintained beyond their normal lifetime of 33 years. Conversely, when demand is slack, vacancy rates will tend to rise, thereby forcing lower rents, so premium housing will filter more rapidly into worker housing.

The influence of upper-income demand for premium housing on premium-housing lifetimes and the influence of labor demand for worker housing on premium-housing lifetimes must be treated separately in order to test their relative influences. Thus the premium-housing-obsolescence multiplier PHOM will be altered to reflect a composite of two influences:

```
PHOM.K=(PHOPD.K)(PHOWD.K)                                    2, A
    PHOM    - PREMIUM-HOUSING-OBSOLESCENCE MULTIPLIER
              (DIMENSIONLESS)
    PHOPD   - PREMIUM-HOUSING OBSOLESCENCE FROM PREMIUM
              DEMAND (DIMENSIONLESS)
    PHOWD   - PREMIUM-HOUSING OBSOLESCENCE FROM WORKER
              DEMAND  (DIMENSIONLESS)
```

Premium-housing-obsolescence from premium demand PHOPD corresponds to the original premium-housing-obsolescence multiplier specified in equations 80 and 80.1 of *Urban Dynamics*:

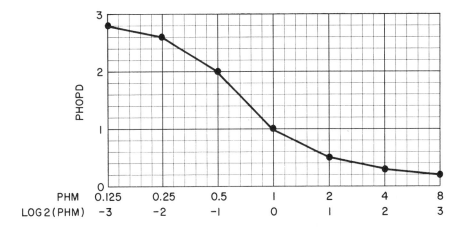

Figure 1 Lifetime of premium housing according to upper-income demand

```
PHOPD.K=TABHL(PHOPDT,1.44*LOGN(PHM.K),-3,3,1)          3, A
PHOPDT=2.8/2.6/2/1/.5/.3/.2                           3.1, T
    PHOPD   - PREMIUM-HOUSING OBSOLESCENCE FROM PREMIUM
              DEMAND (DIMENSIONLESS)
    PHM     - PREMIUM-HOUSING MULTIPLIER
              (DIMENSIONLESS)
```

The point at the extreme left of the table in Figure 1 corresponds to a hypothetical situation in which no managerial-professional population is available to inhabit the city's existing high-income dwellings. Under these conditions there would be little incentive to maintain and operate premium housing; the average premium-housing lifetime is therefore reduced to approximately 11 years. The right-hand side of Figure 1 reflects a rising demand for housing among high-income groups that can cause premium-housing lifetimes to increase up to a limit of 165 years.

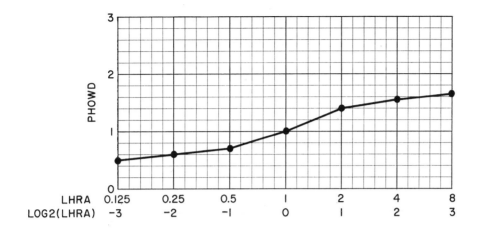

Figure 2 Lifetime of premium housing according to middle-income demand

Premium-housing obsolescence from worker demand PHOWD, which measures the influence of worker-housing demand on premium-housing obsolescence, is formulated as a function of the labor/housing ratio average LHRA. When worker demand for housing is high, premium housing will filter down more rapidly, and conversely:

```
PHOWD.K=TABHL(PHOWDT,1.44*LOGN(LHRA.K),-3,3,1)     4, A
PHOWDT=.5/.6/.7/1/1.4/1.55/1.65                    4.1, T
     PHOWD  - PREMIUM-HOUSING OBSOLESCENCE FROM WORKER
              DEMAND  (DIMENSIONLESS)
     LHRA   - LABOR/HOUSING RATIO AVERAGE
              (DIMENSIONLESS)
```

In Figure 2, the values for premium-housing obsolescence from worker demand have been chosen on the assumption that worker-housing demand is usually a less critical determinant of premium-housing lifetimes than the existing demand exerted by the city's managerial-professional population. For example, in an extended period of urgent demand for both premium and worker housing, the life expectancy of premium housing would in all probability be extended beyond its normal value.[4]

In gauging the profitability of converting premium-housing units into worker housing, owners respond to perceived conversion incentives rather than to actual conditions. It is assumed here that landlords and owners do not respond impetuously to short-term fluctuations in market incentives and that time is required to perceive conditions within the city. Therefore, a smoothed value of the labor/housing ratio LHR has been employed as one indicator of conversion

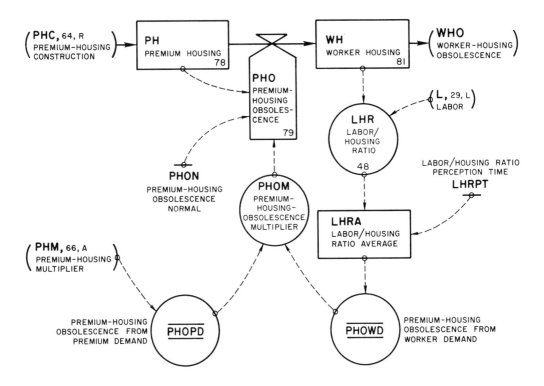

Figure 3   Flow diagram of changes in premium-housing sector

incentives:

```
LHRA.K=LHRA.J+(DT/LHRPT)(LHR.J-LHRA.J)                    5, L
LHRA=LHR                                                 5.1, N
LHRPT=5                                                  5.2, C
     LHRA    - LABOR/HOUSING RATIO AVERAGE
                   (DIMENSIONLESS)
     LHRPT   - LABOR/HOUSING RATIO PERCEPTION TIME
                   (YEARS)
     LHR     - LABOR/HOUSING RATIO    (DIMENSIONLESS)
```

The interactions in the premium-housing sector are shown by the flow diagram in Figure 3, using the standard symbols for levels, rates, and multipliers employed in *Urban Dynamics*.

The rate of worker-housing obsolescence WHO into underemployed housing UH is modeled analogously to premium-housing obsolescence PHO:

```
WHO.KL=(WHON)(WH.K)(WHOM.K)                              6, R
WHON=.02                                                 6.1, C
     WHO     - WORKER-HOUSING OBSOLESCENCE   (HOUSING
                   UNITS/YEAR)
     WHON    - WORKER-HOUSING OBSOLESCENCE NORMAL
                   (FRACTION/YEAR)
     WH      - WORKER HOUSING    (HOUSING UNITS)
     WHOM    - WORKER-HOUSING-OBSOLESCENCE MULTIPLIER
                   (DIMENSIONLESS)
```

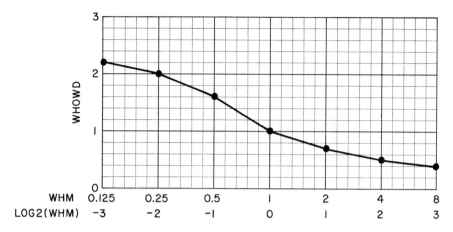

Figure 4 Lifetime of worker housing according to middle-income demand

```
WHOM.K=(WHOWD.K)(WHOUD.K)                              7, A
     WHOM   - WORKER-HOUSING-OBSOLESCENCE MULTIPLIER
              (DIMENSIONLESS)
     WHOWD  - WORKER-HOUSING OBSOLESCENCE FROM WORKER
              DEMAND (DIMENSIONLESS)
     WHOUD  - WORKER-HOUSING OBSOLESCENCE FROM
              UNDEREMPLOYED DEMAND  (DIMENSIONLESS)

WHOWD.K=TABHL(WHOWDT,1.44*LOGN(WHM.K),-3,3,1)          8, A
WHOWDT=2.2/2/1.6/1/.7/.5/.4                            8.1, T
     WHOWD  - WORKER-HOUSING OBSOLESCENCE FROM WORKER
              DEMAND (DIMENSIONLESS)
     WHM    - WORKER-HOUSING MULTIPLIER  (DIMENSIONLESS)
```

Worker-housing obsolescence from worker demand WHOWD has been drawn from equations 94 and 94.1 in *Urban Dynamics*. It measures the impact of worker demand for housing on worker-housing lifetimes. As seen in Figure 4, the average lifetime of worker housing is assumed to increase in periods of high demand for worker housing and to decrease in periods of excess housing availability.

```
WHOUD.K=TABHL(WHOUDT,1.44*LOGN(UHRA.K),-3,3,1)         9, A
WHOUDT=.4/.5/.6/1/1.5/1.7/1.8                          9.1, T
     WHOUD  - WORKER-HOUSING OBSOLESCENCE FROM
              UNDEREMPLOYED DEMAND   (DIMENSIONLESS)
     UHRA   - UNDEREMPLOYED/HOUSING RATIO AVERAGE
              (DIMENSIONLESS)

UHRA.K=UHRA.J+(DT/UHRPT)(UHR.J-UHRA.J)                 10, L
UHRA=UHR                                              10.1, N
UHRPT=5                                               10.2, C
     UHRA   - UNDEREMPLOYED/HOUSING RATIO AVERAGE
              (DIMENSIONLESS)
     UHRPT  - UNDEREMPLOYED/HOUSING RATIO PERCEPTION TIME
              (YEARS)
     UHR    - UNDEREMPLOYED/HOUSING RATIO
              (DIMENSIONLESS)
```

One objective in modeling "demand from below" is to simulate more credibly the process by which landlords decide the profitability of subdividing their worker-housing properties into underemployed housing. Worker-housing obsolescence from underemployed demand WHOUD (shown in Figure 5) measures the contribution of underemployed-housing demand as an input to this

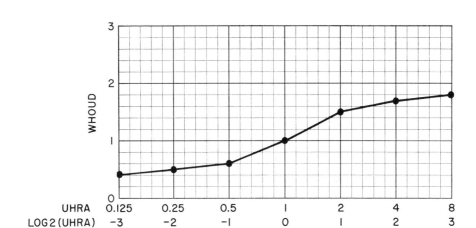

Figure 5   Lifetime of worker housing according to lower-income demand

decision point. The underemployed/housing ratio average UHRA has been employed as a surrogate for underemployed-housing demand.

One minor difference should be noted between the formulation for worker-housing obsolescence WHO and that for premium-housing obsolescence PHO: namely, demand from below is assumed to exert a comparatively greater influence on the lifetime of worker housing than on the obsolescence rate of premium housing. There are two reasons for this. If higher-income persons have an aversion to living in proximity to the underemployed, low worker demand for housing in an area with a high concentration of underemployed may encourage landlords to reduce expenditures for maintenance and repairs and thereby expedite the transition of worker housing to lower-income occupancy. As low-income housing begins to permeate middle-class neighborhoods, relentless "neighborhood effects" and "external effects" may then encourage further accelerated filter rates. A second inducement leading to increased worker housing filter-down is the practice of "block-busting."[5] There do not appear to be any comparable economic or social incentives for owners of premium housing to speed the transition of their properties into worker housing. It should be recalled, however, that the influence of demand from below on premium- and worker-housing lifetimes is here assumed to be somewhat secondary to the corresponding influences of managerial-professional housing demand and labor housing demand.

12.3 Results

With the *Urban Dynamics* model altered as described, we are ready to make computer runs and compare the results with those in the original *Urban Dynamics* model.

For the first run, the only changes made were those already described. The growing city reached an equilibrium after approximately 250 years. The equilibrium values obtained from Run 1 (Figure 6) were remarkably similar to those specified in *Urban Dynamics* (p. 43).

Variable	Urban Dynamics	Modified Model 1	Discrepancy (%)
Underemployed population	377,300	373,900	−1
Labor	392,600	396,000	+1
Managerial-professionals	71,000	71,500	+1
Underemployed housing units	310,100	303,500	−2
Worker housing	335,600	347,000	+3
Premium housing	110,900	110,300	−1
New-enterprise units	4,900	4,900	0
Mature business	7,800	7,900	+1
Declining industry	16,500	16,300	−1

Figure 6 Run 1: Simulation of *Urban Dynamics* growth model with modified housing-obsolescence formulation

In the second run, premium-housing obsolescence from worker demand PHOWD and worker-housing obsolescence from underemployed demand WHOUD were assumed to be more prominent determinants of premium- and worker-housing obsolescence rates, respectively. The intent was to determine the sensitivity of the model to changes in these two variables. As shown in Figures 7 and 8, the range of tables PHOWDT and WHOUDT was increased to

$$\text{T PHOWDT} = .25/.35/.5/1/1.8/2/2.1$$
$$\text{T WHOUDT} = .2/.3/.4/1/1.9/2.1/2.2$$

These two changes are the only further modifications implemented for Run 2. Once again, an equilibrium was obtained after 250 years (see Figure 9).

In Run 1 and in Run 2, the equilibrium underemployed/housing ratio UHR was about 0.82. In the stagnant city, underemployed housing appears to be in excess both relative to employment opportunities and relative to residential need,

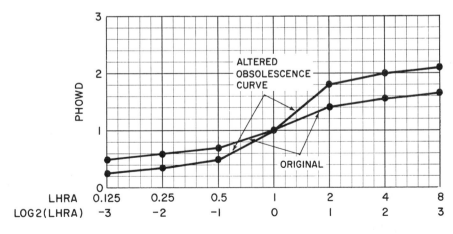

Figure 7 Increased sensitivity of premium-housing obsolescence to worker-housing demand

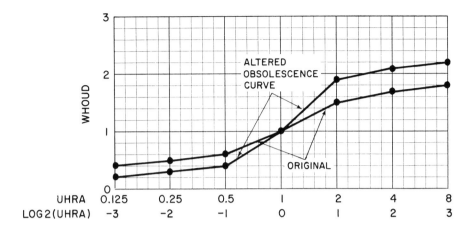

Figure 8   Increased sensitivity of worker-housing obsolescence to underemployed-housing demand

as shown in *Urban Dynamics*. An expanded version of the model would indicate a high local rate of housing abandonment.

For the third run, PHOWDT and WHOUDT were restored to their Run 1 values. But the *Urban Dynamics* revival policies were added to the simulation. New-enterprise construction normal NECN = 0.07 and slum-housing-demolition rate SHDR = 0.05 were implemented at year 300. A new equilibrium was reached at year 360. This equilibrium is summarized in Figure 10, together with the *Urban Dynamics* postrevival mode.

A fourth run, employing the more sensitive PHOWDT and WHOUDT, was made in combination with the revival policies. The results were markedly similar to those of Run 3.

Variable	Urban Dynamics	Modified Model 2	Discrepancy (%)
Underemployed population	377,300	370,000	−2
Labor	392,600	397,200	+1
Managerial-professionals	71,000	70,700	0
Underemployed housing units	310,100	301,400	−3
Worker housing	335,600	354,600	+5
Premium housing	110,900	106,800	−4
New-enterprise units	4,900	4,700	−4
Mature business	7,800	8,100	+4
Declining industry	16,500	16,400	−1

Figure 9   Run 2: Simulation of modified urban model—increased sensitivity to demand from below

Variable	Urban Dynamics Revival	Modified Model 1—Revival	Discrepancy (%)
Underemployed population	335,900	344,100	+3
Labor	600,000	602,900	0
Managerial-professionals	108,700	108,200	0
Underemployed housing units	175,300	183,100	+5
Worker housing	450,600	435,600	−3
Premium housing	152,800	.151,100	−1
New-enterprise units	8,000	7,500	−6
Mature business	12,000	12,000	0
Declining industry	22,200	26,000	+17

Figure 10   Run 3: Simulation of modified urban model—*Urban Dynamics* revival policies

12.4 Conclusions

The similarity of the results obtained from a modified model to those in *Urban Dynamics* indicates that market-induced demand from below is not essential to dynamic considerations of urban decay or urban revival. The addition of this mechanism to the *Urban Dynamics* model does not alter the conditions of excess housing and insufficient employment opportunities described in the book; furthermore, the results affirm the credibility of the *Urban Dynamics* revival policies.

Why do the computer results show that demand from below has such a negligible impact on the development of an urban area? We may examine this issue by analyzing the behavior of the modified urban model when it operates in conjunction with Forrester's revival policies (as summarized in Run 3). When slum-housing demolition is applied to the reviving city, the pressures generated by demand from below induce more worker housing to be converted into underemployed housing. But the increased filter-down causes other reactions throughout the system. In particular, the worker-housing market responds to compensate for the change.

Initially, the labor/housing ratio LHR rises, reflecting a decreased adequacy of the worker-housing stock. The diminished adequacy produces three responses: first, each unit of worker housing is retained longer in that category, so worker-housing obsolescence WHO is reduced. This effect counteracts the pressure (due to demand from below) for worker housing to filter-down at an increased pace. Second, worker-housing construction is augmented whenever the adequacy of worker housing is reduced; finally, increased worker demand for housing causes more premium-housing units to be converted into worker housing. Each effect is by itself minimal. Collectively, however, the three influences operate to restore internal balance in both the underemployed- and worker-housing markets. A similar set of forces readjusts the premium-housing sector. Not surprisingly, the urban model with demand from below reaches an equilibrium almost identical to that of the unaltered model.

In practice, not all structural changes in a dynamic model will evoke significant behavioral changes. The case of demand from below is a compelling illustration of this fact. Housing obsolescence due to demand from below does occur in real-world housing markets. Still, although the addition of demand from below may superficially improve the *credibility* of the *Urban Dynamics* model, it does not improve the *operation* of the model. Under such conditions, good modeling practice would dictate that the omission of demand from below in the *Urban Dynamics* model is justified; its omission avoids excessive model detail and focuses attention on the fundamental dynamic forces governing urban growth and decay.

Appendix: Analysis of Babcock's Formulation

In his thesis, Babcock suggested a formulation for demand from below that differs appreciably from the formulation presented in this paper. When he tested his formulation in the urban model, Babcock found that "the result of the modifications is to substantially eliminate the conditions of excessive underemployed labor force . . . and the shortage of new enterprise NE that Forrester concludes from his model are the inevitable equilibrium condition of the city."[6] Babcock's revisions thus produce behavior significantly different from the results presented in Runs 1 and 2. In view of these outcomes, it seems appropriate to analyze the substance of Babcock's revisions.

It is probably most revealing to examine Babcock's formulation for premium-housing obsolescence PHO, which is given as an inverse function of (PHMO.K/WHMO.K), where

```
PHMO.K=PHEM.K*PHGM.K*PHAM.K*PHPM.K                      1, A
    PHMO    - PREMIUM-HOUSING MULTIPLIER FOR OBSOLESCENCE
              (DIMENSIONLESS)
    PHEM    - PREMIUM-HOUSING ENTERPRISE MULTIPLIER
              (DIMENSIONLESS)
    PHGM    - PREMIUM-HOUSING-GROWTH MULTIPLIER
              (DIMENSIONLESS)
    PHAM    - PREMIUM-HOUSING-ADEQUACY MULTIPLIER
              (DIMENSIONLESS)
    PHPM    - PREMIUM-HOUSING POPULATION MULTIPLIER
              (DIMENSIONLESS)

WHMO.K=WHEM.K*WHGM.K*WHAM.K*WHUM.K                      2, A
    WHMO    - WORKER-HOUSING MULTIPLIER FOR OBSOLESCENCE
              (DIMENSIONLESS)
    WHEM    - WORKER-HOUSING ENTERPRISE MULTIPLIER
              (DIMENSIONLESS)
    WHGM    - WORKER-HOUSING-GROWTH MULTIPLIER
              (DIMENSIONLESS)
    WHAM    - WORKER-HOUSING-ADEQUACY MULTIPLIER
              (DIMENSIONLESS)
    WHUM    - WORKER-HOUSING UNDEREMPLOYED MULTIPLIER
              (DIMENSIONLESS)
```

As explained below, an important element of Babcock's formulation concerns the impact of population composition on housing obsolescence rates, as reflected in the ratio of the terms (PHPM.K/WHUM.K). When the social composition of the city becomes unfavorable, Forrester assumes in *Urban Dynamics* that the area becomes an unattractive location in which to operate high-price residences. As a result, premium-housing construction PHC is reduced; in addition, premium-housing obsolescence PHO is accelerated because of reduced expenditures for maintenance and repair. Both in *Urban Dynamics* and in Babcock's formulation, the influence of the population mix on premium-housing construction is given as follows:

```
PHPM.K=TABHL(PHPMT,MPR.K,0,.1,.02)                    3, A
PHPMT=.3/.7/1/1.2/1.3/1.3                             3.1, T
     PHPM    - PREMIUM-HOUSING POPULATION MULTIPLIER
               (DIMENSIONLESS)
     MPR     - MANAGER/POPULATION RATIO   (DIMENSIONLESS)
```

The worker-housing underemployed multiplier WHUM similarly gives the effect of the population mix on the worker-housing multiplier WHM:

```
WHUM.K=TABHL(WHUMT,LUR.K,0,5,1)                       4, A
WHUMT=.5/.8/1/1.2/1.3/1.3                             4.1, T
     WHUM    - WORKER-HOUSING UNDEREMPLOYED MULTIPLIER
               (DIMENSIONLESS)
     LUR     - LABOR/UNDEREMPLOYED RATIO   (DIMENSIONLESS)
```

In the growth run of the *Urban Dynamics* model, in fact, the premium-housing population multiplier PHPM always assumes the value of 1.3 since the manager/population ratio MPR is always greater than 0.08 (*Urban Dynamics*, pp. 42–43).[7] Thus the manager/population ratio exerts an *unchanging* influence on both premium-housing construction and premium-housing obsolescence. In contrast, the worker-housing underemployed multiplier WHUM declines from 1.3 to 0.8 as the labor/underemployed ratio LUR goes from an initial value well above 2 down to 1.04.

In Babcock's equations, premium-housing obsolescence PHO depends (inversely) on the ratio of (PHPM.K/WHUM.K); as a result, premium-housing obsolescence is *reduced* drastically as the city shifts from growth to equilibrium. We should normally expect both premium-housing and worker-housing obsolescence to increase as the city becomes economically stagnant. Babcock's formulation suggests, however, that premium-housing owners strive all the harder to maintain their properties as the social climate of their city deteriorates.

In effect, Babcock has inadvertently created several negative feedback loops that prevent the population balance of the city from becoming unfavorable. In his formulation, as the population balance of the city shifts toward more underemployed, premium-housing obsolescence is reduced. As a result, the premium-housing stock increases, causing more managers to be drawn to the city. In addition, the filter-down rate of high-quality housing into underemployed housing UH is decreased, and the underemployed population is reduced as a result (Figure 11). Both these effects tend to counteract the initial adverse change

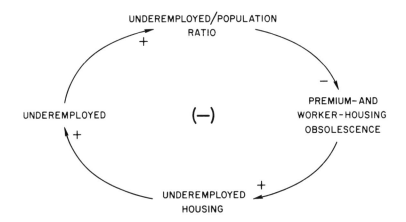

Figure 11   Negative feedback loop governing population balance in Babcock's formulation

in the area's population mix. It seems clear, however, that such mechanisms to rebalance population do not operate in real cities.

Notes

1. The premium-housing sector in the urban model is described in Jay W. Forrester, *Urban Dynamics* (Cambridge, Mass.: The M.I.T. Press, 1969), pp. 170–179.

2. Daniel L. Babcock, "Analysis and Improvement of a Dynamic Model," Ph.D. dissertation, University of California, Los Angeles, 1970.

3. The appendix to this paper analyzes Babcock's formulation of housing-obsolescence rates.

4. The sensitivity of the model to this assumption is examined in Section 12.3.

5. Cf. R. F. Muth, *Cities and Housing* (Chicago: University of Chicago Press, 1969), pp. 108–111. See also Thomas C. Schelling, "A Process of Residential Segregation: Neighborhood Tipping," in *Racial Discrimination in Economic Life*, ed. A. H. Pascal (Lexington, Mass.: Lexington Books, 1972).

6. Babcock, "Analysis and Improvement," p. 137.

7. Renormalizing this multiplier to reflect a reasonable range of the managerial/population ratio has a minimal effect on the computer simulations shown in *Urban Dynamics*.

13
Modeling City-Suburb Interactions

Alan K. Graham

The Urban Dynamics *model gives an aggregate portrayal of the flows of people and industry occurring between an urban area and its external environment. An important criticism of the urban model is that the city's environment subsumes both nearby suburban towns and more distant urban and rural areas, and these should be represented explicitly in an adequate model. The inclusion of a suburban sector in an expanded urban model would certainly extend the range of policy issues addressed by the model. However, before proceeding to develop a suburban model, it is important to examine how commuting and suburban growth might influence the policy implications derived from the original urban model.*

The following paper by Alan K. Graham develops a fairly simple extension of the Urban Dynamics *model to depict city-suburb interactions such as commuting and tax competition. The primary motivation for this study was to determine whether more extensive disaggregation of the original model is warranted. Although the results presented here lend support to the basic structure of the urban model, future efforts to model the dynamics of suburban and metropolitan growth may promise still greater coverage of prominent urban policy questions.*

13
Modeling City-Suburb Interactions

13.1 Introduction

Critics have often faulted *Urban Dynamics* for not explicitly portraying the impact of suburbs or commuters on a city's development. This paper discusses how the *Urban Dynamics* model represents a city's external environment and then shows one way in which commuting and suburban growth can be directly incorporated into the model.

The theory of feedback-system modeling tells us that we need model only a very small part of the real world explicitly and dynamically. Every feedback system has around it a conceptual boundary that circumscribes the elements that interact to produce dynamic behavior. Contained within the boundary should be all the dynamic structure necessary to explain and possibly cure the problem under study. Now, elements within the system can affect elements outside the system. But the system boundary must be drawn so that internal elements cannot influence variables outside the system that in turn exert a significant influence on the system. Stating this positively, all the feedback loops that can alter the overall behavior of the system must be included within the system boundary.

The principle that all important feedback loops must be included within the structure of a dynamic model can lighten the load of the model builder and help direct his efforts; the principle implies that many phenomena need not be explicitly incorporated into a feedback model. Forces that act on the system from outside but are not significantly affected by the internal dynamics of the system are called unidirectional effects; these can be represented satisfactorily by constants or by exogenous inputs. For example, fluctuations in interest rates that influence inner-city business expansion could appear in the *Urban Dynamics* model as a random or cyclic input to the new-enterprise-construction rate. The following section of this paper will give examples of unidirectional phenomena subsumed by constants.

13.2 The Present Urban Model

One of the most difficult concepts in *Urban Dynamics* concerns the interaction of the central city with its "limitless environment." The urban area's environment is actually the rest of the universe. To produce an explicit and detailed model of the universe is of course impossible and indeed unwise; a useful model must at least be tractable. Phenomena should not be modeled explicitly "because they are there"; each proposed piece of structure should be judged by what it contributes to achieving the model's purpose.

The purpose of *Urban Dynamics* is to examine the underlying forces that can account for urban growth and stagnation, and to assist in formulating general policies to achieve urban revival. Toward that end, the model deals with the balance among population, housing, and employment in a fixed urban land area. Thus the question of "how should the environment be represented?" becomes the much more specific question, "how does the environment affect migration and the creation of housing and employment?" The limitless environment in *Urban Dynamics* therefore has two broad influences on the urban area: first, the environment is the source and recipient of flows of people, housing, and economic activity to and from the area. Managers might come from the suburbs of different cities and laborers from the outer city, but all that matters is that these people are available for migration in some part of the city's environment. The urban area's environment is therefore limitless, in the sense that there are more potential migrants than the urban area can possibly contain. Second, the environment functions as a moving reference point with which to compare conditions within the area to govern the flows of people, housing, and economic activity.

Flow rates such as construction, in-migration, and out-migration are all modulated by comparisons of the internal conditions in the urban area with the implicit conditions in the environment. From such conditions as tax rates, employment, housing densities, and land availability, the model computes each of the various flow rates.

For modeling purposes, absolute measures of the attractiveness of the urban area are unimportant. The *Urban Dynamics* model recognizes only factors that differentiate the urban area from its environment. A generally rising standard of living does not significantly alter the relationship of the urban area to its environment; thus the "limitless environment" functions not just as a reference point but as a moving reference point. For this reason, the model need not and does not consider explicitly such effects as technological change, nor does it portray explicitly the dynamics of the national economy.

An example will profitably illustrate representation of the environment in the urban model. The following rate equation gives the number of labor-class people moving into the urban area from the environment per year:

$$LA.KL=(LAN)(L.K)(LAMP.K) \qquad\qquad 41,R$$

$$LAN=.03 \qquad\qquad 41.1,C$$

        LA   - LABOR ARRIVALS (MEN/YEAR)
        LAN - LABOR ARRIVALS NORMAL (FRACTION/YEAR)
        L   - LABOR (MEN)
        LAMP - LABOR-ARRIVAL MULTIPLIER PERCEIVED
               (DIMENSIONLESS)

The equation for labor arrivals has three components: first, the equation assumes that the in-migration rate will be approximately proportional to the number of people already in the city; this gives the term of L.K (labor). The term labor arrivals normal LAN tells what fraction of that labor class population will arrive per year. It is this parameter that describes the fixed relationships between the urban area and its environment.

A large number of phenomena are implicit in the labor arrivals normal LAN. For example, many studies show that intercity distance strongly controls migration, and many critics have noted its apparent absence in the model. However, as long as the nature of the environment (that is, distances and proportional sizes of metropolitan areas) remains constant, the *Urban Dynamics* model can accurately portray the nature of that environment through the normal rate constants in the model. If travel to the particular urban area from other urban areas were particularly difficult, then LAN might be a fairly small number. Similarly, if the urban area were situated in a region favored with great natural beauty, LAN might be large.

The last term of LA modulates the fixed in-migration, (L.K)(LAN), in response to the city's internal conditions. The labor-arrival multiplier LAM is in turn the product of several functions that reflect measurements of the individual internal conditions:

```
LAM.K =(LAJM.K) (LAUM.K) (LATM.K) (LAHM.K) (LAF)          43,A

LAF=1                                                     43.1,C
```

LAM	–	LABØR-ARRIVAL MULTIPLIER (DIMENSIØNLESS)
LAJM	–	LABØR-ARRIVAL JØB MULTIPLIER (DIMENSIØNLESS)
LAUM	–	LABØR-ARRIVAL UNDEREMPLØYED MULTIPLIER (DIMENSIØNLESS)
LATM	–	LABØR-ARRIVAL TAX MULTIPLIER (DIMENSIØNLESS)
LAHM	–	LABØR-ARRIVAL HØUSING MULTIPLIER (DIMENSIØNLESS)
LAF	–	LABØR-ARRIVAL FACTØR (DIMENSIØNLESS)

The equations and graph (Figure 1) that follow describe a function that gives the effect of one single condition, the population density of labor housing, on labor arrivals:

```
LAHM.K =TABLE(LAHMT,LHR.K,0,3,.5)                         47,A

LAHMT=1.3/1.2/1/.5/.2/.1/.05                              47.1,T
```

LAHM	–	LABØR-ARRIVAL HØUSING MULTIPLIER (DIMENSIØNLESS)
LAHMT	–	LABØR-ARRIVAL-HØUSING-MULTIPLIER TABLE
LHR	–	LABØR/HØUSING RATIØ (DIMENSIØNLESS)

All such multipliers have a point at which the multiplier is equal to one. At this "definitional point," the multiplier has a neutral effect on the system flow rate; when all the conditions within the area are at their definitional point, the product of all the multipliers will be equal to one, and the rate will have its "normal" value. The normal constant, in this case labor arrivals normal LAN, gives what migration would be if conditions inside and outside were normalized.

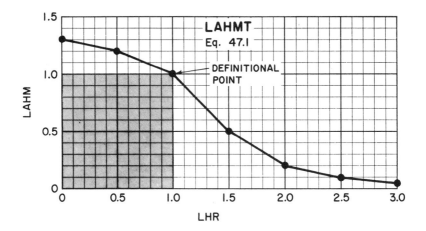

Figure 1 Influence of housing adequacy on labor migration

"Normal" conditions within the area are specified by the location of the definitional points of the multipliers. In this instance, the normal housing condition inside the city is defined so that the labor/housing ratio LHR equals one. Labor arrivals normal LAN reflects the influence of the "normal" conditions outside the area; LAN specifies the migration resulting from the comparison of internal conditions with those outside the area. The multipliers, then, specify the change in labor arrivals LA produced when conditions deviate from their norms. An area need not have ever attained normal conditions; the definitional points are merely convenient reference points by which to specify the formulation of the rate.

13.3 Modeling Commuting

We are now in a position to experiment with city-suburb interactions in the *Urban Dynamics* model by explicitly modeling commuting. The purpose of these experiments was to suggest whether or not the omission of an explicit representation of commuting and suburbs in any way biased Forrester's results, as has been suggested in several published reviews of *Urban Dynamics*. Although the present modifications represent commuting and suburban growth only crudely, the experimental outcomes will indicate the possible worth of more extensive modeling. The appendix to this paper provides the DYNAMO equations for the four major modifications described here:

1. The populations and economic activity surrounding the central city are explicitly represented, although roughly: The population surrounding PS grows, but independently of events in the central urban area. Population and jobs were assumed to be approximately in balance in the surrounding urban and suburban areas, and the composition of the population surrounding was assumed to be constant.

2. All variables that were influenced by the central-city job market in the original *Urban Dynamics* model were made to respond to the metropolitan area-wide job market. Throughout the model, all ratios of central-city population categories to central-city jobs for those categories were replaced by the corresponding metropolitan ratios. For example, the manager/job ratio MR was everywhere replaced by the metropolitan manager/job ratio MMJR, which is just the sum of central-city managerial-professionals MP and surrounding managerial-professionals MPS, divided by the sum of central-city manager jobs and surrounding manager jobs:

$$MMJR = \frac{MP + MPS}{MJ + MPS}$$

Since population and jobs in the city's surrounding areas were assumed always to be in balance, managerial-professionals surrounding MPS appears both in the numerator to represent a population size and in the denominator to represent the number of surrounding jobs. The metropolitan area-wide job ratios for labor L and underemployed U are computed similarly.

3. The distribution of jobs and population between the central city and surrounding areas determined the commuting patterns. Employees and jobs were assumed to be randomly connected within the total metropolitan area, but with a bias toward living and working in the same area.[1] Thus, for example, the fraction of surrounding managers who commute to the central city will be equal to the fraction of the total manager jobs that are in the central city times a bias factor representing the willingness or ability to commute long distances:

$$FSMC-(\frac{MJ}{MJ + MPS})(MICF)$$

where

FSMC–fraction surrounding managers commuting
MJ–central city manager jobs
MPS–managerial-professionals surrounding
MICF–manager in-commuting factor

The underemployed were assumed to commute less than labor, who were assumed to commute less than managerial-professionals.[2]

4. A cost of $60 per commuter per year was added to city's tax needs, reflecting the additional costs of road maintenance and the provision of parking facilities. Figure 2 summarizes the behavior of the modified model. The first column of Figure 2 summarizes the equilibrium conditions of the commuting model when population surrounding PS is held constant at 500,000. Taking these values as the initial conditions and now letting PS grow, the model exhibits the same mode of stagnation as did Forrester's original model: an excess of old housing attracts many underemployed to the central city despite a severe job shortage.

As stated earlier, for simplicity, the population surrounding PS grows exogenously. Since the population surrounding affects commuting patterns and the central-city labor market, the modified model does not reach an equilibrium; for example, in the basic simulation (where no policies are implemented) the

		Time = 0	Time = 50 years	Job Training Program	Low-Cost-Housing Construction	Slum-housing Demolition and New-Enterprise Construction
MP	managerial-professionals	95,580	163,840	158,600	38,730	203,010
L	labor	319,940	268,480	389,520	165,420	467,900
U	underemployed	358,590	375,110	362,880	434,010	310,300
PH	premium housing	151,700	232,320	201,990	39,040	259,590
WH	worker housing	295,980	254,250	312,430	154,340	376,270
UH	underemployed housing	305,100	10,163	300,280	538,980	169,520
NE	new enterprise	3,877	1,776	1,776	26	4,445
MB	mature business	6,205	3,765	4,223	165	8,333
DI	declining industry	14,114	14,518	14,336	15,990	21,512
MHR	manager/housing ratio	1.050	1.175	1.309	1.654	1.303
LHR	labor/housing ratio	1.081	1.056	1.247	1.072	1.244
UHR	underemployed/housing ratio	0.784	0.817	0.806	0.537	1.220
MR	manager/job ratio	2.274	5.620	5.314	2.114	3.628
LR	labor/job ratio	0.953	1.028	1.476	0.868	1.007
UR	underemployed/job ratio	2.076	2.888	3.025	4.454	1.338
UM	underemployed mobility	0.041	0.039	0.090	0.023	0.074
TRN	tax ratio needed	2.312	2.555	2.385	5.380	1.550
LFO	land fraction occupied	0.801	0.833	0.855	0.766	0.874
LD	labor departures	10,526	10,163	20,003	8,067	16,045
UA	underemployed arrivals	15,844	15,425	21,957	15,064	17,942
UD	underemployed departures	15,602	16,122	13,168	16,546	15,037
UTLN	underemployed to labor net	5,562	5,500	15,211	4,013	7,635

Figure 2 Simulation results

central city managerial-professional population grows substantially over 50 years (Figure 2, second column). In Forrester's original model, the managerial-professional population attains an equilibrium due to out-migration, stimulated by serious job shortage in the central city. In the modified model, migration responds to metropolitan area-wide job conditions, so as population surrounding PS grows, central city job conditions become less important in determining the metropolitan job ratios. Thus the shortage of managerial jobs within the central city exerts less of a stimulus to manager departures MD.[3]

The managerial-professional population in the central city therefore grows and, in growing, stimulates premium-housing construction. Eventually, high land occupancy depresses worker-housing construction WHC and new-enterprise construction NEC.

The third column of Figure 2 shows the results after fifty years of a job training program. The training program (as discussed in Section 4.2 of *Urban Dynamics*) converts 5 percent of the underemployed population into skilled labor every year. During the first years of the program, a large portion of the underemployed population is converted to labor, so the underemployed population declines and the labor population increases. However, as the program continues, the central city becomes more attractive to underemployed from outside the central city because of improved job conditions and high upward mobility. Thus underemployed arrivals UA increase, eventually returning the underemployed population close to what it would have been without the training program. Although underemployed upward economic mobility UM is greatly increased, the training program ultimately creates severe employment problems for both labor and underemployed. The tax ratio needed TRN declines slightly, although the decline may be unrealistic, since the training program is assumed in the model to have no direct monetary cost to the central city.

The fourth column of Figure 2 shows the results of applying a low-cost housing construction program (discussed in Section 4.4 of *Urban Dynamics*) to the modified model. The housing program severely depresses the urban area; and the managerial-professional and new enterprise NE labor populations drop significantly. Underemployed upward economic mobility UM is nearly halved, while the tax ratio needed TRN doubles.

The last column in Figure 2 shows the results of applying a policy that Forrester, in Section 5.7 of *Urban Dynamics*, found to improve the economic health of the city substantially. The policy consists of encouraging new-enterprise construction and slum-housing demolition. In the modified model, this revival policy substantially improves the job conditions over what they would have been without the policy. The tax ratio needed TRN falls, and underemployed upward economic mobility UM nearly doubles. The central city functions as an effective economic converter, as it did in Forrester's original simulations. The underemployed population in the city is lowered because of the rapid upward economic mobility into the labor class. The increased flow from underemployed to labor UTL allows more underemployed arrivals UA than in the basic simulation. The ratios of population to housing show modest increases.

It would appear, then, that a spatial job market and commuting per se do not really alter the policy suggestions of *Urban Dynamics*; the qualitative response of the modified model to policies is very similar to that of the original model. Of course, Forrester's model cannot answer all conceivable questions about urban policies relating to suburbs and commuting; undoubtedly issues exist whose resolution would require a far more explicit and realistic consideration of commuting. However, the results presented here indicate that a more thorough representation of commuting would shed little new light on those policy questions addressed in the *Urban Dynamics* book.

Appendix: Documentor Listing of Model Changes.

```
PS.K=PS.J+(DT)(PSG.JK)                                    1, L
PS=5E5                                                    1.1, N
        PS    - POPULATION SURROUNDING (MEN)
        PSG   - POPULATION-SURROUNDING GROWTH (MEN/YEAR)


PSG.KL=PS.K*PSGM.K/30                                     2, R
        PSG   - POPULATION-SURROUNDING GROWTH (MEN/YEAR)
        PS    - POPULATION SURROUNDING (MEN)
        PSGM  - POPULATION-SURROUNDING GROWTH MULTIPLIER
                (DIMENSIONLESS)


PSGM.K=TABHL(PSGMT,PS.K,C,1.25*PSEM,PSEM/4)               3, A
PSGMT=0/1/1.3/.6/0/-1                                     3.1, T
PSEM=2E6                                                  3.2, C
        PSGM  - POPULATION-SURROUNDING GROWTH MULTIPLIER
                (DIMENSIONLESS)
        PS    - POPULATION SURROUNDING (MEN)
        PSEM  - POPULATION-SURROUNDING EFFECTIVE MAXIMUM
                (MEN)


LS.K=PS.K*FLS                                             4, A
FLS=.6                                                    4.1, C
        LS    - LABOR SURROUNDING (MEN)
        PS    - POPULATION SURROUNDING (MEN)
        FLS   - FRACTION LABOR SURROUNDING (DIMENSIONLESS)


MPS.K=PS.K*FMPS                                           5, A
FMPS=.3                                                   5.1, C
        MPS   - MANAGERIAL-PROFESSIONALS SURROUNDING (MEN)
        PS    - POPULATION SURROUNDING (MEN)
        FMPS  - FRACTION MANAGERIAL-PROFESSIONALS
                SURROUNDING (DIMENSIONLESS)


US.K=PS.K*FUS                                             6, A
FUS=.1                                                    6.1, C
        US    - UNDEREMPLOYED SURROUNDING (MEN)
        PS    - POPULATION SURROUNDING (MEN)
        FUS   - FRACTION UNDEREMPLOYED SURROUNDING
                (DIMENSIONLESS)


ELJM.K=TABHL(ELJMT,(SWIN)(MLJRP.K)+(1-SWIN)(LRP.K)        7, A
,0,2,.25)
ELJMT=0/.05/.15/.4/1/1.5/1.7/1.8/1.8                      7.1, T
SWIN=1                                                    7.2, C
        ELJM  - ENTERPRISE LABOR/JOB MULTIPLIER
                (DIMENSIONLESS)
        SWIN  - SUBURBAN SECTOR SWITCH-IN (DIMENSIONLESS)
        MLJRP - METROPOLITAN LABOR/JOB RATIO PERCEIVED
                (DIMENSIONLESS)
        LRP   - LABOR/JOB RATIO PERCEIVED (DIMENSIONLESS)
```

```
MLJRP.K=MLJRP.J+(DT/MLJRPT)(MLJR.J-MLJRP.J)          8, L
MLJRP=1                                              8.1, N
MLJRPT=5                                             8.2, C
    MLJRP   - METROPOLITAN LABOR/JOB RATIO PERCEIVED
                (DIMENSIONLESS)
    MLJRPT  - METROPOLITAN LABOR/JOB RATIO PERCEPTION
                TIME (YEARS)
    MLJR    - METROPOLITAN LABOR/JOB RATIO
                (DIMENSIONLESS)


MLJR.K=(LS.K+L.K)/(LS.K+LJ.K)                        9, A
    MLJR    - METROPOLITAN LABOR/JOB RATIO
                (DIMENSIONLESS)
    LS      - LABOR SURROUNDING (MEN)
    L       - LABOR (MEN)
    LJ      - LABOR JOBS (MEN)

LLF.K=TABHL(LLFT,(SWIN)(MLJR.K)+(1-SWIN)(LR.K),0,2,  10, A
 .5)
LLFT=0/.01/.03/.1/.3                                 10.1, T
    LLF     - LABOR-LAYOFF FRACTION (FRACTION/YEAR)
    SWIN    - SUBURBAN SECTOR SWITCH-IN (DIMENSIONLESS)
    MLJR    - METROPOLITAN LABOR/JOB RATIO
                (DIMENSIONLESS)
    LR      - LABOR/JOB RATIO (DIMENSIONLESS)

LSM.K=TABHL(LSMT,(SWIN)(MLJR.K)+(1-SWIN)(LR.K),0,2,  11, A
 .5)
LSMT=2.4/2/1/.4/.2                                   11.1, T
    LSM     - LABOR-SUPPLY MULTIPLIER (DIMENSIONLESS)
    SWIN    - SUBURBAN SECTOR SWITCH-IN (DIMENSIONLESS)
    MLJR    - METROPOLITAN LABOR/JOB RATIO
                (DIMENSIONLESS)
    LR      - LABOR/JOB RATIO (DIMENSIONLESS)

LAJM.K=TABHL(LAJMT,(SWIN)(MLJR.K)+(1-SWIN)(LR.K),0,  12, A
 2,.25)
LAJMT=2.6/2.6/2.4/1.8/1/.4/.2/.1/.05                 12.1, T
    LAJM    - LABOR-ARRIVAL JOB MULTIPLIER
                (DIMENSIONLESS)
    SWIN    - SUBURBAN SECTOR SWITCH-IN (DIMENSIONLESS)
    MLJR    - METROPOLITAN LABOR/JOB RATIO
                (DIMENSIONLESS)
    LR      - LABOR/JOB RATIO (DIMENSIONLESS)

LCR.K=TABHL(LCRT,(SWIN)(MLJR.K)+(1-SWIN)(LR.K),0,2,  13, A
 .5)
LCRT=0/.5/.9/1.1/1.15                                13.1, T
    LCR     - LABOR CONSTRUCTION RATIO (DIMENSIONLESS)
    SWIN    - SUBURBAN SECTOR SWITCH-IN (DIMENSIONLESS)
    MLJR    - METROPOLITAN LABOR/JOB RATIO
                (DIMENSIONLESS)
    LR      - LABOR/JOB RATIO (DIMENSIONLESS)


MAJM.K=TABHL(MAJMT,(SWIN)(MMJR.K)+(1-SWIN)(MR.K),0,  14, A
 2,.25)
MAJMT=2.7/2.6/2.4/2/1/.4/.2/.1/.05                   14.1, T
    MAJM    - MANAGER-ARRIVAL JOB MULTIPLIER
                (DIMENSIONLESS)
    SWIN    - SUBURBAN SECTOR SWITCH-IN (DIMENSIONLESS)
    MMJR    - METROPOLITAN MANAGER/JOB RATIO
                (DIMENSIONLESS)
    MR      - MANAGER/JOB RATIO (DIMENSIONLESS)

MMJR.K=(MPS.K+MP.K)/(MPS.K+MJ.K)                     15, A
    MMJR    - METROPOLITAN MANAGER/JOB RATIO
                (DIMENSIONLESS)
    MPS     - MANAGERIAL-PROFESSIONALS SURROUNDING (MEN)
    MP      - MANAGERIAL-PROFESSIONALS (MEN)
    MJ      - MANAGER JOBS (MEN)


MSM.K=TABHL(MSMT,(SWIN)(MMJR.K)+(1-SWIN)(MR.K),0,2,  16, A
 .25)
MSMT=2.3/2.2/2/1.6/1/.5/.2/.1/.05                    16.1, T
    MSM     - MANAGER-SUPPLY MULTIPLIER (DIMENSIONLESS)
    SWIN    - SUBURBAN SECTOR SWITCH-IN (DIMENSIONLESS)
    MMJR    - METROPOLITAN MANAGER/JOB RATIO
                (DIMENSIONLESS)
    MR      - MANAGER/JOB RATIO (DIMENSIONLESS)
```

```
EMM.K=TABHL(EMMT,(SWIN)(MMJR.K)+(1-SWIN)(MR.K),0,2,  17, A
 .25)
EMMT=.1/.15/.3/.5/1/1.4/1.7/1.9/2                    17.1, T
      EMM    - ENTERPRISE MANAGER/JOB MULTIPLIER
               (DIMENSIONLESS)
      SWIN   - SUBURBAN SECTOR SWITCH-IN (DIMENSIONLESS)
      MMJR   - METROPOLITAN MANAGER/JOB RATIO
               (DIMENSIONLESS)
      MR     - MANAGER/JOB RATIO (DIMENSIONLESS)

ULJR.K=TABHL(ULJRT,(SWIN)(MLJR.K)+(1-SWIN)(LR.K),0,  18, A
 2,.5)
ULJRT=1.15/.8/.5/.25/.1                              18.1, T
      ULJR   - UNDEREMPLOYED/LABOR JOB RATIO
               (DIMENSIONLESS)
      SWIN   - SUBURBAN SECTOR SWITCH-IN (DIMENSIONLESS)
      MLJR   - METROPOLITAN LABOR/JOB RATIO
               (DIMENSIONLESS)
      LR     - LABOR/JOB RATIO (DIMENSIONLESS)

MUJR.K=(US.K+U.K)/(US.K+UJ.K)                        19, A
      MUJR   - METROPOLITAN UNDEREMPLOYED/JOB RATIO
               (DIMENSIONLESS)
      US     - UNDEREMPLOYED SURROUNDING (MEN)
      U      - UNDEREMPLOYED (MEN)
      UJ     - UNDEREMPLOYED JOBS (MEN)


UJM.K=TABHL(UJMT,(SWIN)(MUJR.K)+(1-SWIN)(UR.K),0,3,  20, A
 .25)
UJMT=2/2/1.9/1.6/1/.6/.4/.3/.2/.15/.1/.05/.02        20.1, T
      UJM    - UNDEREMPLOYED/JOB MULTIPLIER
               (DIMENSIONLESS)
      SWIN   - SUBURBAN SECTOR SWITCH-IN (DIMENSIONLESS)
      MUJR   - METROPOLITAN UNDEREMPLOYED/JOB RATIO
               (DIMENSIONLESS)
      UR     - UNDEREMPLOYED/JOB RATIO (DIMENSIONLESS)

UFW.K=TABHL(UFWT,(SWIN)(MUJR.K)+(1-SWIN)(UR.K),0,4,  21, A
 1)
UFWT=.9/.8/.5/.33/.25                                21.1, T
      UFW    - UNDEREMPLOYED FRACTION WORKING
               (DIMENSIONLESS)
      SWIN   - SUBURBAN SECTOR SWITCH-IN (DIMENSIONLESS)
      MUJR   - METROPOLITAN UNDEREMPLOYED/JOB RATIO
               (DIMENSIONLESS)
      UR     - UNDEREMPLOYED/JOB RATIO (DIMENSIONLESS)

TOC.K=MP.K*FMCO.K+L.K*FLCO.K+U.K*FUCO.K              22, A
      TOC    - TOTAL OUTWARD COMMUTERS (MEN)
      MP     - MANAGERIAL-PROFESSIONALS (MEN)
      FMCO   - FRACTION MANAGERS COMMUTING OUTWARD
               (DIMENSIONLESS)
      L      - LABOR (MEN)
      FLCO   - FRACTION LABOR COMMUTING OUTWARDS
               (DIMENSIONLESS)
      U      - UNDEREMPLOYED (MEN)
      FUCO   - FRACTION UNDEREMPLOYED COMMUTING OUTWARD
               (DIMENSIONLESS)



FMCO.K=(MPS.K/(MPS.K+MJ.K))*MOCF                     23, A
MOCF=.7                                              23.1, C
      FMCO   - FRACTION MANAGERS COMMUTING OUTWARD
               (DIMENSIONLESS)
      MPS    - MANAGERIAL-PROFESSIONALS SURROUNDING (MEN)
      MJ     - MANAGER JOBS (MEN)
      MOCF   - MANAGER OUT-COMMUTING FACTOR
               (DIMENSIONLESS)

FLCO.K=(LS.K/(LS.K+L.K))*LOCF                        24, A
LOCF=.5                                              24.1, C
      FLCO   - FRACTION LABOR COMMUTING OUTWARDS
               (DIMENSIONLESS)
      LS     - LABOR SURROUNDING (MEN)
      L      - LABOR (MEN)
      LOCF   - LABOR OUT-COMMUTING FACTOR (DIMENSIONLESS)
```

```
FUCO.K=(US.K/(US.K+U.K))*UOCF                          25, A
UOCF=.3                                                25.1, C
    FUCO   - FRACTION UNDEREMPLOYED COMMUTING OUTWARD
               (DIMENSIONLESS)
    US     - UNDEREMPLOYED SURROUNDING (MEN)
    U      - UNDEREMPLOYED (MEN)
    UOCF   - UNDEREMPLOYED OUT-COMMUTING FACTOR
               (DIMENSIONLESS)


FSMC.K=(MJ.K/(MJ.K+MPS.K))*MICF                        26, A
MICF=.7                                                26.1, C
    FSMC   - FRACTION SURROUNDING MANAGERS COMMUTING
               (DIMENSIONLESS)
    MJ     - MANAGER JOBS (MEN)
    MPS    - MANAGERIAL-PROFESSIONALS SURROUNDING (MEN)
    MICF   - MANAGER IN-COMMUTING FACTOR (DIMENSIONLESS)

FSLC.K=(LJ.K/(LJ.K+LS.K))*LICF                         27, A
LICF=.5                                                27.1, C
    FSLC   - FRACTION SURROUNDING LABOR COMMUTING
               (DIMENSIONLESS)
    LJ     - LABOR JOBS (MEN)
    LS     - LABOR SURROUNDING (MEN)
    LICF   - LABOR IN-COMMUTING FACTOR (DIMENSIONLESS)

FSUC.K=(UJ.K/(UJ.K+US.K))*UICF                         28, A
UICF=.3                                                28.1, C
    FSUC   - FRACTION SURROUNDING UNDEREMPLOYED
               COMMUTING (DIMENSIONLESS)
    UJ     - UNDEREMPLOYED JOBS (MEN)
    US     - UNDEREMPLOYED SURROUNDING (MEN)
    UICF   - UNDEREMPLOYED IN-COMMUTING FACTOR
               (DIMENSIONLESS)

TIC.K=MPS.K*FSMC.K+LS.K*FSLC.K+US.K*FSUC.K             29, A
MAN=.025                                               29.1, C
MDN=.025                                               29.2, C
    TIC    - TOTAL IN-COMMUTERS (MEN)
    MPS    - MANAGERIAL-PROFESSIONALS SURROUNDING (MEN)
    FSMC   - FRACTION SURROUNDING MANAGERS COMMUTING
               (DIMENSIONLESS)
    LS     - LABOR SURROUNDING (MEN)
    FSLC   - FRACTION SURROUNDING LABOR COMMUTING
               (DIMENSIONLESS)
    US     - UNDEREMPLOYED SURROUNDING (MEN)
    FSUC   - FRACTION SURROUNDING UNDEREMPLOYED
               COMMUTING (DIMENSIONLESS)
    MAN    - MANAGER ARRIVALS NORMAL (FRACTION/YEAR)
    MDN    - MANAGER DEPARTURES NORMAL (FRACTION/YEAR)



TN.K=(TMP*MPFS*MP.K+TLP*LFS*L.K+UFS*TUP*U.K+YCC*       30, A
  (TOC.K+TIC.K))(TCM.K)
YCC=60                                                 30.2, C
    TN     - TAXES NEEDED (DOLLARS/YEAR)
    TMP    - TAX PER MANAGEMENT PERSON (DOLLARS/PERSON/
               YEAR)
    MPFS   - MANAGERIAL-PROFESSIONAL FAMILY SIZE
               (PEOPLE/MAN)
    MP     - MANAGERIAL-PROFESSIONALS (MEN)
    TLP    - TAX PER LABOR PERSON (DOLLARS/PERSON/YEAR)
    LFS    - LABOR FAMILY SIZE (PEOPLE/MAN)
    L      - LABOR (MEN)
    UFS    - UNDEREMPLOYED FAMILY SIZE (PEOPLE/MAN)
    TUP    - TAX PER UNDEREMPLOYED PERSON (DOLLARS/
               PERSON/YEAR)
    U      - UNDEREMPLOYED (MEN)
    YCC    - YEARLY COST PER COMMUTER (DOLLARS/MAN/YEAR)
    TOC    - TOTAL OUTWARD COMMUTERS (MEN)
    TIC    - TOTAL IN-COMMUTERS (MEN)
    TCM    - TAX COLLECTION MULTIPLIER (DIMENSIONLESS)

MAPM.K=TABHL(MAPMT,MPR.K,0,2.5*MPRN,.5*MPRN)           31, A
MAPMT=.1/.4/1/1.3/1.5/1.6                               31.1, T
MPRN=.12                                                31.2, C
    MAPM   - MANAGER-ARRIVAL POPULATION MULTIPLIER
               (DIMENSIONLESS)
    MPR    - MANAGER/POPULATION RATIO (DIMENSIONLESS)
    MPRN   - MANAGER/POPULATION RATIO NORMAL
               (DIMENSIONLESS)
```

Notes

1. Appropriate data on commuting are summarized in Alexander Ganz, "Emerging Patterns of Growth and Travel," Transport Report 68-1 (Cambridge, Mass.: Massachusetts Institute of Technology, Department of City and Regional Planning, 1968).

2. The existence of differential commuting is discussed at length in H. Kassoff and H. Deutschman, "People, Jobs, and Transportation: A Profile of Low Income Households in the Tri-State Region," in *Proceedings of the Conference on Poverty and Transportation* (Brookline, Mass.: American Academy of Arts and Sciences, 1968).

3. The acute excess of central-city managers over central-city managerial jobs in both the original *Urban Dynamics* model and the modified model is scarcely realistic. A reformulation of the equations for manager arrivals MA, manager departures MD, and labor to managers LTM would increase the realism of the managerial-professional sector.

14
Two Modifications to the Tax Sector
of *Urban Dynamics*

Michael R. Goodman

Readers of Urban Dynamics *have proposed diverse modifications and revisions of the structure of the original model. Those suggestions which offer concrete and testable hypotheses comprise a valuable avenue for evaluating the urban model.*

In the following paper, Michael R. Goodman examines two criticisms of the tax sector of Urban Dynamics; *these concern the computation of underemployed tax needs and Forrester's analysis of revenue sharing. Each of Goodman's modifications entails a fairly simple adaptation of the original model equations. Neither change appreciably alters the behavior or equilibrium conditions of the urban model.*

14
Two Modifications to the Tax Sector of *Urban Dynamics*

14.1 Introduction

The tax sector of Forrester's *Urban Dynamics* model relates a city's revenue needs to local tax assessments and collections. In particular, the tax sector illustrates how imbalances between revenue sources and demands can arise as the urban area shifts toward high concentrations of decaying industry or toward large proportions of low-skilled and unemployed workers. Because high local tax rates tend to discourage aggressive construction of new housing and industry, fiscal imbalances may promote urban decline and cause continued erosion of a city's tax base.

This paper describes two alterations to the tax sector of the *Urban Dynamics* model. The first change involves testing a revised financial aid subsidy program within the model; the second change alters the computation of underemployed tax needs. In each instance the model changes are detailed and their effects simulated. The results of these experiments increase confidence in the structure of the tax sector and in the outcome of Forrester's original policy tests.

14.2 Experiment I: Testing a Revised Financial Aid Subsidy Program

In section 4.3 of *Urban Dynamics*, Forrester tests the effects of a revenue-sharing policy that contributes state or federal funds to the city budget. On the basis of the simulations of this policy, Forrester concludes that "financial support from the outside may do nothing to improve fundamental conditions within the city and may even worsen conditions in the long run by causing an unfavorable shift in the proportions of population, housing, and business" (pp. 63–65).

Forrester's examination of the revenue-sharing policy has been criticized because external funds were applied to expand local services rather than to contract municipal debts.[1] Instead, it is argued, federal dollars should be applied to reduce the discrepancy between taxes needed and taxes collected. That is, the financial aid program simulated in the model should *decrease* the city's present tax demands for welfare and public services and retard further increases in tax assessments.

A revised financial aid subsidy program can be modeled very simply—by altering two equations in the original model:

```
TN.K=(TMP*MPFS*MP.K+TLP*LFS*L.K+TUP*UFS*U.K)(TCM.K)        A
    -(TPCSP.K*P.K)

TMP=150                                                    C

TLP=200                                                    C

TUP=300                                                    C
```

TN	– TAXES NEEDED (DOLLARS/YEAR)
TMP	– TAX PER MANAGEMENT PERSON (DOLLARS/PERSON/YEAR)
MPFS	– MANAGERIAL-PROFESSIONAL FAMILY SIZE (PEOPLE/MAN)
MP	– MANAGERIAL-PROFESSIONAL (MEN)
TLP	– TAX PER LABOR PERSON (DOLLARS/PERSON/YEAR)
LFS	– LABOR FAMILY SIZE (PEOPLE/MAN)
L	– LABOR (MEN)
TUP	– TAX PER UNDEREMPLOYED PERSON (DOLLARS/PERSON/YEAR)
UFS	– UNDEREMPLOYED FAMILY SIZE (PEOPLE/MAN)
U	– UNDEREMPLOYED (MEN)
TCM	– TAX-COLLECTION MULTIPLIER (DIMENSIONLESS)

```
TPCR.K=(TC.K/P.K)/TPCN                                        A

TPCN=250                                                      C

    TPCR   - TAX PER CAPITA RATIO (DIMENSIONLESS)
    TC     - TAX COLLECTIONS (DOLLARS/YEAR)
    P      - POPULATION (MEN)
    TPCN   - TAX PER CAPITA NORMAL (DOLLARS/YEAR/PERSON)
```

Taxes needed TN are now defined (in equation 126) as the difference between the revenue needs generated by the city's population and the available external funds. The term (TPCSP.K*P.K) represents the annual contribution of federal or state governments to the local city treasury, measured in dollars per year. Subsidy program revenues thus contribute to lowering taxes needed TN and to reducing the city's tax ratio needed TRN (*Urban Dynamics*, equations 124 and 125, p. 204). In equation 8, the tax per capita ratio TPCR is now defined as the ratio of tax collections TC to population P, divided by the tax per capita normal TPCN.

The results of applying the revised subsidy program to the model in *Urban Dynamics* are summarized in Figure 1. The equilibrium values obtained are quite similar to those of Forrester's original policy test except for the tax ratio needed TRN, tax per capita ratio TPCR, and underemployed to labor net UTLN, which are now reduced by about one-third each. The new subsidy program formulation does not perceptibly improve the stagnant conditions within the urban area; but neither does the program appreciably worsen conditions in the city. Despite these only minor variations, however, the revised program still seems to be a more valid policy formulation and an improved representation of the effects of implementing a local revenue-sharing program.

Variable	Initial Equilibrium Value (Time = 0)	Old Program TPCS = 100 (Time = 50)	New Program TPCS = 100 (Time = 50)	% Change Between Old and New
Underemployed U	377,300	407,000	372,570	− 8
Labor L	392,600	396,800	394,190	0
Managerial-professional MP	71,000	72,700	71,570	− 1
Underemployed arrivals UA	17,300	19,100	17,050	− 10
Underemployed departures UD	17,300	17,500	17,620	0
Labor arrivals LA	7,400	6,800	7,470	+ 10
Labor departures LD	13,200	14,500	12,850	− 11
Labor/job ratio LR	0.97	0.98	0.97	− 1
Underemployed/job ratio UR	1.81	1.97	1.77	− 11
Tax per capita ratio TPCR	1.12	1.52	1.03	− 32
Tax ratio TR	1.97	2.04	1.79	− 12
Tax ratio needed TRN	2.25	2.42	1.51	− 36
Underemployed to labor net UTLN	5,500	7,700	5,300	− 30

Figure 1 Effects of revised city-subsidy program

14.3 Experiment II: Changing Underemployed Tax Needs

The second criticism of the *Urban Dynamics* model concerns the tax needs of the city's underemployed population. Within Forrester's original model, the tax needs per underemployed person are twice those required per management person. This difference is based on the "assumed needs generated by each population class" (*Urban Dynamics*, p. 204) and must be interpreted to reflect costs of welfare, unemployment compensation, public education, transportation, and other support services.

Forrester's formulation might be criticized on the grounds that the tax needs of the underemployed population ought to depend on prevailing job conditions in the city. That is, the tax needs per person should increase with progressively higher local unemployment rates, and conversely.[2]

The hypothesis outlined here can be readily examined within the urban model. The tax per underemployed person TUP is now formulated as a variable depending on the underemployed/job ratio UR. Specifically, TUP is defined as the product of a "normal" tax need of $200 per person per year (equal to the tax per labor person TLP) modulated by the tax per underemployed person multiplier TUPM. As seen in Figure 2, TUPM increases monotonically with an increased underemployed/job ratio UR. The curve was hypothesized so that:

1. When UR=0, and jobs are abundant, the tax per underemployed person TUP equals the tax per labor person TLP.
2. When UR=1.8 (as in "stagnant equilibrium," *Urban Dynamics*, pp. 42–43), TUPM=1.5 and TUP=$300.

```
TN.K=(TMP*MPFS*MP.K+TLP*LFS*L.K+TUP.K*UFS*U.K)(TCM.K)        A

TMP=150                                                      C

TLP=200                                                      C
```

TN	- TAXES NEEDED (DOLLARS/YEAR)
TMP	- TAX PER MANAGEMENT PERSON (DOLLARS/PERSON/YEAR)
MPFS	- MANAGERIAL-PROFESSIONAL FAMILY SIZE (PEOPLE/MAN)
MP	- MANAGERIAL-PROFESSIONAL (MEN)
TLP	- TAX PER LABOR PERSON (DOLLARS/PERSON/YEAR)
LFS	- LABOR FAMILY SIZE (PEOPLE/MAN)
L	- LABOR (MEN)
TUP	- TAX PER UNDEREMPLOYED PERSON (DOLLARS/PERSON/YEAR)
UFS	- UNDEREMPLOYED FAMILY SIZE (PEOPLE/MAN)
U	- UNDEREMPLOYED (MEN)
TCM	- TAX-COLLECTION MULTIPLIER (DIMENSIONLESS)

```
TUP.K=TUPN*TUPM.K                                            A

TUPN=200                                                     C
```

TUP	- TAX PER UNDEREMPLOYED PERSON (DOLLARS/PERSON/YEAR)
TUPN	- TAX PER UNDEREMPLOYED PERSON NORMAL (DOLLARS/PERSON/YEAR)
TUPM	- TAX PER UNDEREMPLOYED PERSON MULTIPLIER (DIMENSIONLESS)

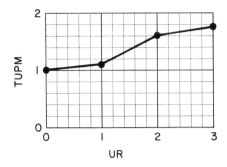

Figure 2 Influence of job availability on tax revenue needs of underemployed

```
TUPM.K=TABHL(TUPMT,UR.K,0,3,1)                            A
TUPMT=1/1.1/1.6/1.75                                     T
        TUPM    - TAX PER UNDEREMPLOYED PERSON MULTIPLIER
                  (DIMENSIONLESS)
        TUPMT   - TAX PER UNDEREMPLOYED PERSON MULTIPLIER
                  TABLE
        UR      - UNDEREMPLOYED/JOB RATIO (DIMENSIONLESS)
```

Figure 3 summarizes the results of applying the preceding modifications to the *Urban Dynamics* model. The changes not only produce virtually no differences in the equilibrium conditions of Forrester's growth model, but lend some additional support to the outcomes described in the *Urban Dynamics* book.

Variable	Old Equilibrium Value	New Equilibrium Value
Underemployed U	377,300	377,580
Labor L	392,600	391,920
Managerial-professional MP	71,100	70,660
Underemployed arrivals UA	17,300	17,100
Underemployed departures UD	17,300	17,500
Labor arrivals LA	7,400	7,270
Labor departures LD	13,200	13,200
Labor/job ratio LR	0.97	0.97
Underemployed/job ratio UR	1.81	1.81
Tax per capita ratio TPCR	1.12	1.11
Tax ratio TR	1.97	1.96
Tax ratio TRN	2.25	2.27
Underemployed to labor net UTLN	5,550	5,400

Figure 3 Effects of implementing the revised formulation of underemployed tax needs on the *Urban Dynamics* growth run model

Notes

1. This criticism was advanced by Professor John F. Kain of Harvard in his review of *Urban Dynamics* in *Fortune*, November 1969, pp. 240–242.

2. To some extent, this influence is already incorporated in the urban model. High employment rates in the city increase the conversion rate of the underemployed into labor (*Urban Dynamics*, equations 17–19), and thereby reduce overall tax needs within the urban area. There is some danger, then, that the modification outlined above involves a "double-counting" or a redefinition of the underemployed and labor population groups. Nonetheless, the modification seems to provide a good illustration of the insensitivity of the urban model to the exact specification of underemployed tax needs.

15
A Dynamic Model of Land Pricing and Urban Land Allocation

Nathaniel J. Mass

Urban Dynamics *offers a detailed theory of the long-term mechanisms by which urban land is allocated between residential and industrial use; the model shows how imbalances between population and available employment are generated over the course of a city's development as a consequence of the filling-up of urban land and the subsequent "filter-down" of local housing and industry.*

To expand upon the market mechanisms contained in the original urban model, the following paper was prepared to examine the influences of land pricing and land zoning on the distribution of urban land. Although the conclusions obtained from experimentation with the pricing submodel are largely consistent with Urban Dynamics, *the expanded urban model with land pricing is able to address broader and more detailed policy questions. The analysis reaffirms the importance of controlling inner-city population densities and shifting urban-land use away from housing and toward industry. It indicates, however, the difficulty in accomplishing this shift through a single policy instrument such as zoning.*

An earlier version of this paper was published in the proceedings of the 1973 Summer Computer Simulation Conference, Montreal, Canada, July 17–19.

15.1 Introduction

Within major urban areas, land prices have followed a consistent pattern of change over the course of each city's development: land prices have increased rapidly along with rising levels of population and economic activity, and they have leveled off or decreased as economic growth within the central city declined. The dynamics of urban-land prices are thus deeply embedded within a city's overall pattern of population growth and industrial development. In turn, land prices have influenced the complexion of most urban areas. Rising land prices have occasioned higher costs of residential development and promoted an intensified use of central-city land.

Because land-price changes are so closely tied to urban residential and industrial growth, an adequate description of the dynamics of land prices requires analyzing the mutual interactions between the market for urban land and the other subsystems of an urban area. Jay W. Forrester's model in *Urban Dynamics* provides one avenue for this analysis. *Urban Dynamics* presents a computer simulation model describing the interactions among population, housing, and industry within a fixed urban land area. In his book Forrester demonstrates how imbalances between housing, jobs, and available labor can arise over the 250-year development of a city.

The research reported in this paper was an attempt to develop a system dynamics model of an urban land market.[1] The model computes *average* land prices for residential and industrial land within a city. As part of ongoing research into the dynamics of cities at M.I.T., the land-pricing model has been incorporated into an expanded urban model along with a detailed zoning sector describing the pressures and incentives for transferring land between residential and industrial use. The following sections of this paper describe the land-pricing sector and illustrate several preliminary simulations of the pricing sector performed on the expanded urban dynamics model.[2]

15.2 Overview of the Land-Pricing Model

An urban land market operates to distribute existing space among competing uses. Because the determinants of residential and industrial land prices are similar in overall structure, the discussion here focuses on the determinants of business-land price. The land-pricing sector consists, essentially, of two coupled negative feedback loops connecting the demand for and supply of urban land; demand and supply interact through the business-land price, as shown in Figure 1.

The substructure portrayed in Figure 1 is, of course, an incomplete representation of an urban land market—there are many determinants of business-land demand and business-land supply other than price. Within the expanded urban dynamics model, for example, industrial construction rates depend on the availability of managers and skilled labor and on local tax rates and economics of scale, in addition to land price and land availability. Also, within the pricing sector of the expanded model, the supply of urban land depends on the available physical supply of open land, expected land prices (as distinguished from current

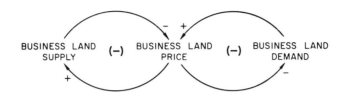

Figure 1 Interaction of business-land price, supply, and demand

·prices) and the holding costs of vacant land. Operating in conjunction with the full urban model, then, the land-pricing sector portrays the effects of local tax rates, labor availability, speculation, neighborhood resistance to zoning, and other factors on the intertemporal allocation of urban land. The expanded urban dynamics model can be applied to study the short-term and long-term forces that allocate urban land between housing and industry.

The pricing mechanism described here differs in several important respects from classical static land-price models. First, the model deals explicitly with the disequilibrium characteristics of urban development, and it formally depicts the mechanisms of price adjustment through which land supply and demand are maintained in balance. Second, the expanded urban model is designed to apply to the exponential growth phase of urban development as well as to the subsequent stages of maturity and population equilibrium. Because the model examines price movements within a city over a long time span, its structure must be sufficiently broad to interrelate the determinants of population movement, industrial location, and residential construction rates. The dynamic pricing model encompasses a wider range of interactions than can be dealt with in a short-term static analysis.

15.3 Model Description

Figure 2 provides a DYNAMO flow diagram of the business-land-price sector.

Business-Land Price. Equation 1 measures the level of business-land price BLP. The business-land price is initialized at $80 per acre at the outset of the simulation.[3]

```
BLP.K=BLP.J+(DT)(BLPC.JK)                        1, L
BLP=80                                           1.1, N
   BLP   - BUSINESS-LAND PRICE  (DOLLARS/ACRE)
   BLPC  - BUSINESS-LAND-PRICE CHANGE  (DOLLARS/ACRE/
           YEAR)
```

The business-land-price change BLPC is formulated as the product of business-land price BLP times the business-land-fractional-price change BLFPC. Changes in land prices occur when supply and demand are imbalanced. For

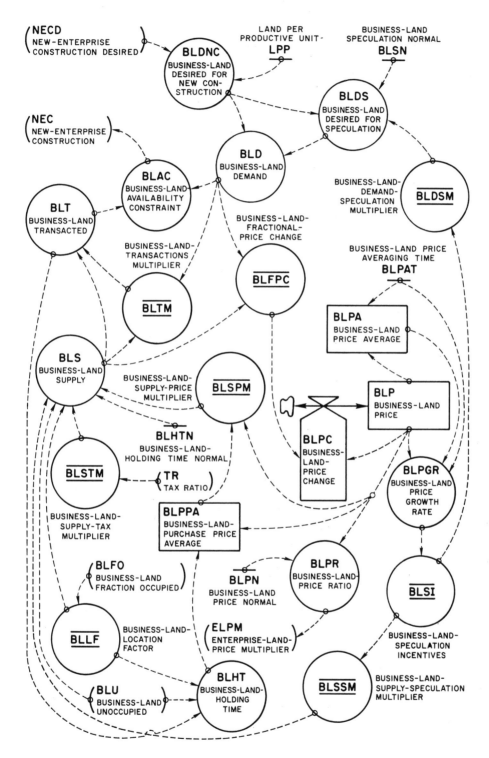

Figure 2 Flow diagram of business-land-price sector

example, an excess demand for land within a city will gradually cause land prices to be bid upward. To simulate the "bidding" apparatus of the land market, the fractional price change has been modeled as a function of the ratio of business-land demand BLD to business-land supply BLS (shown in Figure 3).[4]

At the left of Figure 3, when demand is one-eighth of the current land supply, prices are assumed to be bid downward at a rate of 20 percent per year. As demand rises to one-half of supply, prices are assumed to be bid downward at 10 percent per year; if demand equals supply, prices remain unchanged. At the extreme right of Figure 3, prices are assumed to be bid upward at a rate of 40 percent per year when the demand for business land is eight times the available supply.

```
BLPC.KL=BLP.K*BLFPC.K                                          2, R
   BLPC   - BUSINESS-LAND-PRICE CHANGE   (DOLLARS/ACRE/
              YEAR)
   BLP    - BUSINESS-LAND PRICE  (DOLLARS/ACRE)
   BLFPC  - BUSINESS-LAND-FRACTIONAL-PRICE CHANGE
              (FRACTION/YEAR)

BLFPC.K=TABHL(BLFPCT,1.44*LOGN(BLD.K/BLS.K),-3,3,1)  3, A
BLFPCT=-.2/-.18/-.1/0/.15/.35/.4                     3.1, T
   BLFPC  - BUSINESS-LAND-FRACTIONAL-PRICE CHANGE
              (FRACTION/YEAR)
   BLD    - BUSINESS-LAND DEMAND  (ACRES/YEAR)
   BLS    - BUSINESS-LAND SUPPLY  (ACRES/YEAR)
```

Business-Land Demand. The demand for business land for new industrial construction is a "derived demand, which springs from the demand for the goods and services produced [in the area] ... "[5] For this reason, land desired for new construction is essentially generated outside the pricing sector (although new-

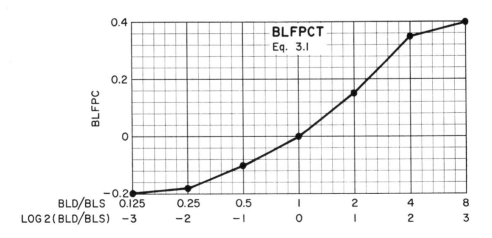

Figure 3 Price changes induced by the balance of business-land demand and business-land supply

enterprise construction desired NECD depends on the price of land in addition to labor availability, local tax rates, the size of the local industrial base, and other factors).[6]

```
BLDNC.K=(NECD.K)(LPP)                              4, A
    BLDNC  - BUSINESS-LAND DESIRED FOR NEW CONSTRUCTION
             (ACRES/YEAR)
    NECD   - NEW-ENTERPRISE CONSTRUCTION DESIRED
             (PRODUCTIVE UNITS/YEAR)
    LPP    - LAND PER PRODUCTIVE UNIT  (ACRES/PRODUCTION
             UNIT)
```

Besides land demanded for new industrial construction, business land may also be demanded for purposes of speculation. For example, a developer may often speculate in land:

> In order to build efficiently, he must make some advance purchases, but many developers clearly buy further ahead than is necessary for continuous operation. All are hopeful that land values will increase while they hold land, and many say that their return for development arises out of their ability to capture the increased land values resulting from the development process rather than from their building activities directly.[7]

```
BLDS.K=(BLDNC.K)(BLSN)(BLDSM.K)                    5, A
BLSN=.25                                          5.1, C
    BLDS   - BUSINESS-LAND DESIRED FOR SPECULATION
             (ACRES/YEAR)
    BLDNC  - BUSINESS-LAND DESIRED FOR NEW CONSTRUCTION
             (ACRES/YEAR)
    BLSN   - BUSINESS-LAND SPECULATION NORMAL
             (DIMENSIONLESS)
    BLDSM  - BUSINESS-LAND-DEMAND-SPECULATION MULTIPLIER
             (DIMENSIONLESS)

BLDSM.K=TABHL(BLDSMT,BLSI.K,0,6,1)                 6, A
BLDSMT=.7/1/1.3/1.75/2.25/3/4                     6.1, T
    BLDSM  - BUSINESS-LAND-DEMAND-SPECULATION MULTIPLIER
             (DIMENSIONLESS)
    BLSI   - BUSINESS-LAND-SPECULATION INCENTIVES
             (DIMENSIONLESS)
```

Business-land desired for speculation BLDS has been modeled as a normal fraction of the land demanded for new construction, modified by the business-land-demand-speculation multiplier BLDSM.[8] This formulation assumes that land speculators gauge the profitability of speculation according to approximately the same set of conditions that determines the profitability of new industrial construction.

Figure 4 assumes that the speculative demand for business land rises slowly at first, with greater than normal incentives, rising more rapidly as the incentives for speculation continue to increase. The particular shape of this curve reflects the composition of speculative demand and appears to be consistent with the results of Milgram's study of northeast Philadelphia. Normally, the speculative market for land will be controlled by professional speculators and land develop-

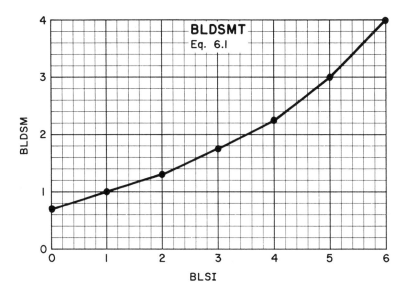

Figure 4 Effects of land speculation on business-land demand

ers. Because professional speculators and developers are "presumably wealthier, with higher incomes, and in less need of immediate money"[9] than other entrants into the speculative land market, they will comprise most speculative activity when incentives are slightly above normal. As the incentives for speculation become more obvious and more compelling, relatively "amateur" speculators will be drawn into the market, and total speculative demand will swell.

Business-Land Speculative Incentives. Speculative profit "is obtained through the mere purchase of land and holding of land *off* the market ..."[10] In terms of economic analysis, then, high incentives for speculative profit produce two effects. First, they raise the quantity of land demanded for speculation; second, they increase the "reservation price" of land so that the supply of land is reduced

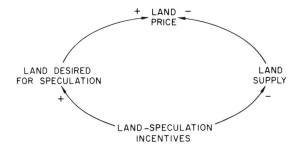

Figure 5 Open-loop view of the effects of speculation on land prices

as land is withheld from the current market. Both of these activities generate an upward pressure on land price. Also, particularly when urban land is scarce, speculation causes a shift toward more intensive land use.[11]

In brief, the incentives for speculation may be said to depend on the expectations of future land profits. In this model of land prices, speculative incentives depend upon an extrapolation of historical land prices as an indicator of expected trends in land prices and the expected profit to be derived from holding vacant land. If, for example, land prices have been rising at 20 percent per year (and are expected to continue to do so) while the holding costs of land are measured at 7 percent per year, then the expected profit rate is 13 percent per year.[12] This general relationship is embodied in equation 7; increases in the growth rate of land prices create greater incentives for speculation.[13]

```
BLSI.K=TABHL(BLSIT,BLPGR.K,-.3,.5,.1)              7, A
BLSIT=.5/.6/.75/1/1.3/1.65/2/2.5/3                7.1, T
     BLSI   - BUSINESS-LAND-SPECULATION INCENTIVES
              (DIMENSIONLESS)
     BLPGR  - BUSINESS-LAND PRICE GROWTH RATE (FRACTION/
              YEAR)
BLPA.K=BLPA.J+(DT/BLPAT)(BLP.J-BLPA.J)            8, L
BLPA=BLP                                          8.1, N
BLPAT=5                                           8.2, C
     BLPA   - BUSINESS-LAND PRICE AVERAGE (DOLLARS/ACRE)
     BLPAT  - BUSINESS-LAND PRICE AVERAGING TIME (YEARS)
     BLP    - BUSINESS-LAND PRICE (DOLLARS/ACRE)

BLPGR.K=(BLP.K-BLPA.K)/(BLP.K*BLPAT)              9, A
     BLPGR  - BUSINESS-LAND PRICE GROWTH RATE (FRACTION/
              YEAR)
     BLP    - BUSINESS-LAND PRICE (DOLLARS/ACRE)
     BLPA   - BUSINESS-LAND PRICE AVERAGE (DOLLARS/ACRE)
     BLPAT  - BUSINESS-LAND PRICE AVERAGING TIME (YEARS)
```

Business-Land Supply. The economic supply of urban land measures the quantity of land that will be offered for sale at any point in time. The supply of land is assumed to depend on a number of factors: the physical land area available for construction; current land prices; the costs of holding undeveloped land; and the

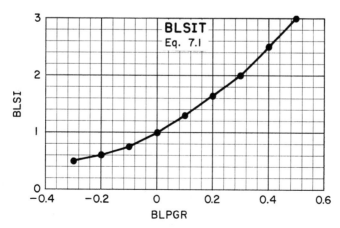

Figure 6 Land speculation incentives determined by the expected rate of increase in land prices

prevailing incentives for land speculation. The interactions among these forces are embodied in the equation for business-land supply:

```
BLS.K=((BLU.K*BLLF.K)/BLHTN)(BLSTM.K)(BLSPM.K)        10, A
   (BLSSM.K)
BLHTN=12.5                                            10.1, C
      BLS    - BUSINESS-LAND SUPPLY  (ACRES/YEAR)
      BLU    - BUSINESS-LAND UNOCCUPIED (ACRES)
      BLLF   - BUSINESS-LAND-LOCATION FACTOR
               (DIMENSIONLESS)
      BLHTN  - BUSINESS-LAND-HOLDING TIME NORMAL (YEARS)
      BLSTM  - BUSINESS-LAND-SUPPLY-TAX MULTIPLIER
               (DIMENSIONLESS)
      BLSPM  - BUSINESS-LAND-SUPPLY-PRICE MULTIPLIER
               (DIMENSIONLESS)
      BLSSM  - BUSINESS-LAND-SUPPLY-SPECULATION MULTIPLIER
               (DIMENSIONLESS)
```

In equation 10, business-land unoccupied BLU measures the quantity of business land remaining vacant. BLU is a function of the total number of business structures within the city and of the total land currently zoned for business activity. (BLU is computed within the zoning sector of the revised urban model.) It represents the city's stock of open land that might be developed for industrial use. Within any fixed urban land area (as portrayed in *Urban Dynamics*), however, not all open business land will be part of the city's "effective" land-market area. If, for example, an urban area were only sparsely developed, then only a small fraction of the city's open land—probably the area adjacent to the core city—would be suitable for development as the core city expanded. The business-land-location factor BLLF attempts to capture this phenomenon by measuring the fraction of open business land that at any point in time comprises the effective market for business land.[14] As shown in Figure 7, BLLF is formulated as an increasing function of the business-land fraction occupied BLFO. As the business-land fraction occupied within the city rises, the remaining (open) business-land area more nearly approximates the effective market for business land; BLLF therefore increases toward a value of unity. The business-land supply BLS, then, is formulated as a product of (BLU*BLLF) divided by the normal holding time of business land, modified by the effects of land price, taxes, and speculative incentives;[15] these three influences are discussed below.

```
BLLF.K=TABHL(BLLFT,BLFO.K,0,1,.2)                     11, A
BLLFT=.02/.3/.6/.9/1/1                                11.1, T
      BLLF   - BUSINESS-LAND-LOCATION FACTOR
               (DIMENSIONLESS)
      BLFO   - BUSINESS-LAND FRACTION OCCUPIED
               (DIMENSIONLESS)
```

The business-land-supply-tax multiplier BLSTM (shown in Figure 8) measures the supply of business land as a function of the holding costs for vacant land. An increase in the tax rate raises the costs of landownership and discourages the

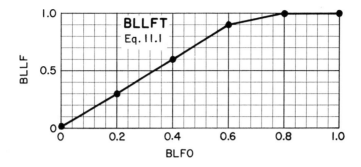

Figure 7 Calculation of the fraction of undeveloped land comprising the effective market for business land

withholding of land from the current market; that is, an increase in the tax rate tends to promote an increase in the supply of land, thereby lowering the average price of land:[16]

> As far as the property tax rests upon the site value of a property, it rests upon the potential earning power of the site, in direct proportion to it, and without consideration of whether the owner develops his property well or poorly. Because the tax takes a portion of land's annual value, whether or not the land is well-used, it discourages, however mildly, the speculation and "withholding" with which planners and developers are constantly faced.[17]

```
BLSTM.K=TABHL(BLSTMT,1.44*LOGN(TR.K),-2,2,1)          12, A
BLSTMT=.5/.6/1/1.2/1.3                                12.1, T
     BLSTM  - BUSINESS-LAND-SUPPLY-TAX MULTIPLIER
              (DIMENSIONLESS)
     TR     - TAX RATIO  (DIMENSIONLESS)
```

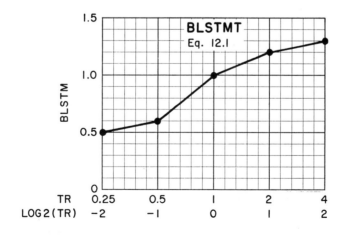

Figure 8 Influence of local tax rate on business-land supply

"As with any commodity, the amount [of land] demanded and that available for sale, up to the limit of all vacant ground in the neighborhood, depends upon the price ... "[18] Equation 13 shows business-land supply as an increasing function of the ratio of the current business-land price BLP to the business-land-purchase price average BLPPA. The latter, which represents the average price at which land *currently being transacted* was formerly purchased, is defined in equation 14. With an increase in land price, for instance, developers may elect to reduce their inventory holdings of vacant land. In contrast, the supply of institutionally held land within a city may be largely unresponsive to changes in price. The business-land-supply-price multiplier BLSPM measures the aggregate effect of land price on land supply. At the extreme left of Figure 9, a zero land price (relative to the purchase price BLPPA) is assumed to reduce the supply of land to zero; at the extreme right, a land price three times the purchase price increases the supply by the factor of 50 percent.

```
BLSPM.K=TABHL(BLSPMT,BLP.K/BLPPA.K,0,3,.5)          13, A
BLSPMT=0/.5/1/1.3/1.4/1.45/1.5                      13.1, T
    BLSPM   - BUSINESS-LAND-SUPPLY-PRICE MULTIPLIER
              (DIMENSIONLESS)
    BLP     - BUSINESS-LAND PRICE   (DOLLARS/ACRE)
    BLPPA   - BUSINESS-LAND-PURCHASE PRICE AVERAGE
              (DOLLARS/ACRE)
```

The business-land-purchase price average BLPPA is an averaged value of the actual business-land price BLP. The averaging time on BLPPA is a variable, equal to the business-land-holding time BLHT. BLHT is defined in equation 15 as the city's effective market area for business land (measured by [BLU*BLLF]) divided by the actual rate of business-land transacted BLT. It measures the delay

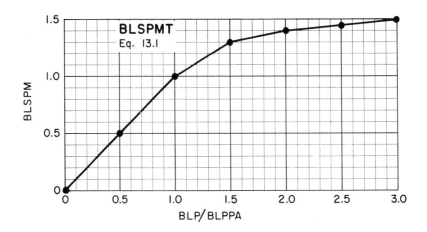

Figure 9 Influence of land price on the supply of business land

between the acquisition and the sale of business land that is currently being transacted.[19]

```
BLPPA.K=BLPPA.J+(DT/BLHT.K)(BLP.K-BLPPA.J)          14, L
BLPPA=BLP                                           14.1, N
     BLPPA   - BUSINESS-LAND-PURCHASE PRICE AVERAGE
               (DOLLARS/ACRE)
     BLHT    - BUSINESS-LAND-HOLDING TIME (YEARS)
     BLP     - BUSINESS-LAND PRICE (DOLLARS/ACRE)
PAGE 3       BUSINESS-LAND PRICE SECTOR    11/21/73


BLHT.K=(BLU.K*BLLF.K)/BLT.K                          15, A
     BLHT    - BUSINESS-LAND-HOLDING TIME (YEARS)
     BLU     - BUSINESS-LAND UNOCCUPIED (ACRES)
     BLLF    - BUSINESS-LAND-LOCATION FACTOR
               (DIMENSIONLESS)
     BLT     - BUSINESS-LAND TRANSACTED  (ACRES/YEAR)
```

Equation 16 illustrates the effects of the incentives for business-land speculation on business-land supply. An increase in the incentives for speculation tends to encourage withholding land from the market, thereby reducing current supply, and conversely.[20]

```
BLSSM.K=TABHL(BLSSMT,BLSI.K,0,6,1)                   16, A
BLSSMT=1.4/1/.75/.65/.55/.5/.5                       16.1, T
     BLSSM   - BUSINESS-LAND-SUPPLY-SPECULATION MULTIPLIER
               (DIMENSIONLESS)
     BLSI    - BUSINESS-LAND-SPECULATION INCENTIVES
               (DIMENSIONLESS)
```

Business-Land Transacted. The previous sections of this paper have discussed the components of the demand for and supply of business land; the pricing

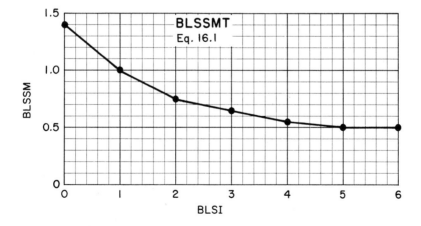

Figure 10 Reduction in business-land supply caused by rising incentives for speculation

mechanism operates, in the long term, to equate the demand for land with the available supply. In the near term, however, how is the current supply of land allocated between new construction and speculative demand?

In equation 17, business-land transacted BLT measures the quantity of land *actually sold* during each time period. Whenever (in the very short term) the supply of land exceeds the current demand for land, then the entire demand may be satisfied; that is, all land desired for new construction or for speculation may, in fact, be obtained. If, however, the demand for land is in excess of supply, the supply of land serves as a constraint on total land transactions.

In equation 17, business-land transacted BLT is given as the business-land supply BLS multiplied by the business-land-transactions multiplier BLTM.[20] BLTM is a decreasing function of the ratio of business-land supply to the business-land demand. This relationship, shown in Figure 11, requires some explanation. In equation 18, when supply equals demand, then BLTM equals one, and business-land transacted simply equals the demand for land. Elsewhere (where land supply does not equal demand), there is either excess supply or excess demand in the marketplace. In the real world, when market supply and demand are imbalanced, adjustment is accomplished not only through price changes but also, for example, through changes in sales effort and terms of sale.

Thus in Figure 11, where supply is greater than demand, increased sales efforts can cause the demand for land to increase somewhat in the short run. Conversely, if the demand for land exceeds supply, landholders can be induced to augment supply slightly in the short run.

```
BLT.K=BLS.K*BLTM.K                                      17, A
    BLT   - BUSINESS-LAND TRANSACTED  (ACRES/YEAR)
    BLS   - BUSINESS-LAND SUPPLY  (ACRES/YEAR)
    BLTM  - BUSINESS-LAND-TRANSACTIONS MULTIPLIER
            (DIMENSIONLESS)

BLTM.K=TABHL(BLTMT,BLS.K/BLD.K,0,6,1)                   18, A
BLTMT=1.2/1/.55/.35/.25/.2/.17                          18.1, T
    BLTM  - BUSINESS-LAND-TRANSACTIONS MULTIPLIER
            (DIMENSIONLESS)
    BLS   - BUSINESS-LAND SUPPLY  (ACRES/YEAR)
    BLD   - BUSINESS-LAND DEMAND  (ACRES/YEAR)
```

The "desired" construction rate of new business structures is converted to an "actual" construction rate through the business-land-availability constraint BLAC:

```
BLAC.K=BLT.K/BLD.K                                      19, A
    BLAC  - BUSINESS-LAND-AVAILABILITY CONSTRAINT
            (DIMENSIONLESS)
    BLT   - BUSINESS-LAND TRANSACTED  (ACRES/YEAR)
    BLD   - BUSINESS-LAND DEMAND  (ACRES/YEAR)
```

The formulation of equation 19 produces two desired effects:

1. At all times the sum of land use for new-enterprise construction plus speculative land use equals business-land transacted BLT. Algebraically, this

NOTE: The equation on page 189 should be corrected to read as follows:

$$\text{Actual land use} = (BLDNC)(BLAC) + (BLDS)(BLAC)$$
$$= (BLD)(BLAC)$$
$$= (BLT)$$

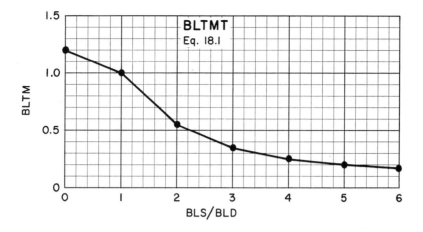

Figure 11 Short-term supply constraint on business-land transactions

may be seen as follows:

```
BLD.K=BLDNC.K+BLDS.K                                    20, A
    BLD    - BUSINESS-LAND DEMAND   (ACRES/YEAR)
    BLDNC  - BUSINESS-LAND DESIRED FOR NEW CONSTRUCTION
             (ACRES/YEAR)
    BLDS   - BUSINESS-LAND DESIRED FOR SPECULATION
             (ACRES/YEAR)
```

$$\text{Actual land use} = (\text{BLCNC})(\text{BLAC}) + (\text{BLDS})(\text{BLAC})$$
$$= (\text{BLD})(\text{BLAC})$$
$$= (\text{BLC})$$
$$= (\text{BLT})$$

2. Increases in business-land desired for speculation BLDS raise speculative demand as a proportion of the total demand for land, and thus lower the proportion of land actually allotted to new industrial construction.

15.4 Model Simulations

As stated earlier, the land-pricing sector was added to Forrester's original *Urban Dynamics* model, along with a zoning sector that transfers land between business and residentially zoned categories. Very briefly, the zoning sector computes the pressures exerted by several factors on the land-zoning rate: neighborhood resistance to zoning; relative prices and availability of business and residential land; and perceived housing adequacy.

Figure 12 illustrates the growth simulation of the expanded urban model. Figure 12*a* exhibits the behavior of the nine major state variables over time, and may be compared with Figure 3-1*a* of *Urban Dynamics* (p. 40). The revised model behaves quite similarly to Forrester's original model (both qualitatively and

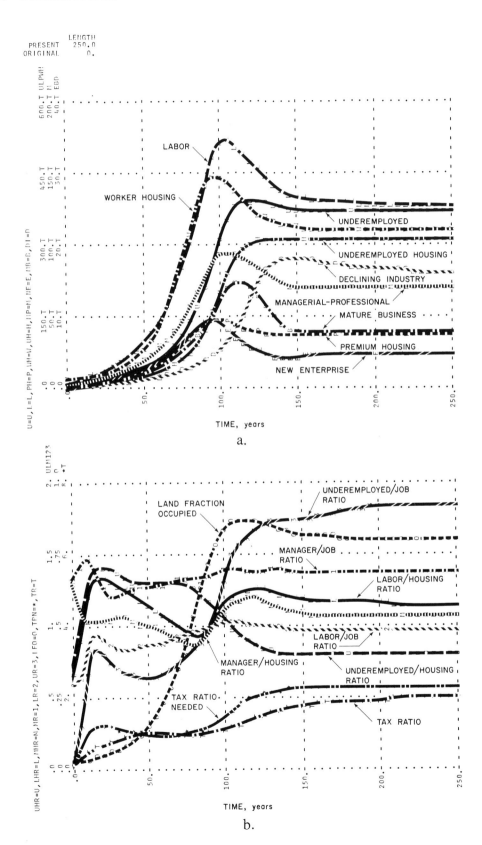

a.

b.

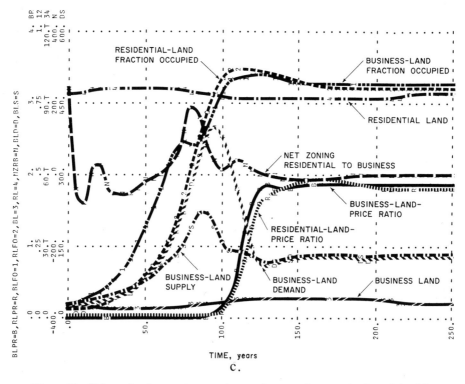

Figure 12 Urban development, maturity, and stagnation—revised model with
land pricing and land zoning

quantitatively). In fact, the similarity of outcomes in the original and revised
models should not be surprising, since the revised model is basically an extended
and more detailed version of the original.

Figure 12*b* exhibits the characteristic symptoms of urban decay described in
Urban Dynamics—an excess of low-quality housing (indicated by the underem-
ployed/housing ratio of about 0.8) and severe job shortage (indicated by the
underemployed/job ratio of about 1.8). Figure 12*c* plots the behavior of several
variables from the land-zoning and land-pricing sectors. In Figure 12*c*, business-
land supply is shown to keep pace with business-land demand during the early
stages of urban growth. As population and economic growth continue, however,
the area's physical land supply is gradually depleted; beginning in about year 80,
business-land supply lags behind business-land demand, and the price of land
rises sharply. Both business-land price and residential-land price attain an
equilibrium value of about $20,000 per acre.[22]

Figure 12, like *Urban Dynamics*, illustrates a land-use imbalance between
housing and industry. Improving the economic base of the city and reducing
unemployment requires shifting the land mix toward increased industrial use.
One means for accomplishing the desired shift might be a deliberate zoning
"bias" that would significantly reduce the rate of flow of land from business to
residential use and would raise the counterflow into business land. Figure 13
illustrates a computer simulation experiment in which such a zoning policy is

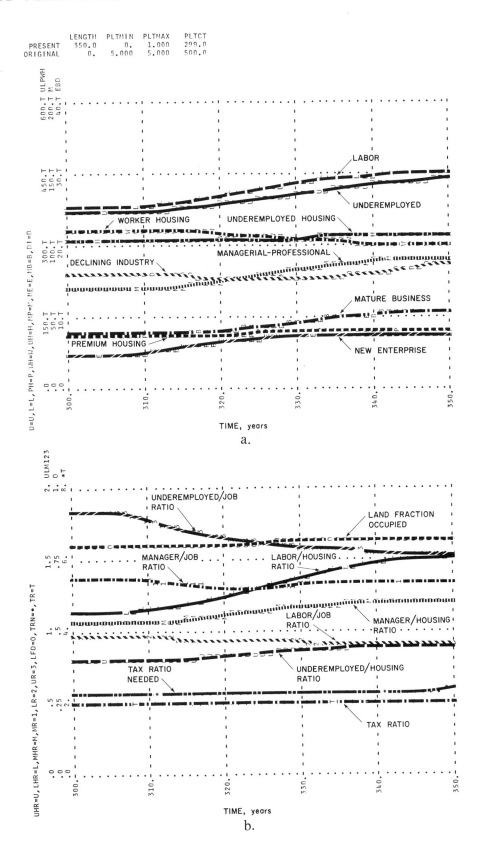

a.

b.

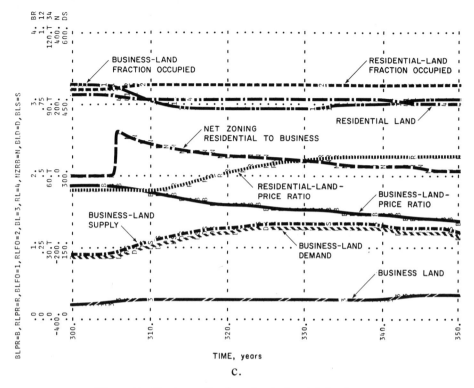

Figure 13 Zoning policy favoring industrial development

examined. For the simulation shown in Figure 13, the expanded urban model was run out to equilibrium, and the zoning policy was implemented beginning in year 305. The policy reduces the flow of land from business to residential use, and it raises the flow into business land, by a factor of five.

Figure 13 illustrates several favorable outcomes stemming from the zoning policy. For example, in Figure 13*b* the underemployed/job ratio declines from 1.8 to 1.5, and the labor/job ratio declines to 0.85. Still, in several respects, the benefits accruing from the zoning policy are not commensurate with the effort applied.

In Figure 13*c*, despite a severe zoning bias favoring business land, the level of residential land declines only slightly. The initial impact of the zoning policy is to place a downward pressure on business-land prices and to increase residential-land prices. Because of lower business-land prices and increased land availability, industrial growth is stimulated, while housing construction is somewhat deterred by the higher costs of residential development.[23] As a result, residential living densities increase (especially for managers and labor; see Figure 13*b*) and the residential-land fraction occupied rises. The increased crowding and higher residential-land prices generate pressures to rezone land for housing and to diminish the flow of residential land into business land. As seen in Figure 13*c*, beginning in year 310 this pressure significantly lowers the net-zoning rate from residential to business land, thus counteracting the zoning policy favoring industry.

Figure 13*a* shows that application of the zoning policy causes a 20 percent rise in the underemployed population of the city; the policy raises job availability and upward mobility for the underemployed by more than it tightens conditions in the underemployed-housing market, leading to a large net in-migration to the city. The increase in the city's underemployed population has several undesirable effects: increased competition for jobs prevents a significant decline in unemployment rates, and rising tax needs within the area leave local tax rates unchanged (Figure 13*b*).

15.5 Conclusions and Interpretation

A more detailed examination of the outcomes described in Figure 13 would require explicitly weighting the costs and benefits deriving from the zoning policy; still, several general points follow from the preceding discussion. First, a zoning policy favoring industrial development by itself may not be highly effective in improving local employment conditions within a city. Figure 13 shows how rising population levels and increased local tax needs tend to reduce or counteract several beneficial impacts of the zoning policy. This suggests that the zoning policy, to become more effective, would need to be combined with other policy measures designed to control urban population. Without such controls, the principal effect of an industry-development program or zoning policy might be to raise the urban population and heighten local competition for jobs and urban services; under such circumstances, the city's residents would gain only marginally.

Far more exploration is needed into the operational mechanisms through which cities may control population and achieve an improved mix of residential and industrial land. Toward this end, land-zoning and land-pricing policies may provide effective leverage points. Such policies as legislated maximum building heights or maximum population densities need to be examined within the framework of dynamic simulation models. Further investigations of the dynamics of urban land allocation should lead to greater understanding of the land-development options open to central cities.

Notes

1. The research reported in this paper was supported in part under HUD contract H-2000-R.

2. Descriptions of the land-zoning equations and the interface of the land-zoning and land-pricing sectors with the urban model are contained in John S. Miller, "Refinement of the *Urban Dynamics* Model for Land Rezoning Policy Analysis," System Dynamics Group Working Paper (Cambridge, Mass.: Massachusetts Institute of Technology, 1973).

3. The initial land price of $80 (measured in current dollars) was estimated roughly based on data cited in Hoyt, pp. 306, 318.

4. As noted, the business-land-fractional-price change BLFPC is intended to simulate the "bidding" process for land. Equations having similar functional form have been developed by economists to study the interactions between unemployment and inflation. R. G. Lipsey (1960), for example, has proposed an equation of the form

$$\frac{\dot{W}}{W} = a \frac{D - S}{S} = a\left(\frac{D}{S} - 1\right),$$

where W is the wage rate; D is the demand for labor; S is the supply of labor; and a is a numerical constant. The formulation developed in this paper differs from Lipsey's equation primarily in that it is nonlinear and, therefore, incorporates such phenomena as asymmetric tendencies toward price increases and decreases.

5. Renne 1947, pp. 29–30.

6. The industrial sector of the *Urban Dynamics* model is described in Forrester, pp. 189–201.

7. Milgram 1967, p. 123.

8. A rough estimate of the business-land speculation normal BLSN was obtained from data presented by Milgram (1967). In a study of the northeastern section of Philadelphia, Milgram found that "somewhat under a quarter (of all land purchased) may have been acquired for long-term price increases or to promote orderly construction by a particular firm. The corresponding figure for long-term holding of non-residential development was slightly higher . . . " (Milgram, p.76).

9. This implies that professional speculators maintain a low discount rate of future profits. See Milgram 1967, p. 124.

10. Fellmeth 1971, p. I–5.

11. Milgram offers a good (static) theoretical analysis of speculative interactions in rural-urban land conversion. See Milgram 1967, pp. 123–129.

12. The 7 percent figure for annual holding costs is cited as typical by Milgram (1967), p. 126. The figure includes both tax costs as well as opportunity costs (the achievable returns from alternative investments in bonds, stocks, or other sources of income).

13. In a more detailed urban model that differentiated between high-density and low-density land use, business-land-speculation incentives BLSI might also depend on the degree of utilization of central-city land. For example, because the demand for office space is relatively price inelastic compared with the demand for lower-density industrial use, increased utilization of an area's business land may raise speculators' expectations of future profit. (Hoyt has documented this process in Chicago during the 1890s. See Hoyt 1933, pp. 149–253.) Therefore, as office buildings begin to predominate in an urban area, speculative forces may cause land to be withdrawn from the current market, thereby driving up land prices and further encouraging office construction over low-density use. This positive feedback loop would produce a shift in the city's employment mix toward increased proportions of white-collar jobs. The effects of this influence on local unemployment and tax rates need to be examined within the context of an expanded urban model.

14. The product (BLU*BLLF) thus measures the unoccupied land area within the business-land market. The factor BLLF is necessary because *Urban Dynamics* portrays the development of a city within a fixed land area. The assumption of a fixed land area implies, for example, that during the initial stages of the city's development the unoccupied urban land area would be quite large; however, the real economic supply of usable land would be much smaller than this, encompassing only the land area adjacent to the growing city. A more detailed urban model in which the city's land area were a variable, and which included both the economic pressures encouraging urban expansion and the physical pressures limiting expansion, might allow a more direct measurement of the city's effective land-market area.

15. In equation 10.1, the business-land-holding time normal BLHTN is set at 12.5 years. Milgram found in her study of northeast Philadelphia that "the land contained in the sample parcels was transacted, on the average, slightly more than once during the study period [18 years], although there was considerable variation in the rate, with almost a quarter not transacted at all and a sixth transacted three or more times" (Milgram 1967, p. 80). Milgram's data would, therefore, imply a land-holding time of about 15 years for northeast Philadelphia between the years 1945 and 1962. To obtain an estimate of BLHTN, this figure was reduced to 12.5 years. This was done primarily because Milgram's sample included a large amount of institutional land, much of which was not transacted at all during the 18-year interval.

16. Actually, an increase in the tax rate acts to lower the land price through *both* the demand side and the supply side: an increase in taxes reduces the demand for industrial land (by diminishing the capital value of land), while increasing the supply. This effect is discussed in Douglas 1936.

17. Rawson 1961, p. 11. Dating back to Henry George, many urban economists have argued that, by taxing land more heavily, cities could promote increased development (See, for example, Milgram 1967, pp. 135–136). The effects of this policy could be readily analyzed with the expanded urban dynamics model.

18. Milgram 1967, p. 124.

19. The floating-reference-point structure embodied in equations 13 and 14 represents landowners' changing perceptions of what constitutes a "fair" or "equitable" price for their land. In determining land supply, landowners are assumed to compare current land prices with the price at which they had previously purchased their land.

20. The effects of speculation on land supply have been modeled as a multiplicative factor, whereas in equations 5 and 6, speculative demand for land is modeled as an additive factor (in total demand). On the demand side, the additive formulation provides a measure of land transactions that do not eventuate in development. (Equation 19 utilizes this measure to determine the short-term supply constraint on industrial construction.) On the supply side, however, the total amount of land supplied is the quantity of interest (rather than the particular source of land).

21. Equation 17 ensures, for one thing, that the city is not built up beyond the capacity of its physical land area.

22. In Figure 12*c*, the business-land-price ratio and residential-land-price ratio represent the actual business-land and residential-land prices, respectively, divided by a "normal" or reference value of $12,000 per acre.

23. In Figure 13*a*, the level of worker housing declines by 10 percent over the course of the simulation.

References

William Alonso, *Location and Land Use: Toward a General Theory of Urban Rent* (Cambridge: Harvard University Press, 1964).

F. C. R. Douglas, *Land-Value Rating* (London: Hogarth Press, 1936).

L. E. Elias, Jr., and J. Gillies, "Some Observations on the Role of Speculators and Speculation in Land Development," *UCLA Law Review* 12 (March 1965): 789–799.

R. T. Ely and E. W. Morehouse, *Elements of Land Economics* (New York: Macmillan, 1924).

Robert C. Fellmeth, ed., *Power and Land in California*, The Ralph Nader Task Force Report on Land Use in the State of California, 1971.

Jay W. Forrester, *Urban Dynamics* (Cambridge: The M.I.T. Press, 1969).

R. O. Harvey and W. A. Clark, "The Nature and Economics of Urban Sprawl," *Land Economics* 41 (February 1965): 1–9.

Homer Hoyt, *One Hundred Years of Land Values in Chicago* (Chicago: University of Chicago Press, 1933).

R. W. Lindholm, "Land Taxation and Economic Development," *Land Economics* 41 (May 1965): 121–130.

R. G. Lipsey, "The Relation between Unemployment and the Rate of Change of Money Wage Rates: A Further Analysis," *Economica* 24 (February 1960): 1–31.

Grace Milgram, *The City Expands*, Prepared under contract with the Office of the Secretary, Department of Housing and Urban Development; Institute for Environmental Studies, University of Pennsylvania, 1967.

Grace Milgram, *U.S. Land Prices—Directions and Dynamics*. Prepared for the consideration of the National Commission on Urban Problems, Research Report no. 13, 1968.

Jerome P. Pickard, *Taxation and Land Use in Metropolitan and Urban America*, Urban Land Institute, Research Monograph no. 12, 1966.

Richard V. Ratcliff, *Urban Land Economics* (New York: McGraw-Hill, 1949).

Mary Rawson, *Property Taxation and Urban Development*, Urban Land Institute, Research Monograph no. 4, 1961.

Roland R. Renne, *Land Economics* (New York: Harper & Brothers, 1947).

Ann L. Strong, "Factors Affecting Land Tenure in the Urban Fringe," *Urban Land* 25 (November 1966): 1–6.

Wilbur R. Thompson, *A Preface to Urban Economics* (Baltimore: Johns Hopkins Press, 1965).

Paul F. Wendt, "Economic Growth and Urban Land Values," *Appraisal Journal* 26 (July 1958): 427–443.

Paul F. Wendt, "Theory of Urban Land Values," *Land Economics* 33 (August 1957): 228–240.

Sidney M. Willhelm, *Urban Zoning and Land-Use Theory* (New York: Free Press of Glencoe, 1962).

Adapting *Urban Dynamics* to Lowell

Walter W. Schroeder III and John E. Strongman

The general theory embodied in Urban Dynamics *attempts to organize the principal economic, social, and political factors that interact to produce urban growth and decline. As yet, this general theory has not been subjected to a rigorous empirical examination. Potentially, however, such examination might take one of two forms: either statistical analysis of individual causal relationships or evaluation of the overall model behavior. As a first step in testing the* Urban Dynamics *theory, the following paper by Walter W. Schroeder III and John E. Strongman compares the output of the urban model with the history of Lowell, Massachusetts. How do the behavior modes projected by the* Urban Dynamics *model compare with the characteristics of a specific city?*

To adapt the Urban Dynamics *model to describe Lowell, only several parameters—for example, land area, population densities, and family sizes—were adjusted to values specific to Lowell. Still, with these modifications, the model closely approximates population growth trends and the shifting balance of population, housing, and jobs observed historically in Lowell. Further tests of the* Urban Dynamics *model structure and output may provide an even stronger foundation for evaluating the underlying theory.*

16
Adapting *Urban Dynamics* to Lowell

16.1 Introduction

Can the *Urban Dynamics* model be adapted to describe a specific city? This question is of considerable relevance to researchers and decision makers interested in applying the model to their city. *Urban Dynamics* was written originally to bring attention to the basic causal structure underlying the processes of urban growth and decline; the model describes all cities, but none in particular. From the viewpoint of the urban decision maker, however, the generic *Urban Dynamics* model may be a less than adequate tool for fully identifying and improving critical policies within his city. How can the model be made a more effective guide for mayors, city manager, department heads, and other urban officials?

This paper was written to illustrate how preliminary efforts to "fit" the *Urban Dynamics* model to Lowell, Massachusetts, were carried out. Those seeking to refine the urban model to portray particular urban areas may find these techniques helpful, or perhaps they will conclude that the changes in the model are only a part of the process required to refine and expand a generic model. To a large extent, the latter conclusion is justified. Considerably more time and modeling effort will be required if the urban model is to address the many day-to-day decisions that confront urban administrators.

The purpose of the preliminary effort described here was to determine the advisability of more extensive model refinements in the future. Does the general theory outlined in *Urban Dynamics* appear relevant in explaining Lowell's past history and the fundamental causes of the city's present problems? If so, then our confidence in this general theory is enhanced. Rather than attempting to "prove" the validity of the *Urban Dynamics* model, the following pages describe a controlled experiment in which the general theory is tested. Theories cannot be proved; only the absense of disproof keeps theories alive. Yet scientific experiments can lend support to theories in specific circumstances. In this case, the test is whether the urban model can adequately describe Lowell.

Lowell was chosen as a test city for several reasons. First, decision makers in Lowell were extremely receptive to the idea of applying the *Urban Dynamics* model to their city. Their cooperation helped in obtaining data on and insights into the city's background and behavior.

Second, as a city founded 150 years ago, Lowell is old enough to permit a key test of the model: does the actual city experience a life cycle of growth, maturity, and decline similar to that of the model?

> The life cycle behavior permits one of the many tests of model validity we can use to establish confidence in the model. If the model operates satisfactorily, beginning with a nearly empty land area, growing, and stabilizing in a sequence of events characteristic of a real-life area, it has passed one of many available tests. [*Urban Dynamics*, p. 50]

Finally, Lowell was chosen for the examination reported here because it exhibits the basic problems of a mature city that are addressed in the *Urban Dynamics* model—high unemployment, industrial disinvestment, inadequate

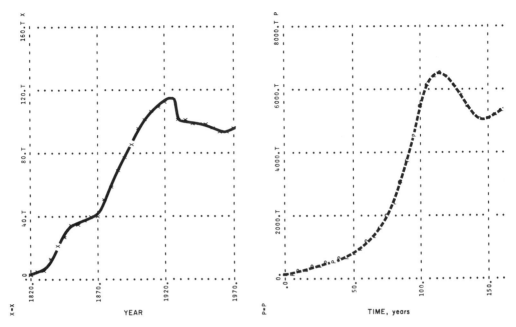

Figure 1   Lowell's growth contrasted with *Urban Dynamics* growth

housing, rising taxes, inefficient land use, and overall socioeconomic decay are all problems that have been evidenced in Lowell for several decades. Because Lowell's problems are similar to those of many mature cities, efforts to adapt the urban model to Lowell should help establish guidelines for adapting it to other cities as well.

16.2 A Basic Comparison: Total Population

In looking for an empirical measure with which to gauge the performance of the *Urban Dynamics* model, one can begin with the population figures for the city. Population data are easily obtained, and can be readily compared with the model's output as a test of its accuracy. Lowell's population is compared with the population curve from the original *Urban Dynamics* growth model in Figure 1.

The similarity of the two curves of Figure 1 strongly suggests that the forces that have produced Lowell's history are also found in the model. The pattern of growth, the sharpness of the peak, and the amount of population decline are strikingly similar in both curves.

Few people seem to realize the extent to which the pattern of exponential growth, stagnation, and decay is characteristic of nearly all U.S. cities. In fact, several critics of *Urban Dynamics* have raised doubts concerning whether cities normally experience a decline in population as they approach old age. Figure 2 makes clear the fact that many major U.S. cities have displayed not only exponential growth but also a declining population as they reach age 150.

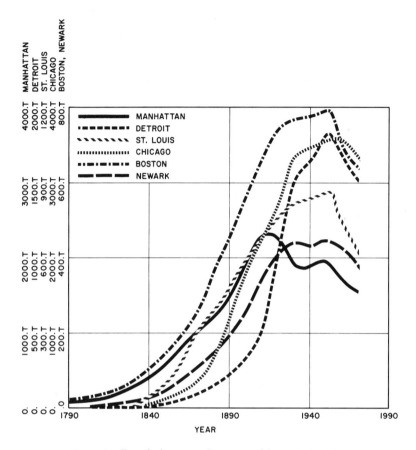

Figure 2 Population growth curves of large U.S. cities

Our familiarity with these major cities should be sufficient to preclude any long discussion of the problems found in each. The cities in Figure 2, some of our oldest, are also among our most troubled. Lowell, although much smaller than the urban areas in Figure 2, appears to have developed in much the same manner as these cities, and is today feeling the same pains that are felt by our larger urban centers.

The common historical pattern of urban population growth suggests that the cause-and-effect mechanisms found in most cities, regardless of size or location, are fundamentally similar. As a result, there is reason to hope that solutions to the problems of one city may be transferable to other cities. This was Forrester's initial assertion, and subsequent empirical findings have lent additional support to the theory that a common urban structure underlies the behavior of cities.

Lowell's Parameters. A brief comparison of the curves in Figure 1 suggests several obvious discrepancies between Lowell and the *Urban Dynamics* "city."

Looking first at the size of the population of each area at its peak, it is clear that Lowell has either a smaller overall area or a lower living density than the *Urban Dynamics* model "city." This is an easy hypothesis to verify.

A recent land use inventory taken by the city planning agency in Lowell proved helpful in defining the city's land area. Whereas the city's legal boundaries encompass an area of 14.1 square miles (or 9,000 acres), only a portion of this total land is "usable" in the sense of being zoned for either residential or industrial use. Only the usable or, as it will be called here, "effective," land area is important from the standpoint of the urban model. Let us define Lowell's effective land area.

Approximately 3,300 acres in Lowell are zoned for residential use. Manufacturing land covers 256 acres, while land for use by trade firms is 236 acres. An additional 5.8 acres are occupied by vacant buildings. Of the remaining 5,150 acres, 2,351 are taken up by roads, utilities, and parking facilities; 725 acres are recreational and quasi-public; 620 acres are public service and charity; and 160 acres are covered by water. Finally, agricultural land is 1,290 acres. Hence Lowell's land use breaks down into two major categories. The first is land upon which people live and work:

Manufacturing	256
Trade	236
Residential	3,332
Vacant	6
	3,830

The second is land that provides amenities but is less essential to the city's job market and tax base:

Rights of way	2,351
Public	620
Recreational and Cultural	725
Water	160
Agricultural	1,288
	5,144

These figures yield a total land area of:

Effective land area	3,830
Other land uses	5,144
Total	8,974

Forrester, in the original *Urban Dynamics* model, implicitly included roads as part of the city's land. We chose to remove roads from consideration, since it is extremely difficult to determine whether they should be considered part of the land used by business units or by housing, or how they should be divided between the two. All cities have roads, and in all cities roads take up approximately 25–30 percent of the total land. It is normally a simple matter to find the exact area taken up by roads, and one does not normally think of his house or business as including a portion of the city's streets. For these reasons, it appears both natural and feasible to exclude streets from the city's effective land area. Because the other land uses in category (2) clearly do not reflect the land uses described in the model, the effective land area of Lowell was taken as 3,830 acres. In contrast, the original model contained an area of 100,000 acres. Our hypothesis that the effective land area would be smaller for Lowell thus appears to be verified.

A survey of the 1960 *Population by Census Tract* data for Lowell revealed an additional set of discrepancies between the parameters of the original *Urban Dynamics* model and those characterizing Lowell. The family sizes in Lowell were smaller than those used in *Urban Dynamics*. The national average family size was approximately 4.1 per family, whereas Forrester had postulated values of 5 for managerial-professionals, 6 for labor, and 8 for underemployed families. Some of these differences can be attributed to differences in definition, but Forrester's figures nonetheless seem too high. The figures for Lowell appear to be closer to the national average.

To determine the parameter values for each of the respective population categories, Lowell's 25 census tracts (a tract is a geographical unit that normally contains about 4,000 people) were separated into three income groups. It was assumed that the three or four upper-income tracts contained primarily managerial-professionals, while the tracts with family incomes near the city-wide average contained labor families, and finally the tracts near the bottom on the income scale contained mostly underemployed. By examining the characteristics of these same tracts, it became possible to determine the family sizes (total population of the tract divided by the total number of families) for each population category within the model.

For example, tracts 14, 15, and 25 in Lowell had the highest median family incomes ($6,909, $7,700, and $7,471, respectively) and contained 3,042 families in a total population of 11,660. Simple calculation shows that there were 3.8 persons per family in these upper-income tracts. This figure may be contrasted with a figure of 5 persons per family in the original *Urban Dynamics* model.

To find the average labor family size, exactly the same procedure was used, only this time for the three tracts whose average family income was closest to the city-wide average. These three tracts had a total population of 12,001 within 3,126 families—yielding 3.9 persons per labor family.

To determine the average underemployed family size, we picked the six tracts with the lowest incomes, and then eliminated the two lowest to avoid any extreme conditions. For example, tract 10, whose median income was $2,144 (almost half that of the next lowest), was eliminated from the sample. Our estimate of the underemployed family size was based upon tracts 1, 9, 11, and 24, which had median incomes of $4,683, $4,512, $4,668, and $4,573, respectively. The total population in these tracts was 9,464, while the total number of families was 2,222. The derived value for underemployed family size, then, is 4.3 persons per family (contrasted with 8 persons per family in the original *Urban Dynamics* model).

In summary, the family sizes for Lowell and for the original model are as follows:

Category	Lowell	Original
Managerial-professional family size MPFS	3.8	5
Labor family size LFS	3.9	6
Underemployed family size UFS	4.3	8

It should be pointed out that there is no reason to believe that these values have remained unchanged throughout Lowell's development. During Lowell's early years, for example, single girls worked in Lowell, and by the model's definition, the family size might have been smaller then than it is today. But, since an important purpose of adapting the model to Lowell is to test policy alternatives for the period 10–30 years hence, the revised model should most closely reflect the present and future of the city rather than its distant past. The values computed here are probably accurate for the past 50 years and are likely to prevail for the foreseeable future. These figures should be used during policy testing.

What about the normal housing densities in Lowell? Several readers of *Urban Dynamics* have suggested that the living densities in the model are far too high. Is this observation accurate for Lowell? Using the same tracts that were used earlier, but this time drawing upon housing statistics from the 1960 *Census Tract* data, some comparisons were made.

As might be expected, the highest proportion (nearly 75 percent) of the housing structures in the low-income tracts were "multifamily." Since in many cases this means *more than two* units per structure, it was assumed that, on the average, there were two units per structure in these tracts. Equivalently, each low-income structure was assumed to house two low-income families, or about 9 people. This figure is considerably lower than the 12 persons per structure proposed in the original model.

In the middle-income tracts, the percentage of multiunit structures dropped to 60 percent—the city-wide average, indicating a slightly lower number of units per structure. A reasonable guess is that 1.75 units per structure are characteristic of middle-income housing in Lowell. This yields a normal worker housing population density of 7 persons per structure—close to the 6 persons per structure used in *Urban Dynamics*.

The number of multiunit structures in Lowell was low (30 percent) in the most affluent tracts. With this in mind, a housing density of 5 people (or about 1.25 families) per managerial-professional housing structure was assumed. The differences between the original *Urban Dynamics* model and the revised model with respect to normal housing densities may be summarized as follows:

Category	Lowell	Urban Dynamics
Premium-housing population density PHPD	5	3
Worker-housing population density WHPD	7	6
Underemployed-housing population density UHPD	9	12

During the process of studying Lowell's housing densities, it became clear that the 0.1 acre per housing structure (LPH) in *Urban Dynamics* is too low to represent Lowell. This 0.1 acre value might be accurate for Manhattan, with its extremely high living density, but not for Lowell. There are, for example, currently 11,000 single-unit homes in Lowell. Simultaneously, 2,196 acres of land are occupied by single-unit structures, yielding a figure of almost exactly 0.2 acre per housing structure.

If the land per housing structure in Lowell is considerably higher than the figure given in *Urban Dynamics*, is not the land per production unit LPP also apt to be greater? Employment data for Lowell indicate that there are approximately 27,000 workers in the city. With 491 acres in use by manufacturing and trade, Lowell currently has a worker density of approximately 55 workers per acre. The original *Urban Dynamics* model, even if it contained 100 percent declining industry, indicates a minimum of 80 workers per acre (there are 16 workers in a declining industry, which, in the model, occupies 0.2 acres). The difference between 55 (Lowell) and 80 workers per acre suggests that productive units occupy considerably more space in Lowell. Changing LPP from 0.2 to 0.3 acres would make the employment characteristics associated with productive units in the model come far closer to representing Lowell. With an LPP of 0.3 acre, the minimum worker density of the city drops from 80 workers per acre to 53 workers per acre—a good approximation to the actual city.

Parameter	Lowell Value	Original Value in *Urban Dynamics*
Area	3,830	100,000
Managerial-professional family size MPFS	3.8	5
Labor family size LFS	3.9	6
Underemployed family size UFS	4.3	8
Premium-housing population density PHPD	5	3
Worker-housing population density WHPD	7	6
Underemployed-housing population density UHPD	9	12
Land per house LPH	0.2	0.1
Land per production unit LPP	0.3	0.2

Figure 3 Parameter changes used to describe Lowell

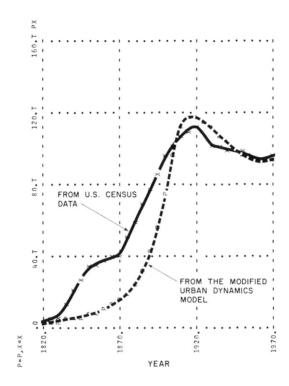

Figure 4   The *Urban Dynamics* model with Lowell parameters

Summary of Parameter Changes.   The nine parametric changes shown in Figure 3, when inserted into the model,[2] produce the computer simulation shown in Figure 4. The actual population curve for Lowell has been superimposed onto Figure 4 to facilitate a comparison between model behavior and the city's history. Although by no means perfect, the "first order" of fit between these curves is significant. The term "first-order fit" refers to the dominant growth pattern, the nearly identical peaks (both in time and in magnitude), and the decay to a nearly identical population value in 1970. From 1900 until 1970, the actual and simulated population curves are never very far apart. There is reason to expect that the revised urban model will be at least as accurate over the next several decades.

16.3 Detailed Comparisons of Model Behavior with Observed Behavior of Lowell
    The fact that the model and the actual city display similar population trends is only one successful test of the model. The urban model appears to have reasonable aggregate behavior. But is the model behavior caused by the same ensemble of forces that have influenced Lowell's development? This section attempts several detailed comparisons of the model with the city of Lowell. In particular, each of the three stages of the urban life cycle (growth, maturity, and

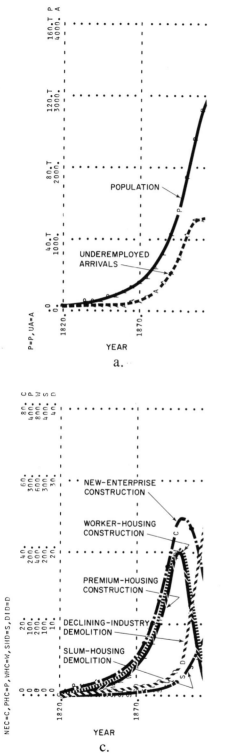

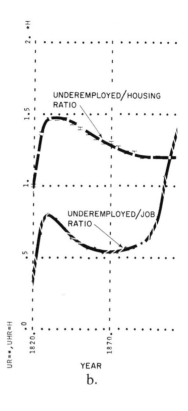

Figure 5 Summary of the growth stage, 1826–1910

decline) will be examined. The phasing, or chronological order of occurrence, of the basic model trends will be compared with the observable trends in Lowell's past. Again, these tests are not intended to "prove" the model's validity. They do, however, present a means for evaluating the model. Each test can be viewed as an experiment. If the output of the model resembles observed behavior, then the underlying theory remains potentially sound. As the number and detail of these tests increase, our ability to assess the strengths and limitations of the urban model will increase as well.

In the following pages, the model's portrayal of the urban life cycle will be examined in detail. For each stage, population movements, migration flows, and measures of employment availability, housing conditions, and construction and demolition activity will be plotted from the same model used to produce Figure 4. Once the trends from the model have been identified, they will be compared with the available data and literature describing Lowell's historical development.

The Growth Stage, 1826–1910.   Figures 5a, 5b, and 5c plot the following variables taken from the growth phase of the model containing the nine parameter modifications for Lowell:

Figure 5a	Total population	(P)
	Underemployed arrivals rate	(A)
Figure 5b	Underemployed/job ratio	(*)
	Underemployed/housing ratio	(H)
Figure 5c	New-enterprise-construction rate	(C)
	Premium-housing-construction rate	(P)
	Worker-housing-construction rate	(W)
	Slum-housing-demolition rate	(S)
	Declining-industry-demolition rate	(D)

The main features of the growth stage of the modified model (as reflected in Figure 5) are as follows:

Population	Rapid population growth due to high rates of inward migration (Figure 5a)
Employment	Expanding employment with a surplus of jobs compared with available labor (Figure 5b)
Housing	Shortage of houses compared with population (Figure 5b)
Construction and demolition	Booms in industrial and residential construction (Figure 5c)

Each of these characteristics will be compared with evidence about Lowell's development:

1. Rapid population growth. The rapid growth of population in the modified model is the result of a rapid in-migration of newcomers. Similarly, rapid population growth in Lowell resulted from the arrival of successive waves of foreign immigrants. Figure 6, constructed from the historical literature of Lowell,

Ethnic Group	Date of Arrival of First Immigrants	Main Period of Immigration	Estimated Total, 1920*
Irish	1822	1820–1850	25,000
English	1826	1830–1850	10,000
French Canadians	1841	1865–1910	35,000
English Canadians	1841	1865–1910	10,000
Greek	1848	1898–1920	20,000
Portuguese	1900	1900–1920	3,000
Russian and East Europeans	1900	1900–1920	3,000

* Includes foreign-born residents and residents with both parents foreign born.

Figure 6 Migration into Lowell
Source: Kengott 1912, Lowell Historical Society n.d.

summarizes the high rates of migration into Lowell between 1820 and 1920. The data effectively illustrate the tremendous attractive "pull" exerted by the growing city during this period.

2. Expanding employment. Employment increases rapidly, with a surplus of jobs compared with workers, during the growth stage of the modified urban model. During this growth phase, the ratio of underemployed/underemployed jobs remains consistently above unity, indicating an abundance of jobs. There is no evidence of any shortage of jobs in Lowell before the 1920s. Instead, there are reports of mill agents canvassing for workers in the 1860s in Canada.

> Prosperity returned [to Lowell] in 1869. The population had been reduced by the [Civil] War and now the corporations were wild for labor. Mill Agents from Lowell were all over Canada trying to induce French Canadians to come. [Lowell Historical Society, p. 57]

Coburn records a similar job abundance in the 1890s,

> . . . before the depression of 1907. Work was then abundant. The Mediterranean steamship service to New York and Boston brought thousands of shepherd boys from Grecian villages, many of whom came to "Lowelmas" to be among fellow countrymen . . . Under the necessity of economizing—often for the sake of financing other members of their families here or in Greece—they slept several in a room with unopened windows. Their hard work in the mills left single men little time or inclination to practice good housekeeping. [Coburn, p. 404]

Coburn further describes an expanding job market in Lowell in the early 1900s, when low unemployment rates occurred even during slumps in the national business cycle:

> Lowell, like most Massachusetts cities, came through the panic of 1907 and the spotty business years that followed with fewer hardships to businessmen and the working class than had been experienced in 1893. The multiplication of industries had become a safety factor. Even in the worst years the building

trades were often active, for it has now apparently become an established principle among New England manufacturers to build new plants at times when business is hardly good enough to keep the old ones running. Even in 1913, when unemployment was general in Eastern manufacturing cities, Lowell showed no such stangnation as was experienced elsewhere. [Coburn, p. 407]

Wage-earners were 29,254 [in 1900]; 46,666 [in 1915]; their earnings rose from $10,853,000 to $33,018,222. [Coburn, p. 413]

3. A housing shortage. The modified urban model indicates the city's growth phase to be a period of housing shortage and overcrowding as residential construction activity tends to lag behind population growth. The late nineteenth and early twentieth century was in fact a time of severe housing shortage and overcrowding in Lowell.

> In 1882 the tenements of Little Canada [a central district in Lowell] were said to be the densest population in the United States except for Ward 4 of New York [Lowell Historical Society, p. 60]

The prevailing housing conditions resulted in large profits to landlords and hazardous living conditions for the tenants. For example:

> One landlord said in cold blood that property of this sort had paid for itself within five years. But the price of such a profit was the health of his tenants. [Kengott, p. 58]
> The danger from fire is great in the crowded tenement districts of the French, Greek, and Portuguese. [Kengott, p. 50]

Overcrowding was common among all ethnic groups and was the dominant characteristic of the housing market in Lowell for several decades:

> A recent publication by the British Government says: "An over-crowded tenement is taken to be one containing more than two occupants per room (bedroom and sitting-room included)." According to this definition, there is much over-crowding in the French, Greek, Polish, and Portuguese sections ... The standard requirement of 400 cubic feet for each adult for twenty-four hours a day, exclusive of the kitchen, is violated on every side in the congested districts named. [Kengott, p. 50]

4. Residential and industrial construction booms. Residential and industrial construction booms underlie the rapid growth in housing and employment in the

Category	Number	Percent
Total number of housing units	25,579	
Number reporting year built	21,908	100.0
Number constructed 1930–1940	287	1.3
Number constructed 1920–1929	1,960	8.9
Number constructed 1900–1919	9,333	42.6
Number constructed 1899 or earlier	10,328	47.1
Number not reporting year built	3,671	

Figure 7 Housing construction data from U.S. Census of Housing, 1940

Year	Estimated Value in $ (1906 Prices)
1906	$300,000
1910	$220,000
1915	$350,000
1919	$500,000
1924	$ 60,000
1927	$ 10,000

Figure 8 Estimated value of industrial permits issued

modified model. The data given in Figure 7 from the U.S. Census of Housing, 1940, indicate that the highest rates of residential construction in Lowell occurred before 1919, that building activity virtually ceased during the 1920s.

Few numerical data are available to measure the rate of industrial construction in Lowell. However, it is evident that the growth period was a time of rapid industrial expansion, since over 15,000,000 square feet of factory mill area were built during the interval. Coburn refers to the growth of industrial capital in Lowell from $45,510,000 in 1900 to $78,714,844 in 1915 (Coburn, p. 413). The data in Figure 8 indicate that the industrial construction boom in Lowell lasted until the early 1920s, but that new industrial construction dropped to almost zero thereafter.

The data contained in Figures 7 and 8 indicate that the residential and industrial construction booms that occurred in Lowell through the early part of the twentieth century ended abruptly in the early 1920s. The modified urban model shows construction rates declining steadily from 1900 onward. The discrepancy between the model output and the evidence about Lowell's history is probably the result of the economic boom in Lowell created by World War I. The wartime demand for textiles and munitions appears to have extended the construction boom for both residential and industrial structures into the 1920s.

5. Summary of the growth stage. There is considerable evidence that the main characteristics of Lowell's growth stage are very similar to those exhibited by the *Urban Dynamics* model. Population growth gave rise to industrial expansion, and industrial expansion encouraged greater population growth. Rapid in-migration caused a tight housing market and a sustained housing boom, which reinforced Lowell's rate of economic growth. For both Lowell and the modified urban model, this was a stage in which growth reinforced growth.

The Maturity Stage, 1910–1930. Figures 9a, 9b, and 9c plot the model's output for the period 1910–1930. Over this interval, the construction boom ends and the model exhibits a stage of transition characterized by the following changes:

1. Population peaks and declines as net in-migration changes to net out-migration (Figure 9a).
2. The supply of jobs peaks and contracts, creating persistent unemployment (Figure 9b).

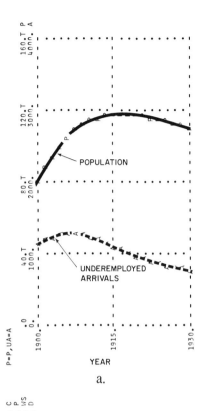

a.

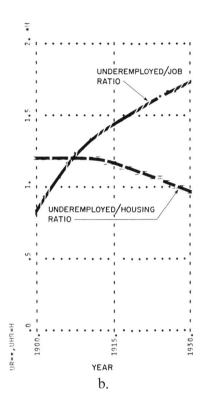

b.

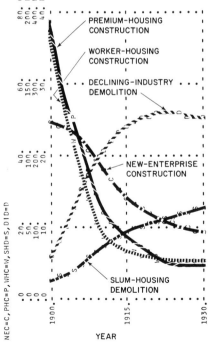

c.

Figure 9   Summary of the maturity phase, 1910–1930

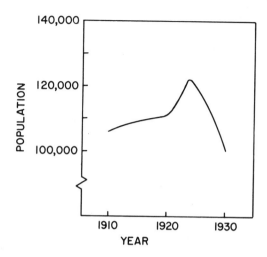

Figure 10 Population change in Lowell, 1910–1930

3. The housing shortage changes to a housing excess; high vacancy rates result (Figure 9*b*).

4. Industrial and residential demolition increases as the city moves into decline (Figure 9*c*).

1. Population peaks and declines. The January 1, 1924, edition of The *Lowell Sun* reported that Lowell's population had increased from 112,759 in 1920 to 124,035, indicating that heavy in-migration continued until about 1924. That year may have been the turning point, however, for on January 3, 1928, the paper estimated that a net of 12,000 people had left the city. The high population inflow during Lowell's growth period changed to an outflow as the city's economy contracted; Lowell's population thus peaked and declined. Figure 10 indicates a period of rapid population change from 1928 to 1930. The change is entirely consistent with the population trend projected by the urban model.

2. The supply of jobs peaks and contracts. It has not been possible to obtain estimates of total employment in Lowell, but detailed information is available about manufacturing employment (the major source of work) in the city from 1904 onward in the annual U.S. *Census of Manufactures*. Total manufacturing employment for the period 1904–1932 is shown in Figure 11.

The following different phases in manufacturing employment can be identified from Figure 11:

1914–1918. Manufacturing employment increased from 30,000 to 40,000, largely due to World War I. In 1916 the largest employer was the United States Cartridge Company (established in 1914), with 7,200 employees in munitions production.

1919–1921. Employment fell to 30,000 in 1919 (equal to the prewar level) and then to 24,500 in 1921.

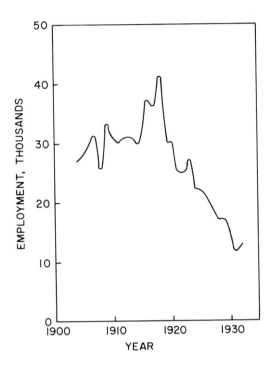

Figure 11   Annual average manufacturing employment in Lowell
Source: U.S. Department of Commerce, *Census of Manufactures*

1922–1923. Employment recovered to 27,000 during a textile boom in 1923.

1924–1928. Employment declined despite a national economic boom.

1928–1932. Employment fell to a low point of 12,000 in 1932 during the national depression. Employment contracted from 1924 onward because the Lowell mills were no longer competitive with newer manufacturers outside the city.

3. The housing shortage changes to a housing excess. On January 3, 1928, The *Lowell Sun* reported a July 1927 study estimating that "ten percent of the floor space in dwelling houses is vacant" (equal to 2,500 apartments), following the exodus of people from 1924 onward. The crowded housing conditions of the growth stage changed to a landscape with many vacant shops and residences. Parker comments: "The commercial and residential areas also give testimony as to recent changes. Vacant shops and vacant tenements are many" (Parker, p. 30). These brief references would indicate that as the population of the city declined, surplus housing began to appear.

4. Industrial and residential demolition increases. The data presented in Figures 7 and 8 indicate that Lowell's construction boom lasted into the early 1920s. By the mid 1920s, however, new building construction was approaching zero. Around this time, demolition activity started to occur. There is no evidence

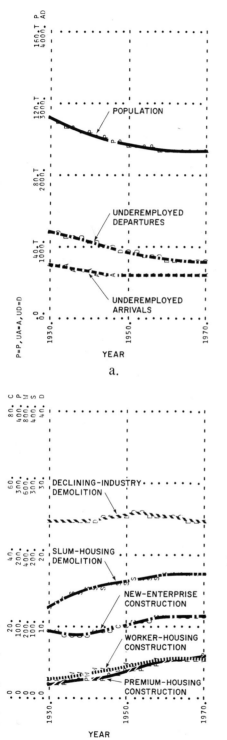

a.

b.

Figure 12 Summary of the equilibrium phase, 1930 to present

c.

of any demolition in Lowell before the 1920s, but many buildings had been razed by the early 1930s.

> Considerable blocks of vacant industrial or residential property have been destroyed to reduce taxes. [Parker, p. 5]

> In Little Canada evidences of loss of population or of its removal from the city, are conspicuous. Once a highly congested district, it is now sprinkled with open plots. [Parker, p. 30]

5. Summary of the transition phase. Lowell's history follows closely the behavior of the modified urban model in the transition from growth to equilibrium. Lowell's population peaked and declined because of heavy out-migration, caused by high unemployment. This, in turn, produced an excess of housing and high vacancy rates. New construction activity declined almost to zero, and industrial and residential demolition became prominent during the transition period.

Equilibrium, 1930 to Present.   The final stage of the urban life cycle is decline into equilibrium, as shown in Figure 12.[5] The main features of the equilibrium period are:

1. Little change in population over time (Figure 12a)
2. Persistent unemployment (Figure 12b)
3. Continuing surplus of old, low-quality housing (figure 12b).

1. Little change in population over time. Lowell's total population since 1930 has been stable, as shown in Figure 13. A slight net out-migration from Lowell continued until the late 1960s when a slight growth trend was reestablished.

2. Persistent unemployment. Unemployment has persisted in Lowell until the present time; it is clearly the major problem facing the city today. Recent data for the Lowell Standard Metropolitan Statistical Area, SMSA (population approximately 200,000) shown in Figure 14 underlines the problem. Although the

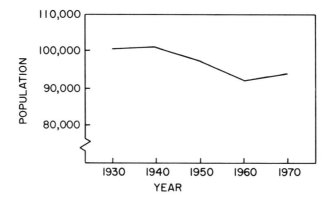

Figure 13   Lowell's population from 1930–1970
Source: U.S. *Statistical Abstract*, 1940–1970.

Year	Lowell SMSA(%)	United States(%)	Ratio: Lowell/U.S.
1958	11.3	6.8	1.67
1960	7.7	5.5	1.40
1962	7.9	5.5	1.44
1964	8.6	5.2	1.65
1966	6.3	3.8	1.67
1968	5.4	3.6	1.50

Figure 14   Unemployment rate in the Lowell SMSA
Source: Greater Lowell Chamber of Commerce, "Economic Fact
File, 1972"; Massachusetts Division of Employment Security, "Massachusetts Trends," May 1971.

unemployment rate within the SMSA increased and fell in a pattern similar to the national rate, it remained between 40 percent and 70 percent higher than the average for the country.

Lowell Chamber of Commerce officials have stated that unemployment is lower in the suburbs of Lowell than in the central city. They estimate that unemployment in Lowell was generally two to three points higher than the SMSA figures given in Figure 14.[6]

Figure 15 plots total private employment and total manufacturing employment in Lowell between 1951 and 1971. As seen in Figure 14, employment levels have been fairly stable over this interval. Overall, however, recent years have been a period of relatively high unemployment for Lowell residents.

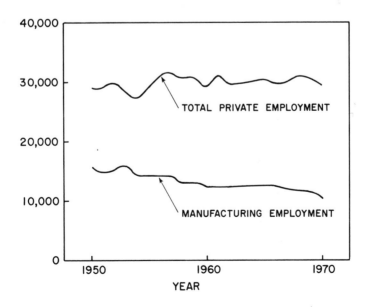

Figure 15   Employment in Lowell 1950–1970

3. Continuing surplus of old, low-quality housing. Is there currently an excess of housing in Lowell? Housing census data for 1970 do not record housing vacancies because of a change in collection procedures. But the following data are recorded in the 1960 housing census:[7]

Total housing units	29,952
Occupied housing units	28,454
Vacant and available for occupancy	1,028
Vacant and not suitable for occupancy	470

From 1960 to 1970, occupied housing units in Lowell increased by 10.7 percent (28,454–31,487) while the population increased by 2.3 percent (92,107–94,239). There is no evidence to suggest any significant change in housing occupancy densities in Lowell. It would seem reasonable, therefore, to draw the inference that there is presently a surplus of well over 1,000 housing units in Lowell—in excess of 3 percent of the total housing stock.

The estimated age profile of Lowell's housing stock is shown in Figure 16. This age profile indicates that two thirds of Lowell's housing stock is over fifty years old. Except for state and federally subsidized housing projects there are few signs of recent residential construction in the central city.

Summary. Available empirical evidence for Lowell shows that the city experienced a clearly identifiable life cycle of growth, maturity, and equilibrium, with characteristics very similar to those of the *Urban Dynamics* model. The comparison is heavily dependent on descriptions found in histories of the city. While the unavailability of precise numerical data prevents a more rigorous comparison between the model and the city of Lowell, the qualitative evidence available about Lowell's past strongly supports the overall behavior of the model.

Year Built	Housing Units
1960 –March 1970	4,000
1950 –1959	2,647
1940 –1949	1,476
1930 –1939	287
1920 –1929	1,960
1919 or earlier	21,109

Figure 16 Breakdown by age of housing in Lowell
Source: Massachusetts, Department of Commerce and Development, "Lowell Monograph," April 1973; United States, *Census of Housing: 1940.*

As a final but important issue, it is interesting to note that the model re-creates Lowell's decline *independent* of exogenous influences. Instead of placing the blame of Lowell's (or any city's) decline on forces at the national or international level, the *Urban Dynamics* model shows how the dynamic interactions within a city's geographical boundary are sufficient to create the historically observed pattern of urban growth and decline.

16.4 The Source of Disparities between the Model Behavior and Lowell's Observed History

The match between the adapted model's behavior and Lowell's history in Figure 4 is less than perfect. There is, for example, a substantial discrepancy during the early growth phase of the city (1830–1850). This discrepancy may seem unreasonably large to someone who considers historical accuracy to be the main criterion for model validity. Yet it is fundamental to system dynamics modeling that this behavioral evaluation not be given unwarranted importance; if the empirical differences are the result of exogeneous forces acting on the real system rather than internal dynamics, then we would not expect the effect of these forces to appear in the behavior of the closed-loop model.

Why did Lowell's population grow by over 300 percent (from 6,000 to 20,000) during the period 1830–1850, while the model grows by only about 30 percent during this same time span? The primary reason seems to have been a unique match between the city's geographical characteristics and the technological needs of the textile industry in the early 1800s. With huge reserves of water power and good access by river for the shipment of raw and finished goods, Lowell was an ideal site for the construction of large textile mills in a period when water power and water transportation prevailed. Within a ten-year span, more than 10,000 jobs were created in Lowell.[8] Simultaneously, factory-owned housing was created to attract workers to the area.

The forces that were responsible for Lowell's early growth were not wholly internal to the city. Lowell benefited early from the match between its resources and the needs of industry but lost its comparative advantage as technology progressed. The *Urban Dynamics* model structure does not adequately reflect such transitory influences. Still, because we would not expect Lowell to develop today (if it were empty) as it did originally, we should not expect a general model designed to improve contemporary Lowell to reproduce perfectly the detailed features of the city's past development.[9]

Many people familiar with Lowell have suggested that the decline of Lowell was not caused by local conditions but by external conditions, especially the growth of the textile industry in the South. Can Lowell's collapse be explained only in terms of increased competition from other regions, or was the decline an inevitable consequence of local trends?

Parker's text, published in 1940, provides a detailed analysis of the causes of Lowell's collapse. She argues that textile production contracted in New England and increased in the southern states because the southern areas had economic advantages of low wages due to an unorganized labor force and a low cost of living, as well as lower taxes due to the provision of fewer urban services.

> The losses of New England in contrast to the gains of the South must, of course, be explained on other bases. The comparisons which have been made point to the differentials in manufacturing costs which have resulted from the South's lower wages, longer hours, and fewer labor regulations as the major factor in this loss. Lower living costs made possible in part by climatic differences and in part by the less densely settled character of the region occupied have contributed to keeping southern wages low. High taxes in the mature industrial communities of New England in contrast to the lower rates which have in general prevailed in the more recently established manufacturing settlements of the Piedmont have increased the differential in manufacturing costs in favor of the South. [Parker, p. 175]

Consequently entrepreneurs often started establishing new plants in the South rather than providing the Lowell mills with the most modern machinery.

> The recency of establishment of many of the southern factories constitutes in itself a factor favoring the South, because the new factories have been equipped in many cases with machinery improved by the latest technological advances. The cotton industry is so highly mechanized that the equipment of a cotton plant requires a large outlay of capital. Exchange of old machinery for new is not to be lightly undertaken. As New England mills in the period under discussion, reached a time when replacement of equipment was needed, they could of course, replace it in New England, but, in view of the difficulties which New England was experiencing from competition with the South, it might be poor judgment to do so. The charge which is frequently made that the cotton manufacturers of New England have been negligent about keeping their plants up to date may in some cases be justified, but in making this charge care should be taken not to confuse negligence with the exercise of common sense. [Parker, p. 176]

A feedback process resulted. Increasingly difficult economic circumstances caused the rate of modernization in the Lowell mills to be slowed. But reductions in modernization served to compound the city's economic difficulties. One can only speculate whether or not a continuous policy of aggressive modernization would have kept the Lowell mills ahead of other producers and hence have reduced the impetus to build new mills in the South. However, there can be little doubt that the failure to modernize prevented Lowell from having any hope of withstanding competition from the newer southern mills.

Parker comments that Lowell had lost competitive advantages to newer communities. "In common with many other New England cities, Lowell is a mature industrial community in which the advantages inherent in a fresh start in manufacturing, and in less highly organized community life, are lacking" (Parker, p. 210).

The three causes of Lowell's decline identified by Parker, namely, high wages, high taxes, and inefficient production techniques are quite consistent with the aging assumptions in the urban model. Although wages are not represented explicitly in the model, they are reflected in the relative tightness of the local labor market (as measured by the labor/job ratio); in this case, the model would indicate relatively high wage rates in Lowell by the stage of maturity that followed a period of sustained full employment and labor shortage during the growth stage. The tax sector of the model is further consistent with Parker's analysis. Taxes increase as the model moves from the growth stage to the maturity stage,[10] indicating, in part, that a young city has lower tax needs and a stronger industrial base than an older city. Finally, the inadequacy of out-dated buildings, facilities, and machinery are directly included in the model's aging assumptions for industrial and residential buildings. Parker's analysis of Lowell's decline seems to provide a specific case study that illustrates the effects of aging, and the internal composition of industrial and residential structures, on a city's economic well-being.

The *Urban Dynamics* model with Lowell parameters declines as a consequence of internal aging. The evidence presented in this paper indicates that internal forces contributed greatly to Lowell's collapse. Growth and maturity resulted in high wages and taxes in Lowell compared with less-developed urban areas. Subsequently, high production costs in Lowell raised the incentives for textile production in the South where wages and taxes were lower. The growth of the southern mills clearly accelerated Lowell's decline but did not alone cause the city to falter. New investment was withheld from Lowell's mills, which lost competitiveness because of outmoded technology as well as high labor costs and tax rates. Aging resulted in rising costs that would have eroded Lowell's economic viability independent of specific changes in the city's environment. Had the city been able to encourage continued investment in Lowell, there is no reason to expect that the dramatic losses beginning in 1920 would have been anywhere near so severe. The rapid decline of industry in Lowell was not only a consequence of the attractive "pull" exerted by conditions in the South but also of the "push" supplied by unfavorable conditions within the city. To attribute Lowell's decline wholly to the pull of external areas is to ignore the important internal mechanisms that have contributed to Lowell's current problems.

16.5 Conclusions

The *Urban Dynamics* model, adapted to Lowell, exhibits a behavior that clearly resembles the history of the city. This paper has presented several tests of the urban model against historical observations. These tests, collectively, lend some additional support to the structure and assumptions of the model. No simple rule exists for converting these tests into quantitative measures of model validity. In the final analysis, each individual must judge for himself the strengths of the model, or those of any equivalent theory.

In the future, the *Urban Dynamics* model may be expanded to portray more closely the characteristics of particular urban areas. A properly constructed urban model can be a valuable tool for separating the causes of a city's ills from its many symptoms. Evaluating alternative policies on more detailed models may help to explain why many past programs in cities have failed. New policies, with far more promising consequences, may begin to evolve. The final result would be a successful application of technological methods to our most fundamental social problems.

Notes

1. In Figure 1, the population growth curve from *Urban Dynamics* was obtained by adding an additional plot card to the model:

$$\text{PLOT } P = P(0, 8E6)$$

2. The model used for making the runs contained in the following pages is the same model contained in the Urban Dynamics text. Slight refinements were made to the obsolescence mechanisms of the original model, but these changes have negligible effects on the model's behavior. For a detailed summary of the obsolescence refinements, see Louis Edward Alfeld, "UD2: Refinements to the Urban Dynamics Model," System Dynamics Group Working Paper (Cambridge, Mass.: Massachusetts Institute of Technology, 1973).

3. To produce the simulations shown in Figure 5, the following plot cards were added to the urban dynamics model equations:

```
PLOT    P=P(0,16E4)/UA=A(0;4E3)
PLOT    UR=*,  UHR=H(0,2)
PLOT    NEC=C(0,80)/PHC=P(0,400)/WHC=
        W(0,800)/SHD=S(0,400)/DID=D(0,40)
```

The simulations show model output for the period 1820-1910 only.

4. To produce these simulations, the identical equations as in Figure 4 (note 3) were added to the urban dynamics model. The simulations in Figure 8 show model output for the period 1900–1930, and the computer plot-period was reduced somewhat to magnify this range.

5. To produce the simulations shown in Figure 12, the identical equations described in note 3 were added to the urban model. The simulations show model output from 1930–1970, and the computer plot-period was reduced somewhat to magnify this range.

6. The following unemployment data are available for the city of Lowell from the U. S. population censuses:

1950–7.0%

1960–5.2%

1970–4.3%

They would indicate that Lowell does not presently have an unemployment problem. However, the data are quite misleading and conflict with the statistics issued monthly by the Massachusetts Division of Employment Security. The latest Division of Employment Security figures for the Lowell SMSA "Massachusetts Trends," March 1973 are:

	Lowell SMSA	Massachusetts
January 1973	10.6%	7.2%
February 1973	10.3%	7.1%

Unemployment is probably the most serious problem facing Lowell today.

7. *U.S. Census of Housing*: *1960*, Series HC (3)-188, "City Blocks" Lowell, Massachusetts: In 1950, the unit of enumeration was the dwelling unit. Although the definition of the housing unit in 1960 is essentially similar to that of the dwelling unit in 1950, the housing unit definition was designed to encompass all private living quarters, whereas the dwelling unit definition did not completely cover all private living accommodations. The main difference between housing units and

dwelling units is as follows: In 1960, *separate* living quarters consisting of one room with direct access but without separate cooking equipment qualify as a housing unit whether in an apartment house, rooming house, or house converted to apartment use; in hotels, a single room qualifies as a housing unit if occupied by a person whose usual residence is the hotel or a person who has no usual residence elsewhere. In 1950, a one-room unit without cooking equipment qualified as a dwelling unit only when located in a regular apartment house or when the room constituted the only living quarters in the structure.

The evidence so far available suggests that using the housing unit concept in 1960 instead of the dwelling unit concept as in 1950 had relatively little effect on the counts for large areas and for the Nation. Any effect on the counts for large areas and on comparability can be expected to be greatest in statistics for blocks and census tracts. Living quarters classified as housing units in 1960 but which would not have been classified as dwelling units in 1950 tend to be clustered in neighborhoods where many persons live alone in single rooms in hotels, rooming houses, and other light housekeeping quarters. In such areas, the 1960 housing unit count for an individual block may be higher than the 1950 dwelling unit count even though no units were added by new construction or conversion.

8. See Walter W. Schroeder III, "Lowell Dynamics: Preliminary Applications of the Theory of Urban Dynamics," Reading 20 in this volume.

9. The most valid modeling action aimed at improving the behavior of the urban dynamics model in this case would be to introduce the early effects of technology as exogenous variables, keeping in mind that the model's accuracy (as depicted in the run in Figure 3) is not greatly enhanced by the presence of these exogenous influences. For example, a model run was made in which normal construction rates of enterprise and housing were substantially increased at year 1824 and then restored to their original values at year 1840 when the surge of actual mill construction ended in Lowell. This run accomplishes the objective of making the model behave more like the city during the growth phase. The exogenous changes in the construction rates tell us nothing new, however, about policy design for today's problems; the changes relate only to Lowell's past behavior and not to future behavior.

10. An analysis of the tax rate is beyond the purpose of this paper. However, Parker's reference to an increasing tax rate as a feature of Lowell's decline is fully consistent with the behavior of the *Urban Dynamics* model.

References

L. S. Bryant and J. B. Rae, *Lowell: An Early American Industrial Community* (Cambridge: Technology Press, 1950).

Frederick Coburn, *History of Lowell and Its People* (New York: Lewis Historical Publishing Co., 1920).

George F. Kengott, *The Record of a City* (New York: MacMillan Co., 1912).

Lowell Historical Society, *The River and Its City: An Outline of Lowell's History*, n.d.

Margaret T. Parker, *Lowell: A Study of Industrial Development* (New York: Macmillan Co., 1940).

Part Four
Applications to Urban Policy Design

Reading 2, "Systems Analysis as a Tool for Urban Planning," pointed out that all urban decisions are made on the basis of models; these may be formal, mathematical models or the "mental" models of city officials. No model can ever be a perfect representation of the system it is designed to portray. Urban administrators are therefore continually pressed to make decisions in the face of imperfect knowledge. Paradoxically, though, the urban mayor or administrator may also have *too much* information in that he is unable to discern which are the important relationships and elements that will have an impact on the eventual outcome of his decision.

Urban Dynamics has contributed to a greater understanding of urban policy alternatives by providing a framework for testing the long-term implications of a proposed policy. Still, translating the general insights and recommendations derived from urban dynamics research into specific legislative and administrative actions represents a major challenge for the future. As a first step in this process, the papers in this section outline several practical implications of the urban dynamics approach for urban management.

17
Self-Learning Revival Policies in *Urban Dynamics*

Nathaniel J. Mass

Urban Dynamics *represents a general theory of the forces that produce the growth, decline, and renewal of an urban area. For several reasons, many of the quantitative relationships within the* Urban Dynamics *model are not currently known with great precision. For example, the model contains many individual causal relationships that have not, as yet, been subjected to extensive study within the social science literature.*

Given the limitations of our current knowledge about cities, an important question bearing on the application of Urban Dynamics (*or any quantitative model*) *to specific urban areas is: how can successful urban policies be formulated using available data and present understanding? The succeeding paper by Nathaniel J. Mass illustrates a fairly simple application of control theory techniques to the problems of urban policy design. It develops an adaptive or "self-learning" revival policy for the* Urban Dynamics *model. Within the physical sciences, methods of feedback control are frequently applied in the development of goal-seeking mechanical and electrical devices. Similarly, experiments with the dynamic policy presented here indicate that shifting parameter values within the urban model do not alter the* general direction *of favorable policy change from that shown in* Urban Dynamics.

Although much research remains to be done in the area of self-learning policies, the development of such policies is a potentially powerful approach for designing effective urban programs. Ultimately, the insights provided by dynamic policies should greatly assist the application of the urban dynamics approach to real cities.

17
Self-Learning Revival Policies
in *Urban Dynamics*

17.1 Introduction

Urban Dynamics presents a theory, in the form of a mathematical model, explaining the growth and decay of an urban area. Professor Forrester devotes Chapters 4 and 5 of his book to an analysis and evaluation of urban management programs that might reverse the path of urban decline. He concludes that urban revival requires the replacement of slum housing with new enterprise.

The recommended policy applied to the *Urban Dynamics* model combines an effort to demolish 5 percent of the city's slum housing each year with a program of business encouragement that increases the city's propensity to generate new enterprise by 40 percent. This combination policy is inserted in the model by increasing the new-enterprise construction normal NECN from 0.05 to 0.07 and by setting the slum-housing-demolition rate SHDR to 0.05. The policy effects substantial improvement in the city; taxes fall, and the favorable economic climate increases the city's effectiveness both in admitting underemployed migrants and in generating economic opportunity. (Changes in a number of significant variables are summarized in Figure 3, columns A and B.)

Urban Dynamics embodies a general theory of urban interactions. The model describes the fundamental processes common to all cities instead of portraying a particular place. Because of this generality, it has been difficult to assess how Forrester's results might depend on the parameters of his model.

In particular, how would the validity of Forrester's proposed policies be affected by changes in model parameters? This paper will illustrate that shifting parameter values do not alter the fundamental direction of desirable policy change; rather, they may influence the *amounts* of enterprise construction and slum-housing demolition needed to support revival. This finding suggests that improvement in a particular city may be obtained through new-enterprise construction and slum-housing demolition. But the necessary amounts of these remedial programs will depend on the parameters of the particular city.

In the *Urban Dynamics* book, the values of enterprise construction and slum-housing demolition selected to revive the hypothetical city, accordingly, reflect the parameters and assumptions contained in that model. We will see that changes in an influential parameter might reduce the efficacy of this exact recommendation. Specifically, we shall reduce the sensitivity of underemployed migration to the availability of housing. Parameter variations of this sort constitute one frequent avenue of validity testing.

This paper introduces a "self-learning" revival policy that adjusts the amounts of enterprise construction and slum-housing demolition toward some objective criteria of revival. The resulting dynamic policy produces improvement in the city irrespective of the magnitude of the housing curve. This application of self-learning policies to the *Urban Dynamics* model is intended to be preliminary. Alternative formulations need to be examined. However, the derived concepts of policy response to parameter changes may be applied profitably to the examination of any dynamic system.

17.2 Revival under an Alternative Assumption

One important relationship in the *Urban Dynamics* model depicts the influence of the underemployed/housing ratio UHR on underemployed migration. Measures of job opportunity, upward mobility, public expenditures, and urban programs on behalf of the underemployed also enter into the migration equation. But the present discussion focuses on the assumed housing influence.[1]

When housing is relatively available (as indicated by a low underemployed/housing ratio UHR), the high attractiveness of the area encourages in-migration. As UHR increases, it indicates a higher degree of crowding and lower incentives for migration.

Let us suppose that underemployed migration into the city were less sensitive to the availability of low-cost housing than the model assumed. The old and new housing curves are shown in Figure 1. We might undertake this parameter change for two reasons. First, we might well suspect that the shape of the curve varies for different cities; for example, residents of an area enjoying a temperate climate might be less easily repulsed by a housing shortage than would residents of an inclement region. Similarly, an excess of housing in a remote area would generate less appeal than a similar abundance in a more accessible area. The second rationale for changing the housing curve is that we may have reservations about the exact appearance of the curve for any one city and therefore desire to test the model over a range of values.

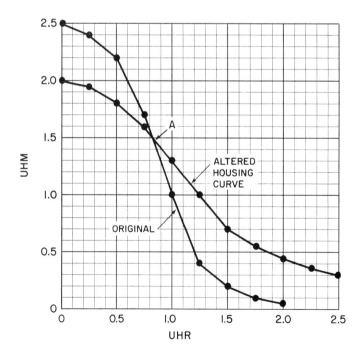

Figure 1 Less influence of housing on underemployed migration[2]

How will this alteration affect the performance of the model? When the city evolves from initially sparse land occupancy, the model equilibrium reached is identical to that of the unaltered growth model; the two equilibria coincide because the two curves of Figure 1 cross at the equilibrium value of UHR at point A. Although it is not necessary (or even to be expected) that the altered curve should pass through point A, this simplification will be particularly instructive. When we apply the revival policies of the *Urban Dynamics* book to the altered model, the comparison with the unaltered model will be facilitated if both sets of outputs emanate from the exact same equilibrium. Assuming that the altered housing curve passes through point A will permit us to focus sharply on the important parameter changes. Of course, if we desired to consider a housing curve that did *not* pass through point A, we could readily do so; its analysis would be somewhat more cumbersome but completely parallel.

When the revival policies in *Urban Dynamics* (NECN = 0.07, SHDR = 0.05) are applied to this new model they are less effective than before (see Figure 3, columns B and C); tax rates decline only slightly and job opportunities are still scarce within the urban area. Furthermore, the underemployed population has risen in size by more than 20 percent, while upward economic mobility has increased only 10 percent.

In view of the outcomes summarized above, it seems quite proper to ask, "Suppose the new housing curve characterized a particular city. Would not the revival policies be relatively less influential in aiding that city?" The answer to this question would be affirmative only if we were to adopt a restrictive view of the revival policies in *Urban Dynamics*; that is, only if we define the revival policies as *always* consisting of NECN of 0.07 and SHDR of 0.05. But such a definition is improper. Forrester states that urban revival requires a shift from slum housing to new enterprise. This delineates the *general direction* of improvement; the particular values chosen for NECN and SHDR depend on the parameter estimates of the model. Given the circumstances, one should apply enough enterprise construction and enough slum-housing demolition to effect the desired change.

To clarify this point, we will introduce a "self-learning" revival policy into the *Urban Dynamics* model. The policy chosen here adjusts continually toward an underemployed/job ratio UR of 1.07 (the value reached in equilibrium by UR in Figure 5-16 of *Urban Dynamics*). New-enterprise construction and slum-housing demolition are augmented whenever the underemployed job ratio average URA is below its desired value, and they are eased when URA is more than satisfactory.[3] Thus attaining revival becomes a process of sequential adjustments to prevailing economic conditions.

The underemployed/job ratio UR was selected as the input to this decision process because it represents a datum that is potentially available to urban decision makers. However, in the real world, UR could never be instantaneously observed. It might be perceived, but only after some period of data collection. Therefore, URA, an exponentially averaged value of UR, has been introduced (1)

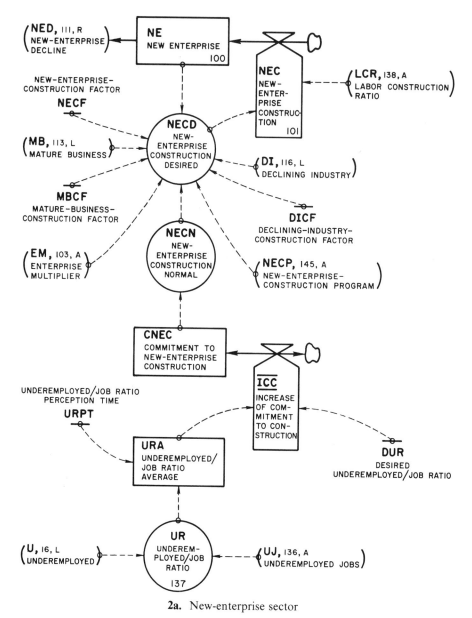

2a. New-enterprise sector

Figure 2 DYNAMO flow diagram for self-learning policy. (For the original structure of the forces governing NEC and SHD, see *Urban Dynamics*, pp. 190, 187.)

in recognition of the time delay in perceiving UR, and (2) to protect against basing policies on short-term fluctuations in UR caused by external events.[4]

A flow diagram for this dynamic policy appears in Figure 2. The DYNAMO equations for the policy, along with a detailed explanation, are contained in the appendix. The reader should note in Figure 2 that both new-enterprise construction normal NECN and the slum-housing-demolition rate SHDR have been made variables.

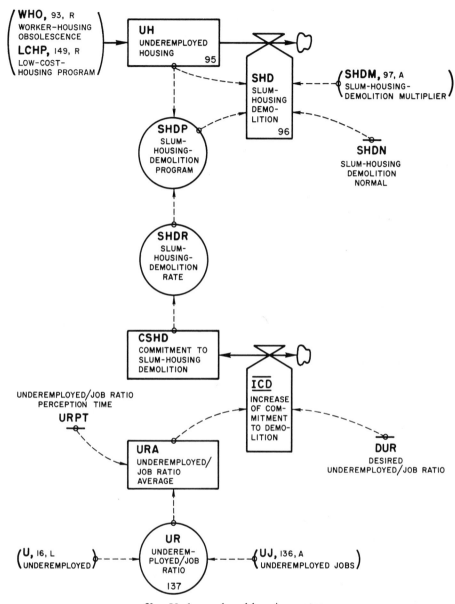

2b. Underemployed-housing sector

Figure 2 (continued)

Figure 3 summarizes the results of applying the new policy to the model (with the new housing curve). Considerable improvement in the city is obtained; resulting changes compare favorably with those achieved by the basic policy on the unaltered model.[5]

A few points should be made with regard to Figure 3. The reader may note that the underemployed/housing ratio UHR reaches a value of 1.96 in equilibrium (compared with 1.28 in revival on the unaltered model, *Urban Dynamics,*

Variable	Symbol	A Value in Stagnant Equilibrium	B Value under NECN = 0.07 SHDR = 0.05 Old UHMT	C Value under NECN = 0.07 SHDR = 0.05 Altered UHMT	D Value under Self-Learning Policy Old UHMT	E Value under Self-Learning Policy Altered UHMT
New enterprise	NE	4,900	8,000	7,200	7,400	8,100
Mature business	MB	7,800	12,000	11,500	11,800	12,900
Declining industry	DI	16,500	22,200	25,800	24,300	34,200
Premium housing	PH	110,900	152,800	151,400	150,500	167,400
Worker housing	WH	335,600	450,600	434,400	446,500	445,000
Underemployed housing	UH	310,100	175,300	181,200	178,700	149,000
Managerial-professional	MP	71,100	108,700	105,000	105,500	123,400
Labor	L	392,600	600,000	582,600	590,100	675,100
Underemployed	U	377,300	335,900	410,000	334,000	437,800
Manager/housing ratio	MHR	1.07	1.19	1.16	1.17	1.23
Labor/housing ratio	LHR	1.17	1.33	1.34	1.32	1.52
Underemployed/housing ratio	UHR	0.81	1.28	1.51	1.25	1.96
Manager/job ratio	MR	1.38	1.36	1.36	1.36	1.34
Labor/job ratio	LR	0.97	0.98	0.96	0.98	0.91
Underemployed/job ratio	UR	1.81	1.07	1.28	1.07	1.07
Tax ratio needed	TRN	2.25	1.50	1.85	1.53	1.79
Underemployed to labor net	UTLN	5,500	9,200	10,100	7,600	16,300
New-enterprise construction normal	NECN	0.05	0.07	0.07	0.07	0.097
Slum-housing-demolition rate	SHDR	0	0.05	0.05	0.05	0.069

Figure 3   Summary of equilibria reached after application of self-learning policy

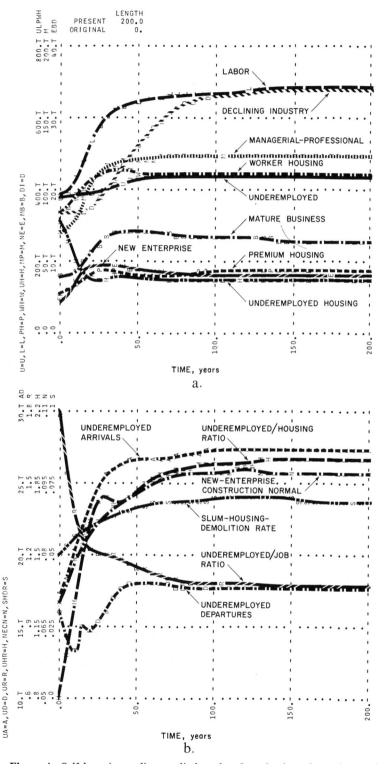

Figure 4 Self-learning policy applied to the altered urban dynamics model

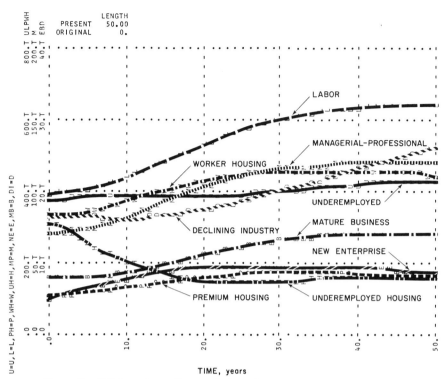

Figure 5a Self learning policy applied to the altered model—first 50 years

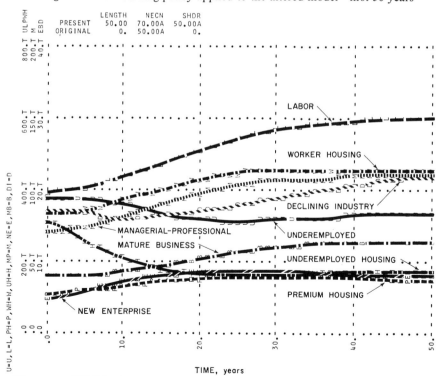

Figure 5b   NECN=0.07, SHDR=0.05 applied to original *Urban Dynamics* model

Figure 5

Figure 5–17). As Professor Forrester explains, some reduction of housing availability is a necessary accompaniment to economic improvement. In the absence of such housing pressure, increased in-migration would drive down the attractiveness of the area to equality with that of its surroundings. Excessive rates of unemployment would still pervade. However, a UHR of 1.96 in this instance does not constitute the imposition of excessive psychological hardship on the underemployed population. In hypothesizing less responsiveness of underemployed migration (and particularly of underemployed departures) to housing, we have said that the hardship imposed by any level of UHR is less than that we had previously theorized. Intrinsically, the housing curve reflects the degree of psychological difficulty imposed upon the underemployed. The reader should note Figure 4*b* in which, for the duration of revival, underemployed arrivals UA always exceed underemployed departures UD. Many underemployed are being attracted to the city despite the tight housing market. But the underemployed population does not rise significantly because many underemployed are being uplifted into the labor category. The city is functioning as an effective socioeconomic converter of underemployed; a city in economic balance is best able to absorb underemployed from its environment and generate economic opportunity for them.

In Figures 4*a* and 4*b*, changes in the variables are measured over a period of 200 years (compared with the 50-year policy analyses in *Urban Dynamics*). The runs were extended to this range to permit the model to reach a condition of equilibrium, allowing the comparison of several runs. The majority of improvement occurs within the first 50 years of the run; over this interval, the underemployed/job ratio UR falls to 1.14, and most level variables have neared their equilibrium values.

Figure 5*a* illustrates the movement of the nine major levels of the altered model over the first 50-year period under the self-learning policy (this plot is a magnification of the first 50 years in Figure 4*a*). Figure 5*b* illustrates the results, over 50 years, of applying the basic revival policy (NECN = 0.07, SHDR = 0.05) to the unaltered model. These two graphs are offered for visual comparison. (A reliable comparison could not be made between Figure 5*a* and Figure 5–16 of *Urban Dynamics* because the vertical scales differ. All the computer outputs in this paper are plotted on the same vertical scale.)

The self-learning policy has been applied in Figures 4 and 5 to regulate employment conditions within the city. This policy is a fairly simple example of an engineering "integral controller." Integral control is a potentially cogent tool for directing social planning.[6]

17.3 Implications of the Dynamic Policy

Urban Dynamics suggests that complex systems are surprisingly insensitive to changes in most parameters. However, as Professor Forrester notes:

> In examining sensitivity of a system to changes in parameters, we should examine three classifications of a parameter:

1. Does it affect either the growth, stability, or equilibrium conditions of the system?
2. Can it be controlled?
3. Does a change in it affect the selection or use of those other parameters or structural modifications that are to be employed to improve the system? [*Urban Dynamics*, pp. 227–229]

In hypothesizing less responsiveness of underemployed migration to housing availability, we have identified a parameter to which the system is insensitive in the context of classification (1) but sensitive in the context of classification (3); that is, the *extent* to which enterprise construction and slum-housing demolition must be applied depends on the shape of the housing curve.[7] Also, we have said, we maintain some uncertainty about the precise shape of the housing curve even for a particular city.

Normally, an uncertain or unmeasurable parameter does not present a hazard unless it is sensitive in the meaning of classification (3). In the present instance, we must direct our analysis toward policy formulations that operate independently of the housing curve. For the purposes of the model presented in *Urban Dynamics*, the proposed revival polices (NECN = 0.07, SHDR = 0.05) are those which are sufficient to achieve renewal subject to the parameter assumptions of the model. When these exact policies are applied to the model containing a different housing curve, they produce some favorable change, although the *relative* desirability of the policy is lessened. We are led, therefore, to conjecture that the policies published in *Urban Dynamics* indicate the direction of improvement rather than the exact amounts of construction and demolition required to assist any city.

This thesis is supported by preliminary experimentation with self-learning revival policies. The policy presented here used the underemployed/job ratio UR as a basis for control action, adjusting enterprise construction and slum-housing-demolition rates continually toward the desired value of UR. Because the policy works independently of the shape of the housing curve, its desirability is independent of the particular curve. It is of course possible that shifts in some other parameter or combination of parameters might also affect policy recommendations; these could necessitate the design of a more elaborate self-learning policy. Future research efforts should investigate this supposition.

The implementation of a self-learning policy has reduced our concern over the shape of the housing curve; thus we may design effective urban-management programs even in the face of uncertain or unmeasurable parameters. However, upon introducing a dynamic policy into the urban model, we raise the possibility of new problems and instabilities. If, for example, a dynamic policy responded too quickly to random noise elements in the system, the resulting instability might deter system improvement. Furthermore, policy response times that are too rapid might cause continual overshoot of equilibrium, thereby entering the model into a state of oscillatory behavior. This latter possibility is illustrated in Figure 6; the self-learning policy with fast response times is here applied to the unaltered urban model.[8] The hastened response times represent the effects of overreaction. In the first years of the run, the underemployed/job ratio UR is high, and new-enterprise construction and slum-housing demolition are increased precipitously; UR declines steadily in response. Eventually, UR overshoots its desired value. Once this occurs, both construction and demolition are relaxed to the point that UR overshoots in the opposite direction. This cycle would tend to repeat itself over time, causing UR to oscillate continuously.

The run in Figure 6 was accomplished by a very pronounced hastening of the policy response times; lesser degenerate modes can arise from slower response times. Further attention and investigative effort should be devoted to improved understanding of these forms of potential instability.

The concepts of system sensitivity developed in this paper apply to a very broad class of systems. Frequently, changing parameter values in a social system can "shift the mode of operation so as to affect the design of new policies" (*Urban*

	ICCT							ICDT
PRESENT	-7.000A	-5.600A	-3.500A	0.	3.500A	5.600A	.7000A	-5.000A
ORIGINAL	-1.000A	-.8000A	-.5000A	0.	.5000A	.8000A	1.000A	-.7000A

							LENGTH	UHMT
PRESENT	-4.000A	-2.500A	0.	2.500A	4.000A	5.000A	200.0	2.500
ORIGINAL	-.5600A	-.3500A	0.	.3500A	.5600A	.7000A	0.	2.000

PRESENT	2.400	2.200	1.700	1.000	.4000	.2000	.1000	50.00A
ORIGINAL	1.950	1.800	1.601	1.301	1.000	.7000	.5500	.4500

PRESENT	50.00A	50.00A
ORIGINAL	.3700	.3000

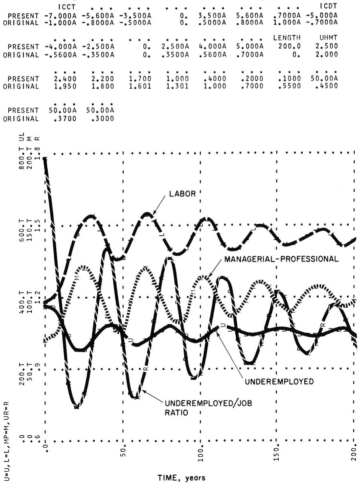

Figure 6 Self-learning policy with fast response times applied to unaltered model

Dynamics, p. 239). A careful search for such influential parameters should accompany any policy design effort. Once an influential parameter has been identified, the analyst should look for ways to make the system insensitive to that parameter. In this light, continued research into self-learning policies seems to be particularly promising.

Appendix: A Description of the Self-Learning Policy

The self-learning policy discussed in this paper uses the underemployed/job ratio UR as a basis for all control action; that is, perceptions of UR guide the direction of policy changes.

But in the real world, UR could not be observed instantaneously by an urban administrator; in any time period, an administrator would necessarily base his actions on a perceived value of UR rather than on its actual value at that exact time. To simulate this effect, we introduce a delayed value of UR:

```
URA.K=URA.J+(DT/URPT)(UR.J-URA.J)              1, L
URA=UR                                         1.1, N
URPT=2                                         1.2, C
     URA    - UNDEREMPLOYED/JOB RATIO AVERAGE
              (DIMENSIONLESS)
     URPT   - UNDEREMPLOYED/JOB RATIO PERCEPTION TIME
              (YEARS)
     UR     - UNDEREMPLOYED/JOB RATIO   (DIMENSIONLESS)
```

Inherently, URPT includes the time necessary to perceive UR and to actuate policy measures. Computer experiments have shown that the behavior of the policy is highly insensitive to the value assigned to URPT.[9] Here we will assume a perception delay of 2 years. When UR is changing, the value of URA will differ from that of UR. However, URA always moves toward UR and attains the same value as UR in equilibrium.

Whenever URA is above its desired value of 1.07, both new-enterprise construction and slum-housing demolition must be augmented in order to generate improved economic conditions for residents of the area. For the enterprise sector, this strategy is accomplished as follows:

```
CNEC.K=CNEC.J+(DT)(ICC.JK)                     2, L
CNEC=.07                                       2.1, N
     CNEC   - COMMITMENT TO NEW-ENTERPRISE CONSTRUCTION
              (FRACTION/YEAR)
     ICC    - INCREASE OF COMMITMENT TO CONSTRUCTION
              (FRACTION/YEAR/YEAR)

ICC.KL=TABHL(ICCT,URA.K/DUR,.4,1.6,.2)         3, R
ICCT=-.001/-.0008/-.0005/0/.0005/.0008/.001    3.1, T
DUR=1.07                                       3.2, C
     ICC    - INCREASE OF COMMITMENT TO CONSTRUCTION
              (FRACTION/YEAR/YEAR)
     URA    - UNDEREMPLOYED/JOB RATIO AVERAGE
              (DIMENSIONLESS)
     DUR    - DESIRED UNDEREMPLOYED/JOB RATIO
              (DIMENSIONLESS)

NECN.K=CNEC.K                                  4, A
     NECN   - NEW-ENTERPRISE CONSTRUCTION NORMAL
              (FRACTION/YEAR)
     CNEC   - COMMITMENT TO NEW-ENTERPRISE CONSTRUCTION
              (FRACTION/YEAR)
```

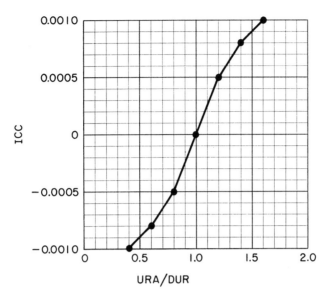

Figure 7 Influence of perceived job conditions on commitment to new-enterprise construction.

ICC is the rate that modulates the level of commitment to enterprise construction. As long as URA is greater than the desired underemployed/job ratio DUR, the level of commitment is supplemented through ICC. To the right of Figure 7, when URA is excessive, the rate of increased commitment is large; the rate of increase diminishes as we move leftward along the table, and it becomes negative when URA is below its desired level. Finally, when URA = 1.07, ICC becomes zero; thereafter, the level of commitment is constant.

CNEC has been initialized to a value of 0.07. This is the value for the new-enterprise construction normal NECN of Figure 5–16 in *Urban Dynamics*. In this policy, NECN is set equal to the value of CNEC.

The structure for the slum housing demolition sector is formulated analogously to the previous structure for the enterprise sector:

```
CSHD.K=CSHD.J+(DT)(ICD.JK)                                    5, L
CSHD=.05                                                      5.1, N
     CSHD    - COMMITMENT TO SLUM-HOUSING DEMOLITION
               (FRACTION/YEAR)
     ICD     - INCREASE OF COMMITMENT TO DEMOLITION
               (FRACTION/YEAR/YEAR)

ICD.KL=TABHL(ICDT,URA.K/DUR,.4,1.6,.2)                        6, R
ICDT=-.0007/-.00056/-.00035/0/.00035/.00056/.0007            6.1, T
     ICD     - INCREASE OF COMMITMENT TO DEMOLITION
               (FRACTION/YEAR/YEAR)
     URA     - UNDEREMPLOYED/JOB RATIO AVERAGE
               (DIMENSIONLESS)
     DUR     - DESIRED UNDEREMPLOYED/JOB RATIO
               (DIMENSIONLESS)
```

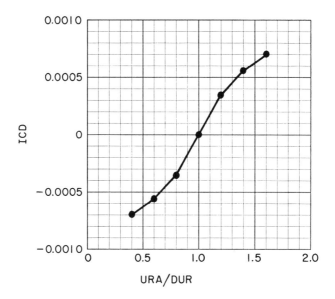

Figure 8   Influence of perceived job conditions on commitment to slum-housing demolition

```
SHDR.K=CSHD.K                                           7, A
    SHDR   - SLUM-HOUSING-DEMOLITION RATE   (FRACTION/
             YEAR)
    CSHD   - COMMITMENT TO SLUM-HOUSING DEMOLITION
             (FRACTION/YEAR)
```

CSHD has been initialized at 0.05, the value of the slum-housing-demolition rate SHDR in Figure 5–16 of *Urban Dynamics*. As with the commitment to new-enterprise construction CNEC, the commitment to slum-housing demolition CSHD is supplemented whenever URA is greater than 1.07 and is reduced whenever URA falls below its desired value. When URA = 1.07, the increase of commitment to demolition ICD is zero, so CSHD assumes a constant value. Finally, the slum-housing-demolition rate SHDR is set to equal CSHD.

Notes

1. The structure of forces governing underemployed migration is illustrated in Figure 2–7, *Urban Dynamics*, p. 24.

2. In Figure 1 the range of UHMT has been extended to function over UHR values greater than 2. Since the altered model may feasibly traverse a UHR of more than 2 under a particular policy, it is necessary to hypothesize values for the table in this range.

3. Because URA is simply a smoothed value of UR, in equilibrium URA = UR = 1.07. When the system is out of equilibrium, URA always adjusts toward UR. In equilibrium, the two values are equal.

4. Appendix E of Jay W. Forrester, *Industrial Dynamics* (Cambridge, Mass.: The M.I.T. Press, 1961), discusses smoothing of information.

5. Figure 3, column D, illustrates the results of applying the self-learning policy to the model with the original housing curve.

6. Integral control devices have frequent and diverse application in the engineering sciences. An example is the roadspeed governor contained in some automobiles. A second application is in chemical process schemes where it is desired to adjust the inflow to a tank so as to keep the interior fluid level constant despite a varying usage rate. Until recently, methods of control theory have had little application to the analysis of social systems. Their potential applicability, however, is considerable. A mathematical treatment of integral control is contained in L. A. MacColl, *Fundamental Theory of Servomechanisms* (Princeton, N.J.: D. Van Nostrand, 1945); A. Porter, *An Introduction to Servomechanisms* (New York: John Wiley, 1950) and G. J. Thaler, *Elements of Servomechanisms* (New York: McGraw-Hill, 1955).

7. It is important to distinguish between the *extent* of change and the *direction* of change. This self-learning policy employs enterprise construction and slum-housing demolition as a mechanism for achieving urban improvement. However, the necessary *amounts* of these may vary with the model parameters.

8. To obtain this run, the following changes were introduced into the equations given in the appendix to this paper.

$$T \ ICCT \ = \ -.007/-.0056/-.0035/0/.0035/.0056/.007$$
$$T \ ICDT \ = \ -.005/-.004/-.0025/0/.0025/.004/.005$$

The effect of these changes is to make system response approximately seven times faster in both construction and demolition.

9. For purposes of brevity, these sensitivity studies have not been included; they are, however, available from the author.

18
Toward a National Urban Consensus

Jay W. Forrester

At the national and local governmental levels, legislative and administrative actions are regularly taken that will mold the character of American cities over the next twenty to thirty years. Today's decisions regarding pollution control or the promotion of economic development may reach their full impact only in the next century. As yet, however, there are no well-accepted tenets underlying urban policy decisions. Many of the papers in this volume illustrate how efforts by local officials to deal individually with urban problems or simultaneously to improve all dimensions of urban life have frequently had outlet in rising urban population densities and increased frustration and dissatisfaction with government. To prevent additional failure, future urban policy makers will need to adopt a long time horizon in their decisions; they will further need to cultivate a holistic view of economic, political, and social interactions within the city.

The following paper by Professor Jay W. Forrester delineates several guidelines for urban policy. It suggests that current city problems are created fundamentally not because of a lack of money but because local fiscal policies, tax regulations, and zoning laws are unintentionally conflicting and inconsistent with long-run objectives. Through interpretation of the concepts contained in Urban Dynamics, *this paper helps to illustrate the use of formal models in structuring an operational theory of urban management.*

18
Toward a National Urban Consensus

This paper proposes steps for reaching a national consensus on redirecting the forces of urban evolution. As background, it first discusses the nature of the urban system and the processes of city planning.

In *Urban Dynamics* I have shown how business, housing, and people can interact to produce the growth and decline of a city. This is done by interrelating fairly noncontroversial assumptions about the urban components in a computer simulation model. The computer then shows the behavioral consequences of the social system that was described in the model. Such a computer model is based on assumptions like the ones we make in our mental models that we use for intuitive reasoning. In general it appears that such assumptions about the behavior of separate parts of a system are sound but that the human mind is poorly adapted to tracing the consequences of the assumptions. In reasoning, even from correct assumptions, we readily mislead ourselves. However, the strength of the computer is the reverse; although it can not provide the structure of a model, it can reliably and completely show the consequences of any assumed set of relationships. A new power in understanding our cities is achieved by combining the newly emerging concepts of system structure and dynamics, the computer to simulate model behavior, and the knowledge of the urban components possessed by those who have had experience in city living and leadership.

The method in *Urban Dynamics*, though not necessarily the particular model, can be used to examine the effect on a city from any proposed policy change. As seen in actual cities and also in the computer model of an urban area, the results from a policy change are often unexpected. Many past efforts to improve the city have been futile or detrimental. Unless we act to understand our social systems better, we can expect the same futility and failure in the future.

18.1 The Nature of Urban Systems

From the study of complex systems we have learned many things:

1. The trouble symptoms of a social system (such as a city, a corporation, or a national economy) are usually produced by the interactions of obvious and well-known parts of the system. Because mental reasoning is unable to deduce dynamic behavior from a knowledge of the separate components, we fail to realize that known policies, actions, and relationships can be the cause of system malfunction.

2. Policy recommendations derived from model simulations are not highly sensitive to the input assumptions if those models properly reflect the structure of our actual systems. The nature of policy recommendations usually do not change when the input assumptions are changed throughout the range of our uncertainty about their true values. But results do depend on proper modeling approaches and do depend on having the proper model structure. (See *Urban Dynamics*, Appendix Section B.3.)

3. Our complex social systems do not behave in accordance with most intuitive reasoning. Very often the "corrections" we undertake to improve a system actually make matters worse. (See *Urban Dynamics*, Chapter 4.)

4. Social systems are self-regulating feedback organizations. As such, they resist efforts from the outside to change their condition. A simple example of this recalcitrant behavior is seen in a room that is too hot because the thermostat is set too high. If someone tries to cool the room by opening a window (that is, he brings in a force for change from the outside), the thermostat turns the heat higher to try to hold the room at the temperature set on the thermostat. (See *Urban Dynamics*, Section 4.2, where job training can increase the number of underemployed; Section 4.3, where a financial subsidy to the city can increase the needed internal tax rate; and Section 5.6, where stricter standards and restrictions on middle-income housing may actually increase the amount of that housing.)

5. A policy change in a social system usually produces a short-run effect that is opposite in direction to the long-run effect. Actions that relieve immediate pressures can reverse their effects at a later time and cause even worse deterioration and stresses. (See *Urban Dynamics*, Section 4.4, where a low-cost-housing program creates a small, brief reduction in unemployment followed by higher unemployment, or Section 4.2, where a job-training program at first reduces the number of underemployed followed by an increase.)

6. Each condition that a city may exhibit has a corresponding set of social or economic pressures. For any urban goal that a city chooses, the citizens must be prepared to live with the corresponding pressures or disadvantages. If the particular pressures are eliminated, the city shifts to a different mode with a different set of pressures. (See *Urban Dynamics*, Section 7.5.)

7. The "attractiveness" of a city is a composite of dozens of factors that give a city its character. The components of attractiveness include housing, job opportunities, tax rates, public services, cultural activities, crowding, prices, pollution, accessibility, safety, location, and weather. (See *Urban Dynamics* p. 117.)

   a. Most components of attractiveness are reduced as the total population and the population density increase above some favorable range of human aggregation.
   b. It is not possible to maintain high values for all components of urban attractiveness. Any area with a high composite attractiveness draws people until the composite attractiveness is driven down to equilibrium with other areas.
   c. If any aspect of an urban area is improved, some other aspect must and will, in time, show a corresponding decline (for example, falling job or housing availability; rising land prices, pollution, and commuting time; or crowding).
   d. Urban planning that fails to choose the negative factors that are to be used to limit population and population density will encounter unexpected negative factors being created by the dynamics of the system in response to population movement.

8. Humanitarian impulses and motives lead to actions that often have only fleeting value. Policies based on alleviating social distress often fall into the class of changes where short-term improvement is followed by long-term deterioration,

even for the group that the policy change is intended to help. Many of our cities are now caught in a vicious circle of worsening troubles created by acting with the best of intent and humanitarian objectives but with results that accentuate the social trapping effect of ghetto areas, actually increase (not just move from place to place) the number of the low-income population, and reduce the chance of economic escape from poverty.

18.2 How We Have Designed Cities

Our cities have not been designed by city planners. What planner would claim to have designed Harlem in New York or Roxbury in Boston as those areas exist today? At best, urban planners launch only the initial phase in a cascade of changes through which an urban area relentlessly falls.

In a very real way, our cities are being designed by the dynamics of the urban structure itself. We have set in motion a self-directing system that is leading us into our "urban crisis." The present procedure for designing an urban system is to respond sequentially to the social pressures that develop. As each pressure arises, we attempt a direct assault on either the symptoms of difficulty or what appears to be the immediate cause.

In searching for causes, we look close in time and location to the symptoms of difficulty. The nature of complex systems produces an *apparent* cause near to the symptoms. But this apparent cause is usually a coincident symptom and is not a lever through which the fundamental difficulty can be corrected. By accepting the apparent cause that the system presents, we are misled into action that merely shifts the symptoms of trouble to another point. We fail to reach the true causes that lie deeper and more remote within the system.

As we act to relieve one set of symptoms, we cause another set of symptoms to arise. The system itself determines a sequence of pressures that lead people from one action to the next, each action creating the next trouble point.

This pattern of reaction to one pressure after another is itself a system design procedure, but it is a defensive procedure. It leads to a result we do not like. We are led through a sequence that is generated by the structure and the policies of the system itself. We are not working toward realizable goals that describe the best kind of city that is possible.

Unless the characteristics of complex systems become understood and recognized in city planning and in our national attitude toward the urban situation, those plans will fail. Most city development plans and national actions violate one or more of the requirements imposed by the fundamental dynamic nature of an urban system. By attempting the impossible, by adopting policies that have the reverse of the intended effect, by seeking utopia with means that produce disaster, and by attacking the very pressures that must accompany desired urban behavior, we sustain the national frustration while the urban crisis worsens.

In stressing the reasons for having arrived at our present urban dilemma, I do not imply either incompetence or lack of good intent on the part of the past urban leaders. Our social systems are so complex and are of such a nature and structure that there has been almost no possibility that effective policies could have been established by judgment, argument, and compromise. Even a person well trained in the dynamics of complex systems does not correctly anticipate the behavior of even a laboratory model system although he may have complete knowledge of the structure and policies of the model. Only by going through extensive computer simulation (that is, examination of the system in the laboratory under a variety of circumstances) does he develop insights about how the components of the system interact.

18.3 Defects in Current Urban Proposals

The following observations about the current urban condition set the stage for discussing future directions:

1. The search for more money dominates almost all discussion of the "urban crisis." But no one stops to explain why we have a system that demands ever more outside support. At one time cities served themselves and the surrounding countryside. There are indications that more money will at best postpone the day when the fundamental causes of urban decline must be faced; at worst, more money can hasten the decline. For example, if traffic delays justify money for central arteries that increase traffic, require more parking garages, bring in more people, force up building heights, produce more traffic, and cause traffic delays, we find "the faster we run, the behinder we get." Any tracing of proposed uses of more money brings us into such circular processes. Money from the outside is probably not a solution except under the impossible conditions of an ever-increasing rate of outside subsidy that can keep ahead of the further demands that the subsidy itself creates. We built our cities in the first place by internal economic processes; why do we believe it is impossible to maintain them? There are indications that cities would revive by themselves and be self-sustaining if we eliminated the positive incentives that cause decline.

2. The desperate effort to raise more money is leading to actions that are self-defeating even from the monetary viewpoint. The graduated state income tax, payroll tax, tax on improvements rather than land, the shift of tax from persons to business, and similar proposals penalize the most mobile parts of the urban community. The result is a selective process that draws to the central city those people and activities which are not self-supporting and repels those people and activities which are most needed to maintain a heterogeneous community, social stability, and economic vitality. This destructive process is widely recognized, but the short-term pressures are thought to be so high that little is done to get off the declining spiral.

3. By reaching beyond the city for suburan and state tax support to compensate for the ill-advised policies that govern our urban areas, we are on the verge of converting whole states to the "urban crisis." The northeast quadrant of the United States is especially vulnerable. This is the old industrial sector. Within the boundary connecting Milwaukee, St. Louis, Washington, D.C., Boston, Buffalo, Detroit and Milwaukee, lie the oldest buildings in the country. Here are

concentrated the declining areas. This entire area is showing symptoms of urban decline. The other three quadrants of the United States are acting as the "suburbs" to this old industrial quadrant. As buildings age and taxes rise, the more mobile and more economically effective segments of business and population are moving to the "suburban" three quadrants of the country. The South and West are showing much more rapid economic growth than the Northeast. The spiral of urban decline then begins to appear as low-income population concentrates in the Northeast quadrant to take the place of those who are moving away. Costs and taxes rise further; the population mix continues to shift in an unfavorable direction and more forcefully drives out those who have mobility.

4. As cities grow and become congested, it appears that total "overhead" costs are growing disproportionately. We should examine optimum size, design, and distribution of activities within a city. It is possible that the trend toward increasing the boundaries of metropolitan government should be reversed.

5. We seem to be in a cycle where communities disintegrate, crime rises, and more police protection is required, but more police remove the need for community self-discipline and indirectly cause more crime. The hypotheses about these social cycles need to be modeled to see which assumptions agree with the observed behavior.

6. The demands for expanded metropolitan government should be questioned. Why do we want larger urban governments? Are the biggest cities free of problems? Is an extended urban boundary a solution to anything? Probably only in the short run. Annexing a suburb that has not yet started its economic decline may give a momentary boost to the tax base, but the action may hasten the decline of the annexed area and enlarge the area of urban blight. Metropolitan water districts and other self-supporting organizations that sell their services at full cost are probably necessary and not to be confused with the expansion of city government. With larger government goes public futility, frustration, and indifference, all of which become more debilitating with time.

18.4 Urban Goals

No achievable goals are guiding our urban planning. Without clear goals of what a city is to be thirty to fifty years hence, there is no basis for choosing between present alternatives. We must think that far ahead because the institutions, buildings, services, facilities, and populations now being established will last that long.

Most organizations, be they corporations or cities, avoid explicit goals because goals imply commitments and, even more important, any clear goal favors one group over another. Most city planning groups refuse to take sides; they want to be all things to all people; they subscribe to all conceivable goals. But if separate steps are taken toward goals that are incompatible, the result may be failure in all the goals.

Many of the "master plans" and "goals for the city" amount to more and better of everything for everyone. As such they set impossible goals. A city cannot be better than its environment in every respect. Try to imagine a city that has less crowding and pollution, more jobs and housing, higher wages, lower rent, and finer amenities than its environment. What happens? People move in until prices rise or the urban system becomes so overloaded that it is no longer superior.

The "attractiveness principle" (see *Urban Dynamics*, p. 117) asserts that if one aspect of a city is improved, another must and will decline. Each improvement will carry with it a negative compensation. I have seen no master plan that specifies the disadvantages that will be made severe enough to control population and population density to compensate for proposed improvements.

The current crop of plans for cities will not alleviate the urban difficulties. They will fail at one of two stages. First, most of them depend on huge infusions of money, money that will probably not be available, so the plans fail by not being implemented. Second, if such a plan is implemented, it will not be dynamically sound. It does not contain the necessary negative counterbalances to the proposed improvements, so the urban system will generate unfavorable factors in unexpected directions. The utopian plans are not viable and contain the mechanisms for their own destruction.

18.5 Directions for Thinking

If the troubles in a social system are *created* by its internal structure and policies (for example, laws, tax regulations, and zoning) and if the external forces to correct the symptoms will usually be defeated, it means that the salvation of the city must originate from the inside. If forces for internal revival are to be established we must reverse our thinking in several crucial areas.

Money. Emphasis should be shifted away from money as the cure-all. In demanding more money as the solution to urban problems, people overlook the fundamental dynamic process now at work in the city. That process: as the city expenditures rise they reduce the pressures for fundamental solutions and allow the underlying causes to generate further demands to match the growing expenditures. In other words, the basic control process is for demands to rise to meet the available revenues. Is it not curious that all the older cities are in approximately the same degree of difficulty regardless of their physical size or the magnitude of their budgets? None are amply funded. None are conspicuously more desperate than the others. There must be a reason for this uniformity of distress that is independent of the size of the budget. The answer is that the problems and the budget grow hand in hand; neither can outrun the other. If the revenue resources get ahead, they are spent in such a way that they generate matching problems. If the troubles get ahead, the pressures rise to increase revenue, or fundamental steps are taken to alleviate underlying causes, or enough population moves elsewhere to reduce the pressures within the particular system. Perhaps the quickest way to force a recognition and correction of the fundamental causes of urban decay would be to remove all expectation of future financial assistance to the cities by state and federal governments. The trend toward interpreting urban problems as a financial demand on higher levels of government must be reversed. Higher levels of government can be most effective by exerting pressures for local action, by altering the tax policies that encourage the perpetuation of old buildings in declining urban areas, and by reversing the policies that favor housing over jobs so that residential construction will no longer rise beyond the economic population-supporting capacity of the area.

Tax laws. The property and income tax laws favor old buildings. The aging of buildings is an intimate part of the urban decline process. The shifting of taxes from real estate to incomes means that the old buildings and the land they occupy need not be used effectively; then can be allowed to decay with little tax penalty. Real estate taxation proportional to market value means that taxes decline as the property ages. This reduces the pressure for the replacement of buildings. The income tax laws allow a building to be depreciated several times against current income; this gives an old building value and helps to keep it in place until it contributes to urban decline.

Population density. Population densities in both residential and commercial zones are allowed to rise in response to the fallacious argument that rising land prices require more intense use. But land prices reflect the permitted use. Under rigid zoning, with no hope of relaxing the restrictions, land prices could not rise too high for the allowed use. Instead, we allow a land-price-population-density spiral to continue until excessive loads are thrown onto transportation, pollution, psychological trauma, and other factors of the urban environment.

Zoning. Zoning has in the past divided land into blocks that are too large and too homogeneous. A large area with housing built all at one time and of a similar quality deteriorates as a whole into a substandard condition. If such an area is large enough, it is avoided by new construction and becomes a slum.

Zoning also allocates too much area for residential use and not enough for industry; this is especially critical when the area begins to age, with the concurrent decline of employment and increase of population. The ratio of residence to industry was satisfactory when the area was first being developed but becomes imbalanced with age. Unless there is rezoning to reduce residence and increase industry, or unless land is held empty initially for later commercial use, the aging area lacks economic vitality to maintain all of its housing stock and the area begins to deteriorate.

The failure to zone so that only forest and agriculture are allowed in rural areas immediately adjacent to urban areas permits urban sprawl to develop and removes the necessity to rebuild and reuse the aging urban areas. Old areas are abandoned rather than revived. This is a direct result of the ease and the lack of legal restrictions in moving onto nearby empty land. The ecological balance between city and agricultural land is destroyed at the same time that the old city is left to deteriorate. A sharp contrast is shown by cities like Copenhagen, Denmark, where open fields lie across a street from multistory apartments. The reluctance to rezone farmland into city land keeps the expansion pressures within the city itself, forcing the maintenance and renovation of old structures and sustaining their effective use until they are replaced.

Selected stresses.   As discussed in *Urban Dynamics* (Section 7.5), each mode of behavior of an urban area will exhibit characteristic pressures. We must cherish and preserve the pressures that go with the chosen style of urban environment. To alleviate those pressures means that the area shifts to a different mode with a change in character and style and a different set of pressures.

Realistic goals.   We must contemplate realistic urban goals that include negative forces powerful enough to limit population and population density. These might be ensembles of policies that can maintain high prices of land and rents, or a housing shortage, or a job shortage (that is the unfortunate control in present ghetto areas), or limited transportation, or limited land area that does not communicate with other areas, or zoning to control density, or a bad array of "quality of life" conditions. The kind of control will determine the character of the city. We should consider the possible kinds of cities having different characters.

18.6 Next Steps

The ideas emerging from dynamic studies of urban systems are so contrary to contemporary thought that they will be accepted only after extensive examination. On the other hand, if they are right, we must not continue along past directions. The *Urban Dynamics* book has already led enough people to doubt the wisdom of present urban policies that a far more serious reexamination of the issues becomes an obligation.

It is now time to clarify further the urban process and to move toward a national urban consensus. *Urban Dynamics* may provide the basis. Three steps appear to be necessary—extending and completing the dynamic studies; interpreting the studies into legal and tax changes; and educating an initial group large enough to maintain momentum toward a change in national attitudes.

First, comments and criticism of the urban dynamics work to date must be carefully solicited and evaluated. Valid suggestions must be incorporated and made a part of the program. Doubts that are not relevant or useful must be explained and dispelled. Other aspects of the urban situation must be examined. New models of social behavior may be needed. For example, the forces, pressures, and motivations in the welfare system should be treated in the same way that *Urban Dynamics* treats the housing-job-population structure. In the welfare substructure we may find that the welfare system is *creating* the welfare cases and may discover that the welfare system is an active part of the social trap that keeps people from becoming self-supporting. Various cities, especially those that appear different from one another in character, should be compared with the urban dynamics findings as a further test of the newly developing urban theory. The additional results must be made available in journal articles and books.

Second, the general directions for change must be interpreted into specific proposals for action. These will be recommendations for modifying state constitutions and laws, city ordinances, real estate and income tax regulations, and national laws and administrative procedures. This step will require participation by lawyers, real estate advisers, tax consultants, and others with firsthand knowledge of how the present social-legal structure motivates people to make decisions that are detrimental to the urban system. This phase would develop specific recommendations for the minimum necessary changes in the tax and legal structure of the country.

Third, the tentative proposals would be exposed to selected people. The participants, perhaps some 500, would be chosen to represent the many viewpoints that must be reconciled in altering our urban social structure. This exposure would be intensive, consisting of documents to read in advance, followed by a one-week series of discussions and seminars conducted in small groups. The purpose would be twofold. First, the comments and reactions would be used to further refine the proposals. Second, the participants should become a cadre of informed proponents who could provide leadership for changing the national attitude toward our cities.

In recommending steps toward a sound national urban policy, we must face the question of city goals and master plans. We will need to clarify the nature of such plans and the conditions necessary to make them achievable. We should deal more fully with the concept of "urban attractiveness" and the assertion that each urban improvement carries with it somewhere a compensating disadvantage. We should then identify the sets of attractiveness-unattractiveness ensembles that look reasonable and possible and that could serve as goals between which cities might choose. In doing so we would be discovering the different characters and atmospheres that a city might have and how to maintain the style, traditions, and quality of life that could distinguish one city from another.

19
Control of Urban Growth

Jay W. Forrester

Many American communities are coming to employ zoning policies and other legislative acts to contain local population and industrial growth. National attitudes, as reflected in the report of the President's Commission on Population Growth and the American Future, are simultaneously shifting toward recognition of the adverse impacts of population growth on resource availability, pollution, crowding, and our political and social institutions.

The following paper by Jay W. Forrester examines the influence of municipal policies and attitudes on urban growth. As Professor Forrester illustrates, technological efforts designed to relieve the symptoms of urban growth have frequently allowed population to expand until social or economic pressures became sufficiently severe to discourage migration to the city. The development of a coherent national urban growth policy in the future will require recognition of the need to control population as a means for preserving desirable urban qualities. However, even for the present, individual communities can exert influence toward limiting urban expansion. This paper outlines several institutional and policy changes that will be necessary accompaniments to successful local and national initiatives.

"Control of Urban Growth" was presented as the keynote address to the meeting of the American Public Works Association in Minneapolis, Minnesota, September 25, 1972.

19
Control of Urban Growth

The theme at this meeting of the American Public Works Association is "A Balanced Approach to Community Development." What does it mean? Ten years ago, "community development" would certainly have meant community growth. But today, community development might imply emphasis on the economic health of the community, or concern for a broad array of issues we call the quality of life. The phrase "community development" is one of those ambiguous terms that means what the listener wants it to mean; it reflects our uncertainty about the future of urban living. The theme speaks of "A Balanced Approach," but the program of the meeting is essentially technological. That too reflects our national attitude and our dependence on technology for the solution of any problem that arises. The program shows sessions on equipment, drainage, solid waste, transportation, water supply, buildings and grounds, roads and streets, and administration. But nothing in the program suggests the close coupling that I believe exists between the strictly public works function and the worsening social stresses that are beginning to face our cities.

19.1 Technology and Public Works

Public works administrators are concerned primarily with the technology of urban living. For more than a hundred years the improvement of technology has been the route to improvement in urban living. Public confidence in technology is deeply ingrained. When there is a problem, the country begins by seeking a technical solution. The reasons are twofold. First, technical approaches in the past seem to have succeeded. Second, technical programs are usually easier to visualize, organize, and execute than are changes and improvements in the psychological, social, economic, and ethical aspects of our existence.

But the faith in technology is being clouded by doubt. Technology has been improving while at the same time many aspects of our social conditions have been worsening. Some people are beginning to wonder if there may not be a connection between the two. Is it possible that the time is past when better technology automatically means better living?

The evidence of faltering confidence in technology is everywhere. People are objecting to more highways because of their harmful impact on families, businesses, and communities, without seeing a lasting benefit as growing population and the increasing distances that must be traveled result, in spite of the additional highways, in as much or more total time being spent in travel. Sewer extensions are being questioned because they imply more houses marching across the remaining open areas. Technology has provided higher buildings that result in more concentrated population and increased social disorders. Urban transit systems are being questioned because they may go hand in hand with economic segregation of the population and the decline of the central city. Taxes are rising, but the technology purchased by taxes seems to be losing the battle.

19.2 Fundamental Social Change

Is it possible that our social system has changed since the days when improved technology did lead to improved living? Can a social system undergo changes in its apparent character so that yesterday's *solutions* to problems become the *causes* of tomorrow's problems? I suggest that indeed such changes in the behavior of our social system are possible, and that they are occurring.

A social system can change its behavior when the restraints under which it operates become different. In the past, the production of material goods was primarily determined by and limited by the availability of capital and labor. To say that production was determined by capital and labor implies that it was not limited by anything else. Our traditions and rules of thumb for social and economic management developed in a period when the inputs to production from nature were, for all practical purposes, unlimited. There was no significant shortage of agricultural land, water, natural resources, energy, or pollution dissipation capacity. But times have changed. In every direction human activity is now being limited by the maximum capacity of the natural environment. When the constraints shift from human effort, in the form of labor and the creation of capital, to a different set of limits, the entire character of the social system can seem to change. Our economic system is undergoing such a transition. Under the new conditions, remedies that worked in the past are apt to be disappointing in the future.

When there are no geographical or environmental limits, economic growth can run ahead of population growth to increase the public well-being. During the growth phase, the many goals of society tend to be independent of one another and can be separately pursued. In the past, if an individual wanted more personal freedom, he could move to the unsettled frontier, while at the same time improving his standard of living by farming rich and virgin agricultural land. But as space fills up, all the social goals begin to interact more strongly with one another. More and more the system begins to offer only trade-offs and compromises. If one wants a higher population, he must accept less personal freedom. If there is to be more industry, there will necessarily be more government regulation and more social groups to intervene in each step and action. If agriculture is to become more capital intensive, there will be more pollution and more long-term damage to the productivity of the land. As population rises against the environmental limits, there will necessarily be higher unemployment and more welfare, with rising governmental costs that divert resources away from additional capital investment.

The change to a new kind of behavior in our socioeconomic system is a consequence of population and economic growth. In the past, when land and natural endowments were unlimited compared to our needs, few restraining pressures were reflected back from nature as a result of exponential growth. But as the natural limits are approached, countervailing forces develop ever more strongly. More and more effort is used in merely overcoming the limitations of the environment rather than, as earlier, in producing effective human benefit. For a while, by expending enough physical effort and capital, the barriers set up by nature can be pushed back somewhat. However, if we follow the route of fighting nature's limits we will exhaust ourselves. The limits can be pushed some, at ever-increasing cost, but they cannot be eliminated.

19.3 Social Stress from Growth

The detrimental consequences of continued growth are appearing not only as environmental damage. In fact, environmental damage from growth is probably one of the lesser threats to society. The greater threats may be psychological as frustration rises, as the individual perceives himself as powerless to affect his future, and as discord increases. Growth is bringing pressure on every facet of existence.

Imbedded in our folklore is a belief that larger size leads to greater economic efficiency. Up to a point, that probably has been true. But now in cities, even medium-sized ones, the economies of scale no longer favor additional growth. The cost per capita for the operation of a city rises steeply as the total population and the population density increase. At some point, and the largest cities have arrived at that point, the rising costs pull down the vitality of the entire socioeconomic process, making further growth all but impossible.

When growth generates costs faster than benefits, we find ourselves in the position where "the faster we run, the behinder we get." Many people are beginning to recognize the futility of solving growth-created problems by further growth but, strangely enough, there is as yet little attention to the possibility of "catching up by stopping." If we could slow the growth of population and population density in a city while adopting policies to generate continuous renewal and revitalization, it would be much easier to increase the standard of living and the quality of life. But under the existing circumstances, improving the services of a city after a while leads not to improvement in the quality of life but, instead, to larger size with the additional services being swallowed up by more people who demand more of the municipal administration.

The underlying cause of today's social pressures is growth.[1] The changing attitude toward economic growth shows how completely our world is changing. Until ten years ago, everyone promoted growth. Boosterism was the central theme. States had development commissions to promote industry and to attract population. Towns and cities had chambers of commerce to promote growth. But times have changed.

In the present transition period, the prevalent attitude is to accept growth with resignation as a burden to be borne. But that resignation is giving way to opposition. More and more there is active resistance to growth. Oregon, Vermont, Colorado, California, Florida, and Delaware have, in various ways, taken steps to limit the expansion of population and industry.

19.4 Leadership for Major Redirection

Not only is the national attitude faltering toward growth as the solution to social problems, but the country is also unclear on where to expect leadership in setting new social directions. Is the leadership for facing fundamental changes in society to come from the federal government or from local leadership? Can the federal government set new directions, or is it limited to attempting minor improvements on the old patterns?

The ambiguity in federal government leadership is illustrated by the "Report on National Growth 1972" from the president to Congress. The report acknowledges the multiplicity of problems associated with population and economic growth. But it nowhere faces squarely the need for slowing down those growth processes that are creating ever more difficult problems. In noting the difficulties associated with growth, the report uses such phrases as

> responding to the challenges of growth ... coping more effectively with growth ... to deal with the problems of growth ... Increasing population in metropolitan areas has intensified problems of air, water, and noise pollution and other forms of environmental degradation. Forests, streams, swamps, shorelines, wetlands, open space, and scenic areas have been consumed by metropolitan development ... The problems associated with growth, by any definition, include many of the most intractable social and governmental concerns of this country.

But federal policy cannot take a stand for which a public constituency has not yet been established. So the report is politically unable to depart from the past national tradition of depending on growth for the solution of all problems. Rather than clearly facing growth as the cause, and raising the issue of slowing growth as the long-term solution, the report pays homage to the national idol of growth in such phrases as

> formulating a growth policy ... Population growth recovered rapidly in the 1940's ... Urbanization also benefited the Middle Atlantic States; after 1900, they were able to reverse their steadily diminishing share of the total population ... This growth, in the form of population changes, technological development, economic expansion, and individual initiative, will almost certainly continue during the foreseeable future ... The Federal government can do much to set the tone and provide leadership and new directions for the Nation in preparing for growth ... This is especially true in the economic area. Fiscal and monetary policy, prudently conducted, can do much to keep the Nation's economy growing at its full potential. Similarly, Federal support for research and development can help accelerate the pace of technological advancement, which is so necessary to a growing economy.

So the federal policy at the moment is, in effect, to attempt to relieve the pressures that result from growth while at the same time attempting to accelerate that growth. This is not said as a criticism of the national administration.

Until new trends in thought are well established and widely recognized, there is no constituency to support a national government in a major reversal of past social beliefs. Our national political system does not permit a federal administration to exercise effective leadership in new directions that break sharply with past traditions. Leadership in small things can come from the federal government. Leadership in big things must start with individuals and local governments.

The United States is now in one of those major periods of reorientation that occasionally face a society. Probably not since the founding of the country and the writing of the national Constitution has so much been at stake and so much unfettered and innovative thinking been necessary. The clichés, the folklore, and the Horatio Alger stories of the past must be shaken off as we face the fact that continuing growth, far from solving problems, is the primary generator of our growing social distress. But there is reason for hope and confidence.

The issues are being faced squarely by many individuals, groups, and even to some extent by cities and states. Many are beginning to see that the rising social and natural pressures will make it impossible to maintain the present quality of life if population and industrialization continue to grow. Instead of running ahead of the growth wave, it is becoming clear to many that ways must be found of facing the issue and learning how to restrain the expansionary forces that are coming to dominate society. The implications are staggering. The ramifications will extend into corporate and governmental organization, into the legal structure, and into values, goals, and ethical beliefs.[2]

19.5 The Attractiveness Principle

Why can public services not get ahead of demands? Why do the best of intentions for improving a city lead, instead, to greater social pressures, more commuting delays, increased drug addiction, higher crime rates, and greater welfare loads? The answer lies in what we have come to call the "attractiveness principle" (see *Urban Dynamics*).

The attractiveness principle states that, to any particular population class, all geographical areas tend to become equally attractive. Or perhaps more realistically stated, all areas tend to become equally unattractive. Why do all areas tend toward equal attractiveness? It is because people move from unattractive areas to areas of greater attractiveness. I use "attractiveness" to encompass every aspect of a city that contributes to its desirability or undesirability. Population movement is an equalizing process. As people move toward a more attractive area, they drive up prices and overload the job opportunities, the environmental capacity, the available housing, and the governmental services. In other words, rising population drives down all the characteristics of an area that made it initially attractive.

To illustrate the attractiveness principle, imagine for a moment the ideal city. Perhaps the ideal city would be one with readily available housing at low cost, a surplus of jobs at high wages, excellent schools, no smoke or pollution, housing located near one's place of work, no crime, beautiful parks, cultural opportunities, and to this list the reader can add his own preferences. Suppose such a city existed. What would happen? It would be perceived as the ideal place to live. People from everywhere would move into the ideal city until the advantages had been so swamped by rising population that the city would offer no net attractiveness compared with other locations.

19.6 Quantity versus Quality

There is a necessary and fundamental compromise that must be accepted between growth and quality. To hope otherwise is to delude oneself. A White House report carried the title "Toward Balanced Growth, Quantity with Quality." The phrase "Quantity with Quality" is inherently a contradiction. It is a political transitional phrase that lies between the old concept of "growth is good" and the future realities in which growth is seen as the fundamental cause of rising social problems.

The fundamental conflict between quality and quantity arises after quantity has grown beyond a certain point. It appears that the United States is now beyond that point. Further growth in population and industrialization means declining quality. How is the compromise between quality and quantity to be struck? Is it to be done uniformly for everyone, or is there to be a local choice between quality and quantity? Returning to the theme of this meeting, "balanced development" means the choice between quality and quantity.

A society has many goals. These impinge on one another more and more heavily as an economic system approaches the end of growth, enters the transition period, and eventually moves into some form of equilibrium. The multiple goals have the characteristic that no one of them can be maximized without unacceptable losses in one or more other goals. Some of the goals are material, others are social and psychological, but they all impinge on one another. We want freedom, but not at the expense of extreme economic hardship. We want to build more housing, but cannot forever at the expense of agricultural land. We want more capital investment to increase productivity and control pollution, but not to the detriment of governmental services.

Many people seem to assume that control of growth will circumscribe our freedoms but that continued growth will not. Nothing could be further from the truth. The fallacy is illustrated by a paragraph again taken from the President's "Report on National Growth 1972," where we find,

> In many nations, the central government has undertaken forceful, comprehensive policies to control the process of growth. Similar policies have not been adopted in the United States for several reasons. Among the most important of these is the distinctive form of government which we value so highly in this country. Ours is a *federal* system, with powers shared between the States and National Government. This system preserves the ability of citizens to have a major voice in determining policies that most directly affect them. This voice is sustained by keeping government close to the people.

But it is becoming more and more apparent that growth in population, industrialization, pollution, unemployment, welfare costs, inflation, and imbalanced trade is undermining local and state freedom. The symptoms resulting from growth are being attacked mostly from the national level, with the result that national policies and the terms of national funding impose nationally determined values on all areas. Federal laws to cope with the results of uncontrolled growth restrict local choice. The higher the social stresses from growth become, the more governmental machinery will be assembled to fight the symptoms. On the other hand, growth can be controlled in many ways, some of which would also destroy freedom, but other ways can be devised to preserve freedom. However, the alternative of continued growth runs only in one direction—toward less individual and local freedom.

19.7 Compromises between Goals

A whole set of pressures is now beginning to inhibit growth. The country faces an oil shortage. Pollution is no longer merely an industrial problem; to reduce pollution created by the individual, his automobile now has less performance, more maintenance, and a higher gasoline consumption. As a result, automotive emissions have been somewhat reduced, but the national oil shortage has worsened and our dependence on other countries has increased. Pollution has also become a major issue in agriculture, as fertilizers and the wastes from animal feed lots pollute rivers and lakes. At the social level, rising crime, drug addiction, mental stress, and community breakdown are all exerting pressure against further growth. Many pressures are developing to stop growth; some we can influence, others we cannot. A most important question is how we would like to have the growth-suppressing pressures distributed.

Pressures to slow the growth process will continue to rise. They will tend to develop from every direction. Some of the pressures can be alleviated. But do we want to alleviate, where we can, the pressures arising from growth? Or, do those pressures serve a valuable purpose?

Unless ever-rising exponential growth can go on forever, and that is generally accepted as impossible, then some set of pressures will eventually stop growth. From whence should the growth-suppressing pressures come? Should the pressures be distributed throughout our society, or should they be concentrated in only a few places within our socioeconomic system? This choice between concentration or distribution of pressures is of the greatest importance. The question arises because we have the power to alleviate pressures in some sectors of the society but not in others. If we alleviate pressures where we can do so, growth will continue until it produces a further rise in the pressures that we cannot control. The way we react to present pressures determines the nature of future pressures.

One set of pressures, such as water shortages and crowded streets, can be alleviated by technological means. We are very good at handling technology, and we can eliminate those pressures if we wish. A second set of pressures, such as job availability, can be alleviated by economic means, and those we know less about but can still influence. A third set of pressures are of a social nature—crime, civil disorder, declining mental health, war, drug addiction, and the collapse of goals and values. These are the ultimate pressures with which we know not how to cope.

If we alleviate the pressures that can now be overcome, those pressures no longer contribute to slowing the growth process. Growth then continues until higher pressures are generated in other sectors. This process has been going on. The first pressures to arise were dealt with technologically by increasing building heights, improving transportation, bringing water from greater distances, developing new sources of energy, and improving medical treatment. As a result of such technological successes, growth continued until a variety of economic malfunctions began to appear—rising unemployment and welfare, worsening balance of trade, and inflation. To a small extent, the economic pressures have been alleviated and their consequences delayed. Growth has thereby continued until the social deterioration resulting from crowding and complexity has begun to manifest itself in serious ways.

In this sequence of technology—solving one problem only to produce an insolvable problem later—is buried the reasons for the antitechnology attitude that has begun to develop. In the past, technology appeared to be solving our problems. The technologists became self-confident. The public came to depend on them. The attitude took root that all problems could be solved by an ever-improving technology. Instead, the rising technology, with its consequent growth in population and industrialization, has carried the society to a complexity and a congestion that are producing rising symptoms of distress in the economic and social sectors. The very fact that technology succeeds in meeting its narrow goals produces greater difficulties in other parts of our social system. The antitechnology feeling grows because of the repeated cycle in which pressures develop, technology produces an excellent solution within its narrow self-perceived goals, the social system becomes more compressed and frustrating and the public perceives that the overall quality of life has failed to respond to the technical solution. The failure to satisfy society results because meeting the subgoals of the technologist is less and less likely to enhance the composite value of all the social goals. For each technical goal that is improved, some social or economic goal is forced to decline.

Growth has continued past the point where suboptimizing is satisfactory. Suboptimizing means the meeting of a local goal without attention to consequences in other parts of the system. During the past period of our industrial growth, the various facets of the technical-social-economic system were sufficiently uncoupled that suboptimizing was a satisfactory procedure for decentralization. Suboptimizing allowed different groups to pursue their own ends independently, with confidence that the total good would thereby improve. But as the system becomes more congested, the solution of one problem begins to create another. The blind pursuit of individually laudable goals can create a total system of degraded utility.

19.8 Determining the Future Quality of a City

What does this discussion of technology and social goals mean for the American Public Works Association? It means that in the past those who dealt with the technological aspects of urban life were free to suboptimize. The public well-being was increased by the best possible job of drainage, waste disposal, transportation, water supply, and the construction of streets. But it is no longer true that improving each of these will always improve a city. By solving each of these technical problems the technologist risks becoming a party to increasing the population of a city and the densities of the population. He may start social processes that eventually reduce the quality of life. The public is recognizing that improved technology does not always bring an improved society. As a result, men who have sincerely dedicated their efforts to the public good, but perhaps have not foreseen the diversity of social consequences, have already begun to feel the backlash of public criticism.

So far I have developed several propositions. First, pressures are rising that will inevitably stop growth. Second, the national commitment to growth is too strong for the federal government to lead the country in a new direction until a broad constituency for changed expectations has been formed. Third, if the stress-creating nature of growth is to be recognized, and if experiments are to be carried out to find a satisfactory way of moving from growth to a society that can accept a future equilibrium, leadership must come from the local and state levels. Fourth, technical accomplishments no longer appear to be capable of solving our mounting social problems; instead, technology, as now being used, may often lead to expansion in urban population and living densities that become the cause of rising social difficulties. Fifth, all cities do at all times tend toward equal attractiveness in which no one city can remain significantly more attractive to in-migration than other cities. Given this set of propositions, what freedom of action is left to a city?

A city can choose, to a substantial extent, the mix of pressures under which it wishes to exist. There are many components of urban attractiveness, and if one of these is decreased, others can be improved. One cannot create the ideal city. But one can create certain ideal features if he is willing to compensate for them by intentionally allowing other features to worsen. In the past we have improved the technological aspects of cities and have thereby unintentionally contributed to the rise of many of the economic and social problems that plague cities today. There are many facets to a city. There are many things that the public and an urban administration can do. One thing they cannot do is produce the perfect city. They can, however, exercise a wide choice among imperfect cities.

I suggest that a valid goal for local urban leadership is to focus on improving the quality of life for the residents already in the city, at the same time protecting against the kind of growth that would overwhelm the gains. In short, one might raise the attractiveness of a city for the present residents while, at the same time, decreasing the attractiveness to those who might inundate the system from the outside.

Such statements, I recognize, lead to ethical and legal controversy. I am saying that a city should look after itself first. Its own welfare should come ahead of concern for others who are taking no steps to solve the fundamental problems for themselves. If enough cities establish successful policies for themselves, there will be two results. First, a precedent will have been set for coping with the fundamental underlying source of difficulties. Second, the larger the number of areas that solve their problems for themselves, the sooner and more forcefully will the remaining uncontrolled growth impinge on other parts of the country and the more quickly will the nation realistically face the long-range issues of stress arising from excessive growth.

So what can a city do? It can influence its future by choosing among the components of attractiveness. The attractiveness components of a city fall into two categories according to whether they operate more forcefully on the quality of life in the city or on inward migration and growth. These two categories are the "diffuse" and the "compartmentalized" characteristics of a city. The objective should be to maximize the diffuse characteristics of the city in order to improve the quality of urban life while controlling the compartmentalized characteristics in order to prevent the expanded population that would defeat the improvement for present residents.

The diffuse characteristics, such as public safety and clean air, are shared equally by all; their effect is not limited to particular individuals; and they apply alike to present residents and those who might move in. The compartmentalized characteristics of a city, like jobs and housing, are identified with particular individuals; they can be possessed by present residents but are not necessarily available to others from the outside.

Every diffuse characteristic of a city that makes it more attractive for the present residents will also make it more attractive for those who might move in, who would increase the population and density. Therefore, every improvement in the diffuse categories of attractiveness must be accompanied by some worsening in the compartmentalized categories of attractiveness to prevent self-defeating growth. The attractiveness characteristics of a city should be categorized in terms of whether they affect all residents or primarily potential newcomers. For example, the vitality of industry, a balanced socioeconomic mix of population, the quality of schools, the freedom from pollution, low crime rates, public parks, and cultural facilities are all desirable to present residents. If there is no counterbalance to restrain an expanding population, such attractive features tend to be self-defeating by causing inward migration. But the compartmentalized characteristics of a city primarily affect growth without necessarily reducing the quality of life for present residents. The number of housing units and the number of jobs tend to be compartments in the sense that they have a one-to-one correspondence with individuals rather than each being shared by all. The absence of an unoccupied house or a job can be a strong deterrent to in-migration, without necessarily driving down the internal quality of life.

I see no solution for urban problems until cities begin to exhibit the courage to plan in terms of a maximum population, a maximum number of housing units, a maximum permissible building height, and a maximum number of jobs. A city must also choose the type of city it wants to be. To become and remain a city that is all things to all people is impossible. There can be many uniquely different kinds of cities, each with its special mix of advantages and disadvantages. However, the policies that create one type of city may destroy another type. A choice of city type must be made, and corresponding policies must be chosen to create the combination of advantages *and disadvantages* that are characteristic of that type. One might have an industrial city, a commercial city, a resort city, a retirement city, or a city that attracts and traps without opportunity a disproportionate number of unemployed and welfare residents, as some cities are now doing. But there are severe limits on how many types of cities can be created simultaneously in one place. When the choices have been made, and when effort is no longer dissipated in growth, there will be an opportunity to come to grips with social and economic decay.

Why do I bring this message to the American Public Works Association? Because the members are at the center of the two most important issues I have raised. First, leaders in public works are the custodians of the technological aspects of the urban environment. Those responsible for the physical aspects of a city can continue to solve the technological subgoals of roads, water, waste, and transportation and thereby sustain the growth process and cause a continual shifting of pressures into the social realm of rising crime, increasing psychological trauma, growing welfare costs, and accelerating community breakdown. Or, they can move to reverse the growth attitudes that in the past we considered good, but are good no more, and help halt further expansion of that part of our technological base on which the urban crisis is growing. A second reason for these issues to be important in public works comes from the unique influence that public works has over what I call the compartmentalized characteristics of a city. Public works actions directly affect the number of streets that are built, the number of houses that are erected, and the number of industrial locations that are established. Such physical actions, backed up by zoning and municipal policy, determine the kind of urban growth and whether or not there is to be growth. Through the judicious use of, and indeed the appropriate limitation of, water supply, drainage, building heights, waste disposal, road building, and transportation systems, a city can influence its future.

The reader may be thinking that planning and controlling the size and composition of a city and the migration to it are undemocratic or immoral. It may even seem that I am suggesting control where there has not been control before. Neither is true. Every city has arrived at its present size, character, and composition because of the actions that have controlled the city's evolution in the past. By adding to the water system, sewers, and streets, a city has, in effect, decided to increase its size. By building a rapid transit system a city is often, in effect, deciding to change the composition of its population by encouraging new construction in outlying areas, allowing inner areas to decay, and attracting low-income and unskilled persons to the inner ring at the same time that job opportunities decline. In other words, a control of growth and migration has been exerted at all times, but it has often been guided by short-term considerations, with unexpected and undesirable long-term results. The issue is not one of control or no control. The issue is the kind of control and toward what end.

The interurban control of population movement is the internal counterpart of international control of population movement. Except for the legal, coercive, psychological, and economic deterrents to human mobility, the standard of living and the quality of life of all countries would fall to the level set by the population group that accepts the lowest standards. No group can be expected to exert the self-discipline now necessary to limit population and the environmental demands of industrialization unless there is a way to keep the future advantages of such self-discipline from being swallowed up by inward migration. If the control of international movement of population is ethical, then some intercity counterpart must also be ethical. Or, if the justification is only that of practical necessity, then the internal necessity arises in a country that is reaching its growth limit without having established a national means to implement a compromise between quantity and quality. Between nations, countries exert restrictions on population movement that are not allowed internally between urban areas. Even so, the policies of each city have a powerful effect on mobility and on the resulting character of the city. Because controls are implicit in every action taken and every urban policy adopted, a city should understand the future consequences of its present actions. A city affects its local choice between quantity and quality mostly by how it handles the diffuse versus the compartmentalized components of attractiveness.

The difference between diffuse and compartmentalized control of urban population can be illustrated by two extremes of policies that might govern the availability of water. Depending on how it is managed, the availability of water might be either a diffuse or a compartmentalized control on growth. Consider a city with a limited water supply—more and more this will be the actual situation. To illustrate diffuse control, one could distribute water freely and equally to everyone, both present and future residents. New houses could be constructed, new industries could be encouraged, growth could be continued, and the water could be divided among all. If no other growth limits were encountered, growth would continue until the low water pressure, occasional shortages, and the threat of disaster from drought had risen to the point where out-migration equaled in-migration. Under this circumstance of unrestricted access to water, net growth would have been stopped, but the equally distributed nature of the water shortage would have reduced the quality of life for all residents. The water shortage would be diffuse; it would be spread to all, former residents and newcomers alike. Alternatively, the opposite water policy illustrates compartmentalized control. Building permits and new water connections could be denied so that water demand is constrained to lie well within the water supply. Water would be available to present, but not to new, residents. Under these circumstances, the quality of life for the present residents would be maintained, but growth beyond the limit of satisfactory water supply would be restricted.

I believe that such a choice between present residents and potential in-migrants is inherent in a practical solution of our urban problems. Unless control through such self-interest is acceptable, and ways are available to exercise control, there is no incentive for any city or state to solve its own problems. Its efforts will be swamped from the outside. There must be freedom for local action, and the consequent differences between areas, if social experiments are to lead to better futures and if there is to be diversity in the country rather than one gray homogenized sameness. If there is to be any meaning to the president's hope of preserving "the ability of citizens to have a major voice in determining policies that most directly affect them," local areas must be able to control their destinies in different ways and toward different ends.

If people are to influence the policies most affecting them, it follows that policies will be different in different places, and the resulting trade-offs between growth and the quality of life will be different. If there is to be any substance to local choice, there must be differences between localities.

In the policies for a city that I am proposing, the ethical and legal issues are substantial. A city, in looking after its own well-being, will no doubt be accused of being selfish because it discriminates against nonresidents. But what are the alternatives? Must it discriminate against its own present residents instead? Must it discriminate against its own long-term interests? Must it be forced to take only a short-range view of its future? Must it be a party to delaying the day when the nation faces the fundamental choice between quality and quantity? Our past policies have not been so successful that they should persuade us against new experiments.

If a sufficient number of cities find new ways of controlling their own destinies in spite of national policy and what other cities do, then pressures to work toward the long-term well-being of the country will be quickly generated. If some cities and states take effective steps to establish an equilibrium with their natural surroundings, and to maintain a viable and proper internal balance of population and industry, then the remaining growth in the country will quickly descend on those communities and states that have taken no such action. A national consensus to establish a viable balance with the capacity of the environment will quickly develop out of the contrasts between those who have and those who have not dealt with the basic issues of overcommitment.

In summary, I believe that the country is now heading more deeply into economic and social difficulty. Technological solutions will no longer suffice. There is no national consensus strong enough to support an effective national policy nor to ensure national leadership in solving the problems that are arising from growth and overcommitment of the nation's long-term capability. But, fortunately, the problems are solvable piecemeal at the local level independently of other areas and of the national government. Local action can set a precedent for the country as a whole. Those in public works are in a uniquely influential position for exerting that leadership.

Notes

1. See Jay W. Forrester, *World Dynamics* (Cambridge, Mass.: Wright-Allen Press, 1971), and Donella H. Meadows et al., *The Limits to Growth* (New York: Universe Books, 1972).

2. Jay W. Forrester, "Churches at the Transition between Growth and World Equilibrium," Chapter 13 in *Toward Global Equilibrium: Collected Papers* (Cambridge, Mass.: Wright-Allen Press, 1973).

20
Lowell Dynamics: Preliminary Applications of the Theory of *Urban Dynamics*

Walter W. Schroeder III

Efforts to apply the Urban Dynamics *model to Lowell, Massachusetts, originated in June 1971, when Walter W. Schroeder III began working with James Sullivan, city manager of Lowell. The summer project in Lowell eventually led up to the current urban dynamics research program at M.I.T. sponsored by the U.S. Department of Housing and Urban Development. (The preliminary efforts to modify the model to describe Lowell are discussed in Walter W. Schroeder III and John E. Strongman, "Adapting* Urban Dynamics *to Lowell," Reading 16 in this volume.)*

The following paper isolates several decision points that may inadvertently be contributing to a short-term planning horizon and to a widening imbalance between population and available employment opportunities in Lowell. The examination of Lowell's current assessment and taxation policies within the framework of the Urban Dynamics *model illuminates several forces behind the city's diminishing job base and expanding supply of low-quality housing. Several potential areas for policy intervention in Lowell's job and housing markets are also examined.*

This paper is abstracted from Schroeder's 1972 M.I.T. Sloan School of Management M.S. thesis of the same title.

20
Lowell Dynamics:
Preliminary Applications
of the Theory of *Urban Dynamics*

20.1 Introduction

This paper is a summary of preliminary efforts to use urban dynamics in order to define, analyze, and propose solutions to the major problems facing Lowell, Massachusetts. Beginning in June 1971, a research project was begun to determine whether the modeling process could in fact make a useful contribution in an actual urban setting.

To bring the *Urban Dynamics* model into a specific city's decision-making structure, Professor John F. Collins, former mayor of Boston, encouraged me to spend the summer working with James Sullivan, the city manager of Lowell, to determine the feasibility of a successful application of the model. Specifically, we hoped to answer several quesions:

1. Is there a need for a mathematical model of Lowell; are the problems ones that require additional analytic tools?
2. Can the *Urban Dynamics* model be modified and refined to fit Lowell's particular characteristics and needs?
3. What policies and programs might the *Urban Dynamics* model suggest that would be appropriate for alleviating Lowell's problems?

These questions are given preliminary treatment in the following pages. Section 20.2 describes Lowell's development from a town of 600 in 1820 to its present role as the center of a large metropolitan region. By first learning about Lowell's past, we may better understand its present problems. A look at present-day Lowell will help illustrate the conflicts and trade-offs inherent in the urban system. Despite a well-qualified professional administration, many of the city's problems remain acute. Lowell seems to defy even the best efforts designed to restore local economic vitality.

Section 20.3 examines a number of present and proposed city policies. With the help of the urban dynamics framework, possible inconsistencies in present doctrines are brought to light. Policies that at first seem to be expedient may have unexpected secondary effects that counteract the policy's desired effects, and may even contribute to worsening the city in the long run. With a better understanding of the urban system taken as a whole, several new directions for policy changes are proposed in Section 20.4. They are presented not as final recommendations but as the starting point for efforts that may ultimately produce a clear definition of Lowell's problems and a strategy for attacking the causes of those problems. Since Lowell's problems appear to be characteristic of many medium and large cities, the efforts reported here are likely to have a high degree of transferability to other cities.

20.2 The Growth and Decline of Lowell

Lowell, Massachusetts, incorporated in 1824, was once the center of textile production in the United States. Today, economic growth and vitality have been replaced by stagnation and decay. The population fell from a high of 118,000 in 1920 to 93,000 in 1970. The origins of the city's problems lie deep within its history.

LOWELL MANUFACTORIES.

STATISTICS OF LOWELL MANUFACTURES, JANUARY 1. 1837.

COMPILED FROM AUTHENTIC SOURCES.

CORPORATIONS.	Locks and Canals.	Merrimack.	Hamilton.	Appleton.	Lowell.	Suffolk.	Tremont.	Lawrence.	Middlesex.	Boott Cotton Mills.	Total.
Capital Stock,	600,000	1,500,000	1,000,000	500,000	500,000	450,000	500,000	1,500,000	500,000	1,000,000	8,050,000
Number of Mills,	2 shops and a smithy.	5 and Print Works.	3 and Print Works.	2	Cotton & Carpet Mill, 1 building.	2	2	5, another or bleachery preparing.	2 and Dye-House.	4, two in operation, and 2 going into operation the next season.	27, exclusive of Print-Works, &c.
Spindles,	·	35,704	21,228	11,776	5000 cotton besides woollen.	11,264	11,520	31,000	4620	14,016	146,128
Looms,	·	1253	620	380	144 cotton 70 carpet.	352	404	910	38 broadcloth, 92 cassimere.	404	4667
Females employed,	·	1400	860	470	375	470	460	1250	350	450	6085
Males,	500	437	230	65	200	70	70	200	185	70	1827
Yards made per week,	·	186,000	110,000	100,000	2500 carpet, 150 Rugs, 55,000.	90,000	125,800	200,000	6500 cassimere, 1500 broad-cloth.	73,000	950,250
Bales Cotton used in do.	1250 tons wrought and cast iron yearly	120	100	95	76	86	90	180	None.	60	807
Pounds Cotton wrought in do.	·	44,000	39,000	33,000	30,000	82,000	34,000	64,000	600,000 lb. wool per ann. and 3,000,000 teasels.	21,000	297,000
Yards dyed and printed do.	·	165,000	70,000	None.	None.	None.	None.	None.	None.	None.	235,000
Kinds of Goods made,	Machinery, Cars and Engines for Railroads.	Prints and Sheetings, No. 29 to 40.	Prints and Drillings, No. 14 to 40.	Sheetings and Shirtings, No. 14.	Carpets, Rugs, and Negro Cloth.	Drillings, No. 14.	Sheetings and Shirtings, No. 14.	Printing Cloths, Sheetings, & Shirtings, No. 14 to 30.	Broadcloths and Cassimeres.	Drillings, No. 14; Shirtings, No. 40.	
Tons Anthracite Coal per annum,	20 chaldrons smith's coal; 200 tons hard coal.	5200	2800	300	350	330	329	650	500	300	10,759
Cords of Wood per annum,	300	1500	1250	300	500	70	60	60	1000	70	4510
Gallons of Oil,	2300	8700	6500	3375	Olive, 4000. Sperm. 4000.	3840	3692	8217	Olive, 11,000 Sperm. 2500	3500	59,324
Diameter of Water Wheels,	13	30	13	13	13	13	13	17	17 and 12	17	
Length of do. for each mill,	14	24	42	42	60	42	42	60	46 and 21	60	
Incorporated,	1792	1822	1825	1828	1828	1830	1830	1830	1830	1835	
Commenced operations,	1822	1823	1825	1828	1828	1832	1832	1833-4	1830	1836	
How warmed,	Hot Air.	Hot Air Furnace.	Hot Air Furnace.	Hot Air Furnace.	Hot Air Furnace.	Hot Air Furnace.	Hot Air Furnace.	Steam.	Wakefield Furnace and Steam.	Hot Air.	

Figure 1   Statistics of Lowell Manufactures
Source: L.S. Bryant and J. B. Rae, *Lowell: An Early American Industrial Community* (Cambridge, Mass.: Technology Press, 1950).

Situated at the junction of the rapids of the Merrimack and Concord rivers, Lowell was a typically lazy farm town with a population of 600 in 1820. These rapids, because of their tremendous reserves of waterpower, attracted the attention of Francis Cabot Lowell, who was hoping to develop the first large textile mill in the United States.

> In 1822, a site for the new mill was selected in East Chelmsford [Lowell] and the Merrimack Manufacturing Company was incorporated on the sixth of February in that year, with a capital of $600,000 . . . The Hamilton Manufacturing Company was incorporated in 1825.[1]

The early growth of the area's economy was truly impressive. Census data show that from 1830 to 1840 the population of the city more than tripled, increasing from 6,500 to over 20,000. The prime force behind this growth can be found in Figure 1, which roughly itemizes the more than 8,000 new jobs created from 1822 to 1836. So rapid was the industrial development that, "[by] 1839, the land and water-power which the original company had for sale was wholly taken up by the ninth factory to be established."[3] Boarding houses were quickly erected by the mill owners to accommodate and "induce the American girls from the farms and country villages to work in the mills."[4]

In the *History of Lowell* by Frederick Coburn, the city's early growth is summarized as follows:

> An industry . . . [fixed] upon a locality as suitable for exploitation of resources and employment of the local labor. Capital, in other words, has seen an opportunity for favorable investment. New machinery is set up in factories or workshops, and work that pays better, at least in point of cash disbursements, than that previously available begins to tempt people from the adjacent farms.[5]

Soon after Lowell was founded, and throughout the remainder of the nineteenth century, the mills had to rely on attracting workers from farther and farther away.

> Presently, however, as it becomes increasingly difficult to induce the sons and daughters of the farm to work at the wages paid under competitive conditions in the urban workshops, and as at the same time the growing demand for the city's products tends to exhaust the local supply of labor, employers, thus situated, reach out for the help of immigrants.[6]

Growing at an exponential rate, Lowell drew workers from an ever-increasing distance:

> From every part of New England, and presently from the British Isles and Canada, they began to arrive . . . Lowell [was] practically the only town of its kind in North America, [and] it naturally secured the very pick of aspiring young manhood.[7]

Toward the end of the nineteenth century, however, the city's vitality, as measured by the growth in population (Figure 2) began to falter. Even before the period of growth had actually ended, people in the city had become aware that their city was changing.

Today [1890], youths of similar ability often turn to one of the newer and presumably more progressive industrial centres of the West or South. An opinion is sometimes expressed to the effect that Lowell in its first years was a more stimulating place to live than today.[8]

Why did Lowell begin to lose its early prosperity? One factor was the decreasing strength of the city's economic base. During the last half of the nineteenth century Lowell entered a "bitter struggle for existence against Southern competition"[9] in the cotton industry. The more efficient, newer mills in the South were winning, economically, against the less productive mills of Lowell.[10] As a result, most firms began cutting back on employees and production. Others wisely diversified when possible.[11]

The California Gold Rush also had an impact on Lowell. Approximately 1,500 young men (over 5 percent of the total labor force) left Lowell for the West in 1849.[12] An equally large number of young men were affected by the Civil War, for "Amidst the extensive enlistment and the departure of individuals and families [to the West], the population fell from 36,827 in 1860 to 31,000 in 1865 according to the state census."[13]

When the Civil War ended, Lowell gradually regained some of its earlier livelihood. Still,

While progress was steady and continual in many directions, this [1870–1890] was not a time of sensational developments or so much display of enterprise and initiative as had characterized the first years of the community ... [14]

Many of the gravest problems of the twentieth century city first became acute in the last decades of the nineteenth century; deterioration of originally inadequate housing facilities for the working class; indifference to city planning for the future; neglect of the welfare of newly arrived immigrants ... [15]

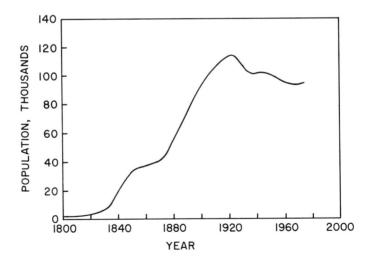

Figure 2 Lowell's population since 1800

By 1920 the problems of Lowell had become even more apparent. Many immigrants still came to Lowell, seeking opportunities that no longer existed. Evidence of the lack of opportunity is the fact that from 1920 to 1930 (a period of national prosperity) the population of Lowell *dropped* by 15 percent to 100,000. Lowell was no longer a unique city. Other, newer, cities had gained the upper hand.

The depression of the 1930s inhibited many people from leaving Lowell because they had neither the money nor the incentive to move elsewhere. It is doubtful, for the same reasons, that many moved *to* Lowell during this same period. Census data provide the only support for this proposition, since the decline in population of modern Lowell appears to have been interrupted by the depression and World War II—both of which served to inhibit intercity migration during the 1930s and early 1940s. Since World War II, Lowell has gradually settled to a population of about 94,000.

During recent years Lowell has suffered a severely stricken economy. Foreign competition all but wiped out the last of the mills in the late 1940s, and unemployment has remained well above the 6 percent level for the past thirty years. Lowell's unemployment rate in August 1971 was 14 percent. Once a thriving city, Lowell now consists primarily of half-empty factories. The erosion of the city's industry and commerce has resulted in a dramatically rising tax rate (Figure 3) and an inadequate, overpriced housing supply. Present unemployment conditions in Lowell are frequently blamed for a rapidly rising crime rate. With too few wage earners in the city, retail trade has also suffered.

What are the forces that have produced Lowell's decline? How can they be reversed? The project attempted to answer these questions with the help of local officials and the theories underlying the *Urban Dynamics* model. Among the many people in Lowell who enthusiastically volunteered their time to the program were

Fiscal Year	Gross Charges	Credits	Net Amount Raised by Taxation	Valuation	Tax Rates
1970	32,528,687.66	9,413,755.16	23,114,932.50	154,099,550.00	150.00
1969	29,399,294.28	9,550,639.08	19,848,655.20	150,368,600.00	132.00
1968	28,080,102.13	10,143,832.93	17,936,269.20	147,018,600.00	122.00
1967	26,638,236.01	10,517,035.59	16,121,200.42	143,427,050.00	112.40
1966	25,609,207.92	10,094,812.80	15,514,395.12	141,554,700.00	109.60
1965	22,988,288.43	7,607,717.65	15,308,570.78	140,333,675.00	109.60
1964	21,050,820.83	7,703,993.27	13,346,827.56	137,880,450.00	96.80
1963	19,614,202.11	7,140,460.91	12,473,741.20	132,163,800.00	94.00
1962	18,244,296.31	7,143,557.35	11,100,738.96	130,311,450.00	84.80
1961	16,905,027.38	6,705,951.63	10,199,075.75	127,161,250.00	79.80

Figure 3 City of Lowell tax rate and tax levies
Source: City of Lowell, *Annual Report of the City Auditor*, 1970, p. 71.

the following:

The city manager
Several city planners
The editor of the *Lowell Sun*
Nearly all of the city councilors
The city solicitor
A past city manager of the city
The assistant to the president of the Chamber of Commerce
The Model Cities Director
A mill owner
The president of the Lowell Housing Authority
The housing inspector
The president of a local bank

A series of interviews with these people revealed several important features of Lowell that relate to the concepts embodied in *Urban Dynamics*. Perhaps most evident from the interviews is the extent to which the many problems of the city are interconnected. City officials were quick to agree with the basic *Urban Dynamics* model structure that interconnects such problems as underemployment, housing inadequacies, high tax rates, inefficient land use, industrial disinvestment, low upward economic mobility, and overcrowding.

Although city officials agreed that Lowell's problems are interconnected, they substantially disagreed on which problem was the most critical. Of fifteen interviews, ten separate problems were considered to be "the most critical for Lowell." These ten problems, when considered from the perspective of the city

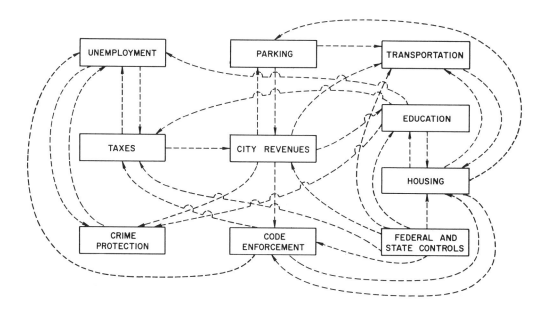

Figure 4 Lowell's interrelated problems (simplified)

manager, have identifiable ties that are diagrammed in Figure 4. This figure is much too simple to encompass all the city's problems, but even this representation portrays the nearly impossible task of making good decisions for a system in which everything affects everything else.

To illustrate some of the trade-offs within the urban system suppose, for example, that the School Committee exerts pressure on the city manager for a larger share of the city's revenues. Making this increase allocation would have both favorable and unfavorable results. The increased school expenditures may cause the quality of education to rise; ultimately, a better skilled and more knowledgeable public may help reduce the city's high unemployment rate by attracting high-paying industry. A better educational system may also help lower the city's crime rate. But a number of negative side effects would also be generated as a result of higher educational outlays. Because fewer revenues would be available for maintaining and improving transportation and parking facilities, upgrading code enforcement capabilities, and supporting programs aimed at directly reducing unemployment (such as job training) or improving urban services (police protection, health care, and public works), the adequacy of each of these other city components may diminish. Or, more likely, the increased school allocation would simply be passed along to city taxpayers in the form of a higher tax rate.

Less obvious is the likelihood that the extra school budget allocation, even if it successfully raises the quality of education in the city, might stimulate new pressures that would directly worsen other problems. For example, people may move to the city to take advantage of better educational opportunities for their children. These new families will require sewerage and solid waste facilities, contribute to traffic jams, and ultimately place more demands on the educational system that attracted them in the first place. These new burdens on the city may wind up *worsening* the city's imbalance between revenues and expenses.

The *Urban Dynamics* model helps to explain why actions designed to deal with separate city problems may be costly or counterproductive. In cities like Lowell, where resources of time, manpower, and money are constrained (few if any cities do not qualify for this category), problem trade-offs tend to dominate over real system improvement. The job of running a mature city can often be described as an attempt to keep bad problems from getting worse rather than an attempt to solve problems. Most important city measures today are taken to control the unanticipated effects of yesterday's measures.

Lowell's officials, in perceiving a multitude of problems, are trying to "solve" each problem as it arises. But this type of "crisis management," which shifts from one problem to the next, can be effective over the long run only if each problem can be individually dealt with and forgotten. *Urban Dynamics* suggests, however, that compartmentalized urban decision making is ineffective because a city's problems are not independent of one another. Moreover, crisis management, instead of solving all problems, tends to produce action only after the problems have become so severe and complex that they defy simple and direct solutions.

The chief objective of an *Urban Dynamics* modeling effort in Lowell is to begin moving the city out of the crisis management mode and toward a set of clear, feasible goals. The fact that there are ten "number one" priorities guiding Lowell decision makers explains why each agency finds itself trying to grapple with problems that are at least partly the result of other city agencies and departments; efforts designed, for example, both to increase job availability and to improve housing adequacy are inherently conflicting. Each of these actions tends to encourage increased population and, thus, increased demands for jobs, housing, and urban services.

Because the city of Lowell has no single set of long-term goals, the ties between the planning and management functions have atrophied. Immediate problems receive just as much attention as more deeply rooted ones that are far more serious in terms of their long-range impact. The lack of clear goals and priorities is the only possible explanation for the fact that while the city's unemployment rate was 14 percent in 1971, the directors of Lowell's city planning agency cited "downtown parking" as the area in which most of their attention was directed.

In his description of the forces that produce current urban problems, Forrester outlines the shortcomings of crisis management. As the focus of decision makers grows more short term in nature, the "system" of forces that influence urban behavior is given essentially free reign.

> In a very real way, our cities are being designed by the dynamics of the urban structure itself. We have set in motion a self-directing system that is leading us into our "urban crisis." The present procedure for designing an urban system is to respond sequentially to the social pressures that develop. As each pressure arises, we attempt a direct assault on either the symptoms of difficulty or what appears to be the immediate cause.
>
> In searching for causes, we look close in time and location to the symptoms of difficulty. The nature of complex systems produces an *apparent* cause near to the symptoms. But this apparent cause is usually a coincident symptom and is not a lever through which the fundamental difficulty can be corrected. By accepting the apparent cause that the system presents, we are misled into action that merely shifts the symptoms of trouble to another point. We fail to reach the true causes that lie deeper and more remote within the system.
>
> As we act to relieve one set of symptoms, we cause another set of symptoms to arise. The system itself determines a sequence of pressures that lead people from one action to the next, each action creating the next trouble point ...
>
> Unless the characteristics of complex systems become understood and recognized in city planning and in our national attitude toward the urban situation, those plans will fail. Most city development plans and national actions violate one or more of the requirements imposed by the fundamental dynamic nature of an urban system.[16]

The implication of these statements for Lowell is very direct. The problems of a city appear to result as much from conflicts between local (and controllable) decisions as from forces beyond local control. But if the causes of city problems are in part local, then so are the solutions. The next two sections attempt to identify several decision-making areas in the city that may be inadvertently aggravating rather than reducing Lowell's problems.

20.3 Shortcomings of Some Currently Proposed City Programs

To revitalize a city, one must first understand its illness. Treating symptoms in biological systems has often proved fatal (consider the early medicine man who placed his fever victim in cold water); treating the symptoms of urban problems may be no less dangerous.

This section analyzes some of Lowell's current urban-management policies from the perspective of the urban dynamics approach. The analysis will show how the city's present assessing, demolition, housing, and zoning policies may be having undesired and unforseen effects. New policies, based upon preliminary insights from the model's logical framework will then be proposed.

The objective of this analysis is to illustrate the scope of policy testing that could be carried on with a dynamic simulation model. It must be emphasized that the original *Urban Dynamics* model can be used effectively only to identify broad directions of favorable policy change. A more detailed model will be required before policies can be precisely specified and their results fully simulated.

Keeping in mind not only the present state of the model but also the political realities of Lowell, desirable urban policies should be not only technically sound but also relatively painless to implement. "Relatively painless" refers in this case to two basic factors. First, the amount of disruption that a policy change will impose upon the city must be considered. People will not change long-followed traditions overnight. Policy changes that rely upon altering well-entrenched social norms have little chance of real or early acceptance. Second, the cost of the change to the city (in dollars and cents) must be taken into account. Lowell's skyrocketing tax rate is evidence of the critical financial shortage facing the city. The city has few available funds for even the most promising plans. Thus, in designing policies for Lowell, the strategies considered must be evaluated within the framework of the city's fiscal, social, and political constraints.

Direct Mill Demolition. An example of a potentially good policy that fails in one or more of these practical criteria is the demolition of old mills. If some of the mills were demolished, the vacated land could be offered to industrial developers who would, with near certainty, put the land to more efficient use. The *Urban Dynamics* model suggests that part of Lowell's problem is that the desirable land in the city is nearly fully developed. Old mill structures are choking off new, more productive development. Furthermore, these old mills contribute very little to the city's tax base because, as the assessor stated, nearly all of the mill owners have received substantial tax abatements.

Because the mills do house *some* industrial activity (and employ some workers), demolition would initially cause higher unemployment in the city. In addition, mill owners are apt to oppose strongly any forced demolition or major renovation as evidenced by the fact that none have demolished their buildings voluntarily in the last several years.

The most compelling argument against a mill demolition policy, however, is financial. The mills are large, well built (at their base, many are six feet thick), and extremely costly to demolish. Private owners cannot absorb this expense, nor can the city presently afford to do so. Federal or state money for industrial demolition does not exist except as a portion of an urban renewal plan. In short, because of fiscal constraints, the mills in Lowell are apt to survive in their present state a while longer.

With the city convinced that the mills have outlived their usefulness, new firms are discouraged from locating in the mills because of an ever-present threat that the structures will be removed in the near future. It seems likely that public criticism of the mills is virtually guaranteeing their marginal use and small contribution to the city. New private investment in these old structures might be both desirable and possible if there was strong confidence that this investment would not be wasted on a soon-to-be-demolished factory. To reverse the almost self-fulfilling nature of this negative criticism, new approaches are necessary.

Old factory buildings can be primary spawning grounds for new products and new firms. They can make great contributions to an industrialized urban area. But in Lowell, the desired balance between new and old firms located in the mill buildings has not been maintained.

One possible use of Lowell's mills might involve the conversion and subdivision of existing large plant facilities to several smaller industrial condominiums. These condominiums would offer a number of alternatives not presently available to developers in Lowell. First, small-scale (perhaps one floor or less) development, rather than factory-wide renovation, would make it financially possible for small, young firms to locate in these structures. Second, the potential would exist for firms to expand into additional units. Finally, since the condominiums would be organized such that none of the units could be demolished without the consent of the other occupants, the threat of forced relocation in the near future would be significantly reduced.

The current mill situation is not an easy one for Lowell to endure. Potentially valuable central-city land is being underutilized. Low industrial rents, a small assessed value, and minimal worker densities now characterize these aged buildings. Many experts in Lowell feel that the key to improving the city's land use is through direct demolition. Others insist that demolition is infeasible. The latter group contends that the problems and costs associated with demolition are excessive, and there may be reason to keep some of the city's mills intact.

Because of the controversy and frustration surrounding the future of the mills, it seems inadvisable to advocate any demolition plans without a more complete analysis of the impacts of such action. A detailed urban dynamics model might prove useful in this investigation. Should it become clear that some demolition is critical to the city's revival, the model might also be helpful in directing a more effective attack on those leverage points in the city system that influence demolition.

Service Tax Plan. Another policy espoused by urban administrators both in Lowell and elsewhere is a "service tax" on currently untaxed property in the city. Officials complain that while churches, charities, private schools, and all other nonprivately owned properties pay no taxes to the city, they receive police, fire, waste disposal, and other services from the city. The service tax plan calls for properties currently not paying local taxes to begin paying a service charge to the city as a reimbursement for services received.

The plan might seem to hold significant promise from the practical perspective, since it is not a drastic change, nor would it directly penalize many people, although the tax would place greater burdens on tax-exempt property. Many people see the service tax plan as a major step in narrowing the disparity between city revenues and expenses. In the long run, however, there may be outcomes that make this policy extremely undesirable.

The proposed service tax plan appears to be a perfect example of the kind of policy that exhibits long-run effects that are counter to its positive short-run impact. Like many other proposed schemes to alleviate the financial plight of the city, it overlooks a deeply rooted mechanism of the urban system.

> In demanding more money as the solution to urban problems, people overlook the fundamental dynamic process now at work in the city. That process: as the city expenditures rise they reduce the pressures for fundamental solutions and allow the underlying causes to generate further demands to match the growing expenditures. In other words, the basic control process is for demands to rise to meet the available revenues. Is it not curious that all the older cities are in approximately the same degree of difficulty regardless of their physical size or the magnitude of their budgets? None are amply funded. None are conspicuously more desperate than the others. There must be a reason for this uniformity of distress that is independent of the size of the budget. The answer is that the problems and the budget grow hand in hand; neither can outrun the other. If the revenue resources get ahead, they are spent in such a way that they generate matching problems. If the troubles get ahead, the pressures rise to increase underlying causes, or enough population moves elsewhere to reduce the pressures within the particular system. Perhaps the quickest way to force a recognition and correction of the fundamental causes of urban decay would be to remove all expectation of future financial assistance to the cities by state and federal governments.[17]

The service tax plan, as it generates extra revenues, allows city administrators to "take the lid off" some expenditures. The net outcome may be a bigger city budget and a tax rate as high or higher than would exist without the plan.

20.4 Some New Directions for an Old City

The project in Lowell was intended to discover policies holding significant promise of having a positive long-run effect upon the city. The elusive "leverage points" for improving the city do not, however, appear to lie within the realm of a service tax plan. Where, then, do they lie? Judging from the lack of success of urban experts to find them, the areas of important urban trade-offs appear to be extremely difficult to locate. *Urban Dynamics* points to one area of possible sensitivity in the urban system—housing. The book shows how changes in a city's housing policies may have important positive impacts upon the area as a whole. It is proposed here that the preliminary insights of the book can help develop new policies to attack the causes of Lowell's interlocking problems. Because several Lowell officials also consider there to be a "housing problem" (each with his own different definition) in the city, there is the strong possibility of a change in city policies that impact upon housing.

The housing market in Lowell is similar to that of most other medium-sized cities. There are slums. There are abandoned and condemned buildings. The central-city area contains mostly high-density rental units in the lower-income category. These are also the oldest residential structures. The filter-down process (the normal conversion of aging upper-income homes into multiple lower-income apartments) is evident in Lowell. The growing pool of low rent, substandard housing created by this process has been cited by several city officials as being responsible for the rapidly growing in-migration of poor to the city.[18] The worsening imbalance between rich and poor, between old and new, in the city will almost certainly widen the gap between the city's needs and its resources.

The remainder of this section describes a set of policy changes that, together, may aid in reversing the course of Lowell's decline. These policies will not be expensive, nor are they impractical. Designed from a qualitative analysis of the city and the *Urban Dynamics* model, they are necessarily only a "first cut" at providing the city with policy alternatives that will raise the quality of life in Lowell.

The first policy concerns the current imbalance between residential and commercial assessment. The second policy treats a similar assessing imbalance between homeowners and apartment dwellers. The third policy deals with establishing new priorities for demolition (both residential and industrial). The fourth policy deals with the problems associated with the city's traditional approach to subsidized and public housing. Finally, the fifth policy suggests that Lowell's current zoning procedures may be inconsistent with its long-term goals, and points to new directions for zoning. Because these policies are the result of a city-wide systems approach rather than the commonly used segmented or subsystem approach to problem resolution, they differ substantially from past practice.

Commercial and Industrial versus Residential Assessments. There is a strong chance that current assessing policies in Lowell are subtly contributing to the city's major problems. One possible example is found in the difference between residential and commercial assessing. A discussion with one of the city's assessors revealed that residential structures are assessed at 37 percent of their "fair market value." In Lowell, a house purchased for $24,000 would be assessed at $9,000, or 37 percent of its fair market (purchase) value.[19] The current tax rate ($156.00 per $1,000 assessed value in 1971) is then multiplied by the assessed value to determine a homeowner's yearly tax bill to the city.

For commercial and industrial structures, assessing is performed differently. Instead of working with the vague "fair market value" concept, the city taxes income-producing structures on the basis of gross yearly income. The results of the income taxation plan have been, in the assessor's words, to "penalize commercial and industrial activity by making it pay a relatively large share of the city's taxes." In other words, if a numerical comparison were possible, it would show that industrial assessments run well above 37 percent of their fair market value to perhaps 45–50 percent.

Nearly all Massachusetts cities, for a variety of reasons, exhibit this same type of disparity between residential and industrial assessing. Perhaps the primary reason is that all homeowners feel directly the effects of property tax increases, whereas only the upper management of firms feel the direct effect of increased taxes on industry. As a result, city officials, following the "path of least resistance," have through the years been placing more and more of the local tax burden upon firms. Yet an analysis of the effects of this policy from a city-wide perspective suggests that perhaps a more equitable balance in assessing (taking some of the tax burden off industries) would be good for everyone concerned. Why?

Lowell, and most other Massachusetts cities, may be discouraging the construction of commercial and industrial buildings because of the relatively higher taxes that must be paid here. Another city in another state may be assessing differently, so that the tax bill for the same building in that area is significantly lower. If Lowell and this other city are similar in all other important respects, then most new industrial development that occurs will take place in the other city.

At the same time, if the two cities have equal revenue needs, then Lowell's assessing policy on housing will favor its construction in Lowell for the same reasons that industrial construction would be favored in the other city. The resulting pressures on new development from Lowell's current assessing practices, if continued over several years, could produce a significant imbalance in the number of people that the city can house relative to the number of people that the city's industries can employ. The by-products of this imbalance might include a rising unemployment rate, an increasing tax rate, and a rising incidence of poverty within the city. With a less healthy economy and fewer jobs for its inhabitants, the city offers fewer opportunities and freedoms to its poor. The middle and upper classes, meanwhile, may choose to leave the city as conditions become less tolerable. Such out-migration may serve to aggravate Lowell's problems still further. There is a downward economic spiral here that seems to be predominant in most depressed urban areas. We need a better understanding of the forces that produce this negative spiral and should take action to contain this trend through new, more effective policies.

A change in assessment practices in Lowell could help generate a positive impact on the local quality of life. As taxes are lowered on commercial and industrial structures, the area will become a more attractive site for development.

The cost associated with this policy change is, of course, a higher assessment on residential structures. But as industrial development progresses, additions to the city's tax base will begin to offset the increased tax burden placed upon the homeowner. Within a few (perhaps 5–10) years, the city may find that the cost of reducing commercial taxes is totally financed by the additional local taxes received from new industrial development.

Over the short run, the increased property taxes on housing may discourage new housing construction. Cutting back on housing expansion may help the city to curb the influx of people that presently seems to be placing greater and greater demands upon the city's limited resources. A combination policy of stimulating industrial expansion and diminishing in-migration may help push Lowell in the healthy direction of balancing the city's overall ratio between housing and jobs. As unemployment drops, the costs of providing social welfare to the city will also diminish, adding to the list of positive benefits resulting from the policy change. Because city costs may be lowered by this assessing change, the city will become less constrained in its efforts to solve other potentially significant problems.

An imbalance between housing and industry arises in nearly all older cities. The forces in Lowell do not appear unique. Meanwhile, the social and economic pressures that have forced this imbalance are likely to get still stronger as decay worsens. It is no accident that a city such as Lowell has a bias in assessment that favors housing and allows the city to house more people than it employs (resulting in high unemployment).

While jobs in Lowell are becoming fewer, the city's housing stock is actually increasing. In 1960 there were 29,861 housing units in Lowell proper (14.1 sq mi), whereas in 1970 there were 31,474 units—an increase of 5.4 percent. At the same time, the number of jobs in the city dropped by 4 percent (from 24,037 in 1960 to approximately 22,000 in 1970). The increased unemployment rate (from 8 percent to 11 percent) is consistent with these trends. An important point to note is that while jobs in the city declined over the ten-year period, the population of the city increased slightly (by about 1 percent). The increase can be explained only by the fact that enough housing was built to offset the area's falling attractiveness due to the poor employment picture. Because housing appears to play an important role in shaping a city's aggregate balance of population and jobs, further examination into housing trends in Lowell will be useful.

What do current trends toward increased housing and lower job availability in Lowell portend for the future of the city? Discussions with Lowell officials indicated that excessive housing availability was shifting the problems of other areas (Boston, New York, and Puerto Rico) to Lowell as large numbers arrived from these areas. They complain that Lowell's inability to meet the needs of a rapidly growing number of poor is worsening conditions not only for the poor already in Lowell but for the rest of the city's inhabitants as well. If a good measure of a city's viability is its ability to accommodate the needs of all its people, then the current status of housing in Lowell may be undermining that viability.

To avoid unwarranted criticism, it is emphasized that by no means is any of the blame for Lowell's problems to be placed on its assessors. Their work is as complex and ambiguous as that of any agency of any city. The fact that nearly all Massachusetts assessors are currently following the same broad guidelines is evidence that Lowell's assessors are consciously looking for a guidance but are receiving very little. Unfortunately, tried and tested assessing practices are no longer sufficient.

New assessing policies should be designed with careful recognition of their potential future impacts. The current assessing policy appears to respond to financial and political pressures in such a way that unhealthy long-term trends are produced. Although the exact details of a more appropriate assessing balance between commercial and residential structures cannot yet be determined, the need for change in assessing practices as an influence upon this balance is clear.

The Trend toward High-Density Living—Assessing Rental Living Space versus Privately Owned Homes. Lowell (again, like most cities) has been moving consistently in the direction of high-density rental apartment living. The downtown section of Lowell is now nearly 100 percent renter occupied, and the percentage of total housing units rented in Lowell has reached 57 percent. The rental housing stock in Lowell grew 8 percent from 1960 to 1970, while the number of private homes grew by only 3 percent. This may be another unhealthy trend produced by the forces normally operating in urban areas.

The growth figures for homes and apartments in Lowell illustrate how the housing market in the city has reacted to current demands and pressures. It is doubtful whether any conscious policy has ever been established to oversee the development of the city's housing stock. Instead, a loose implicit policy of "let the chips fall as they may" pretty well summarizes the average city's housing policy. As before, a closer look at the situation reveals that more careful planning and control of housing development may have promising long-run effects for Lowell.

The trend toward high-density living allows progressively more people to live in a fixed geographical land area. To the extent that problems in cities are correlated with the size of the urban population, these problems are aggravated by increasing the living density in an area. Cities certainly do not always enjoy a desirable relationship between housing and industry. In fact, the number of people living in a city may be increasing while the number employed there is dropping. Increasing housing densities may be partly responsible for increasing unemployment. Why does this trend predominate?

> Population densities in both residential and commercial zones are allowed to rise in response to the fallacious argument that rising land prices require more intense use. But land prices reflect the permitted use. Under rigid zoning, with no hope of relaxing the restrictions, land prices could not rise too high for the allowed use. Instead, we allow a land-price-population-density spiral to continue until excessive loads are thrown onto transportation, pollution, psychological trauma, and other factors of the urban environment.[20]

Several good arguments exist for the need to control the extent of high-density living in a moderate-sized city such as Lowell. The simple fact is, however, that the financial incentives for residential construction strongly favor apartments. Again, this stems from an assessment practice that taxes the average homeowner far more than the renter. The result is higher profitability in apartment development than in home construction. To illustrate this point, a comparison will help.

It is difficult to equate a privately owned home and an apartment, since different advantages are associated with each. The current real estate practice is to equate a $200 per month apartment with a $24,000 home in Lowell. As noted, the home gets assessed at 37 percent of its "fair market value," or $9,000, while the apartment gets taxed at 23 percent of the gross yearly rental income. With Lowell's $156 tax rate, the homeowner pays ($9,000)($156/$1,000), or $1,400 per year in local taxes, while the landlord pays (0.23)($2,400), or $600 per year in taxes on the equivalent apartment. Even though the homeowner can deduct his local taxes on his federal and state income tax returns, not until he reaches something like the 50 percent tax bracket does the inequity vanish. The average citizen will find himself paying a 25–30 percent higher local tax bill if he owns his own home. This difference in property tax costs helps explain the rapid growth of apartments in Lowell, as well as the lack of capital investment by the renter. Designed to aid the assessor, the income-taxation plan on residential units is producing a strong bias favoring high-density living over homeownership.

It is unlikely that current housing trends in Lowell are working to the city's benefit. What is needed now is a more cautious look at rental assessments that could help redirect the city's future. Instead of taxing 23 percent of a unit's gross yearly rental income, we may conclude that the figure should be considerably higher, perhaps 35 percent or more.

Rebalancing the tax burden between homeowners and renters will also ease the short-run problems encountered with the residential versus commercial assessing adjustment that was discussed previously. It was pointed out that taxes would have to be raised on residential structures to meet the short-run cost of reducing corporate assessments (and to keep city revenues constant). However, this second proposed policy change suggests that most of the extra residential tax load should be placed upon the renter rather than the homeowner. These first two policies, if implemented together, may produce more desirable results than either policy operating by itself.

New Priorities for Demolition and Code Enforcement.   The preceding two policy recommendations were designed to alleviate two observed problems in Lowell:

1. Too much housing is being built in Lowell.
2. The large proportion of high-density housing being built is detrimental to the long-term interests of the city.

Implicit in these recommendations is that Lowell must gain control over the amount and type of housing being developed within its boundaries. By controlling this development, the city's housing stock may eventually fall back within viable limits that define a healthy city. Besides limiting new housing construction, there is another, equally effective, mechanism for regulating the size of the city's pool of housing. Not only can the inflow rate of housing be lessened but also the outflow of undesirable housing can be accelerated through increased demolition. This latter alternative is often considered inferior to the former, since demolition is regarded to be costly, destructive, and full of negative connotations, whereas new development is looked upon as constructive, optimistic, and exciting. The unfortunate fact is that increased demolition may often be both cheaper and more effective in bringing about a city's revival.

Many of Lowell's problems can be attributed to the normal processes of aging and housing filter-down. The most run-down housing in the city is also the oldest. The worse this housing gets, the less there is for the landlord to recover from his investment. As a result, rents are extremely low. Usually located near the central business district, these run-down properties could be extremely valuable, but their decayed condition renders them nearly worthless. Aged housing contributes little to the city's tax base or to its socioeconomic vitality.

In Lowell, there are presently 4,000 substandard housing units. Of these, almost 1,400 units are vacant; they represent a full 10 percent of the total rental units in the city.

The large stock of substandard housing, coupled with a significant number of low-entry-point jobs in the city, provides a strong pull on low-income families from other nearby cities (Boston, Providence, New York, Montreal) who learn about these opportunities from their peers already in Lowell. The recent upsurge in the number of Blacks, Puerto Ricans, and French Canadians lends support to this hypothesis. As long as some unskilled jobs and cheap housing are available in Lowell, this influx is likely to continue. Unhappily, the new migrants to Lowell often lose enthusiasm for their jobs, since upward movement within the "secondary labor force" is extremely limited. Low-skilled workers in the city often search for new opportunities, find none, and go onto unemployment and welfare rolls. This process is currently imposing a significant burden in direct and indirect costs for both the city and the state.

An accelerated demolition of Lowell's substandard housing would not only prevent these migrants from living in utter desolation but would also help keep the pool of substandard housing from remaining at the presently unhealthy level. The city's current demolition rate is well below the rate at which formerly good housing "filters down" as it ages to become housing for middle- and lower-income families. As a result, the size of the pool of inadequate (if not substandard) housing grows daily. This growth threatens to draw increasing numbers of poor into the city. Demolition of the vacant units would place a natural constraint on in-migration.

The benefits of demolition do not end with having controlled in-migration. In fact, this control is only a means to a far more important and promising end. Demolition opens the city's land to new development. New industrial and residential structures would pose valuable additions to the city's tax base, thus helping to ease the city's tax burden. As taxes fall, further industrial development may take place, which would begin to reduce unemployment and enhance the upward mobility for the poor. Demolition may not only erase one problem; it also paves the way for a solution to other problems.

The prime factors behind the lack of adequate demolition to date in Lowell appear to be, first, a lack of public awareness of the need for more demolition; second, the reluctance to tamper with housing because of the difficulties involved with relocation; third, the lack of funds. To illustrate that money is not the only factor, however, it should be noted that Lowell has used only $40,000 of the original $140,000 demolition grant received from HUD in the fall of 1970.

An extremely subtle factor inhibiting the removal of a building by either the owner or the city is the use of tax abatements. In an effort to ease the burden on the owners of old decaying structures, the city has frequently granted abatements (a one-time lowering of the assessed value), which significantly reduce the local taxes paid by the owner. These abatements have side effects, however, that are of serious consequence. Because taxes on their buildings are lower, owners can afford *not to* demolish them. It may be easier for an owner to incur a small loss (made smaller by an abatement) than to pay the substantial costs of demolition. If taxes on apartment structures were maintained at their original level, losses might often be severe enough to induce voluntary demolition by the owner. Should the owner fail to demolish, at least the more rapid buildup of back taxes would warrant the city taking a lien on the property before it loses all of its market value. Delaying private demolition of old structures is likely to be poor urban policy. New and better-quality housing is kept out of the city because space is blocked by the old, while the value of the old housing continues to slide. Abatements may frequently have the effect of reinforcing this trend.

Encouraging accelerated demolition may tempt some readers to conclude that the concept of controlling urban in-migration through the pressures supplied by limited housing availability is unethical and prejudicial against the poor. This notion is unwarranted. In fact, the policy changes outlined here will have significant and enduring benefits for the city's poor. Critical to the argument of accelerated slum demolition is the distinction between driving out the poor (or in some way limiting their freedom) and limiting the influx of more poor to an area. Our goal in solving Lowell's problems is not to force its poor elsewhere; rather, it is to produce viable plans for helping the city to meet the needs of its present population. Experience tells us that such positive programs may require that population inflows to the city be constrained. In general, urban programs designed to improve the quality of life for the city's poor have a secondary effect of drawing more poor into the city from outside. These programs contain the seeds of their own destruction. In-migration will continue until the city, on the average, falls back to the level of attractiveness of other nearby urban areas.

To solve Lowell's unemployment problem, the city not only needs to create new jobs, but it also needs to establish some "negative counterbalance"—some constraint or limitation on migration to the city. A city's most effective negative counterbalance may be a tight housing market. Demolition of Lowell's 1,400 vacant substandard housing units will force no one from the city. Further demolition, when coupled with increased job availability will help raise average income levels and the average quality of housing throughout the city—again, with no forced out-migration. By helping to raise the average quality of life in Lowell, this policy may significantly aid the city's poor.

A program of accelerated demolition would also help control the spread of blighted housing in Lowell. One decaying building in a neighborhood is often sufficient to prompt even the most responsible members of the community to move out. As residents depart the area, local businesses fail, and the community may deteriorate into a slum. Early demolition is easily seen to be more effective (and a good deal cheaper) than massive rehabilitation later on.

Suppose, for example a healthy urban housing situation is defined as one in which less than 6 percent of the total housing stock is substandard. Currently, Lowell's housing stock, with 4,000/31,000 or 13 percent substandard housing, is well beyond this limit. To move back to a healthy housing mix through new construction, the city would have to double its housing supply. On the other hand, the city could also reach its objective by demolishing half of its already existing substandard housing. There is not enough vacant land in Lowell to double the housing stock, nor is there reason to expect that developers would want to undertake such an effort; demolition appears to be a far more realistic entry point for shifting the balance of new and old housing in Lowell.

Current policy in many cities is directed toward "diluting" urban blight through a wave of new development. Less costly and more effective may be a new plan that "extracts" rather than "dilutes." Like a malignancy, urban blight will not be cured until its source is removed. Any other action may postpone the day of reckoning but will not cure the disease. Immediate demolition is far more desirable than the social and economic ills (higher crime, unemployment, and lower quality of education) that promise to result if current attitudes toward demolition in Lowell continue.

Should the city decide that such a program would be beneficial, an accelerated demolition of substandard housing can evolve if any or all of the following policies are adopted: first, a reduction in the delay involved in processing demolition papers (often six months or more). Presently, getting a building demolished by the city is an extremely slow process. Second, a set of more rigid codes should be enforced. The current practice of code enforcement in the city uses condemnation as a "last resort" rather than as an active means of controlling urban blight. Third, a policy of not granting abatements to aging housing structures should be strictly adhered to. Fourth, a policy that combines demolition of substandard or condemned housing with new construction would allow the city to gain control over the proliferation of low-income and substandard housing in the city.

The potential benefits of increased demolition may not only affect the housing market but also the industrial base in Lowell. How will this benefit be realized? Essentially, the removal of old, underused industrial structures will free city land, making it possible to retain younger, growing firms that might otherwise expand outside the city.

Industries either in Lowell or in other cities behave according to one of three basic patterns. One pattern is growth. Growing firms need space. Cities, by definition, are seldom able to provide unlimited room for growth. As a result, healthy firms continually leave the city to expand elsewhere.

A second pattern is decay. Dying industries also take up valuable land, but only temporarily.

Third, firms can stagnate. This behavior mode characterizes much of the industry found in decayed urban areas. The stagnating firm is normally a marginal operation with small profits. Worker densities have been lowered to improve the marginal productivity of labor and raise competitiveness. No longer healthy, and seldom capable of offering their workers any significant potential for advancement, these firms add little to the city's economic base. Unlike the dead firm, the stagnating firm continues to occupy nearly all of its former space. The development of new firms and the expansion of healthy ones are blocked by this stagnation.

Changes in local taxation policy and in industrial code enforcements may be able to control the spread of stagnating firms. The result would be a city with lower unemployment, higher average incomes, and greater competitiveness. With a better blend of newer industries, Lowell would reap better harvests from its industrial land.

How does an area such as Lowell come to be dominated by high concentrations of aging industrial structures? Forrester points to a general explanation that seems to be accurate for describing Lowell:

> The property and income tax laws favor old buildings. The aging of buildings is an intimate part of the urban decline process. The shifting of taxes from real estate to incomes means that the old buildings and the land they occupy need not be used effectively; they can be allowed to decay with little tax penalty. Real estate taxation proportional to market value means that taxes decline as the property ages. This reduces the pressure for the replacement of buildings. The income tax laws allow a building to be depreciated several times against current income; this gives an old building value and helps to keep it in place until it contributes to urban decline.[21]

Lowell's current practices of assessing industrial and commercial properties on the basis of gross yearly income and of granting numerous abatements are having the undesirable long-term effects of smothering new growth. Instead, assessing doctrines must change to require more effective use of the city's land by local industries.

Federal Housing Programs. One of the most perplexing elements of today's urban life is the coexistence of a shortage of adequate housing for the poor (a tight housing market) an a simultaneous high vacancy/abandonment rate. In response to the question "what is Lowell's most serious problem?" several city officials mentioned housing, but in widely varying contexts. For example, the city solicitor was primarily concerned by the city's 4,000 substandard units (13 percent of the total housing supply). A big problem, according to the solicitor, is that this abundance of cheap housing destroys the economic balance of the city by drawing excessive numbers of poor into Lowell. This growing imbalance is placing extra loads upon the city's school system, police force, and social welfare system.

The solicitor emphasized that he wasn't out to infringe upon people's basic rights, nor did he want to make strong value judgments. But he felt that there was an excess of the type of housing that is attractive to low-income families who are not presently residents of Lowell. Rising population densities and increased revenue needs place a severe burden on the city. The final outcome of the trend, the solicitor projected, will be an overworked city system in which everyone—both present and future residents—is worse off. He strongly argued for more stringent code enforcement in the city. With stronger codes, substandard housing units would be either upgraded or condemned. Either way, the influx of the very poor to Lowell would be reduced in magnitude. Evidence that the current influx is disproportionately large is that the number of poor Black and Puerto Rican families in Lowell doubled between 1969 and 1971.

The city solicitor felt that until one can control the processes that breed urban blight, the problems will worsen. Lowell, once a proud city with large one-family homes, is no longer proud, and its homes have been split into two- and four-family apartments. An increasing housing supply (not in quality, but quantity), when coupled with the city's weak economic base, lies behind Lowell's unemployment problem. The solicitor was convinced that this unhealthy trend could be brought back into a better balance if the city's housing codes were strengthened and better enforced.

Whereas the city solicitor blamed the city's problems on an excess of low-income housing, an essentially opposite view was expressed by the president of the Lowell Housing Authority (LHA). His agency's purpose is to maintain the existing 1,600 units of subsidized housing in Lowell and to build more as it becomes necessary. A brief look at the operations of the Lowell Housing Authority will show, however, how the decisions and actions taken in one area of the city can produce results that conflict strongly with the objectives of other functional areas. The conflict is not the fault of the people within the LHA. Rather, it is an inherent problem of the social and governmental structures in nearly all cities.

The Lowell Housing Authority continually places eligible residents of Lowell onto a waiting list for subsidized housing. These are people who qualify for housing assistance, but for whom housing is not yet available. In 1971, the list contained 650 families. On the basis of the number of people on this list, the LHA applies to HUD for funds to construct additional units. Generally, an application will be to house one-third of the current list, or, in this case, approximately 200 additional units. In fact, during the summer of 1971 an application for these 200 new units was approved by HUD.

This is all fine and good for the LHA, but what happens to the rest of the city? As the city's supply of good quality, low-income housing is increased, there are bound to be families who move to Lowell to take advantage of the opportunity to improve their life styles. Ninety-nine percent of those who move into the new subsidized housing are already Lowell residents. But these residents, as they relocate, create vacancies in the private housing market. Rents in these private units are held down by the expanding supply of public low-rent housing. The availability of low-cost housing for the new resident virtually ensures that one by-product of building housing for a city's poor will be to add to the total number of poor in the city. In addition, unless an increased demolition rate of aged structures is initiated, the size of the pool of "bad" housing will grow, lengthening the LHA waiting list, and creating more pressure to build still more subsidized housing.

To compound the problems, most cities (including Lowell) currently evaluate their housing authorities on the basis of how much housing is produced and how well it is maintained. The limits of responsibility of the LHA are presently drawn too narrowly. The effects of present LHA policies, if continued, will place an increasing strain upon the city's already faltering economic and social strength. The city must structure such major activities as housing development to take into account not only the immediate consequences of actions (more housing), but also the long-run consequences (such as higher crime, worse education, and higher welfare costs). New priorities and evaluative criteria need to be developed in all cities with regard to subsidized housing. Until then, we cannot fault the city's housing authority for fulfilling its own (albeit potentially countereffective) responsibilities.

The conditions that lead to a shortage of good quality low-income housing and a simultaneous high vacancy rate are rooted at the very heart of an area's economic and social system. A housing problem, in its fullest definition, extends far beyond the city's housing market. In general, the lack of good jobs and incomes, more than any other factor, gives rise to blight and abandonment in cities.

The tenant who loses his job can no longer continue to pay his former rent. When whole neighborhood populations lose their jobs (because of a large cutback of a nearby firm, perhaps), landlords are compelled to lower rents if they wish to keep tenants from moving out and creating costly vacancies. To help finance his rent drop, the landlord must reduce his normal maintenance expenditures. Soon the building deteriorates visibly, and those who can afford to move out will do so. The character of the neighborhood shifts, and attitudes toward education, crime, and community cohesion rapidly decay. Like an economic trap, the city in economic decline tends to accumulate poor families that cannot afford to move to other areas with more promise.

Federal housing programs have attempted to bring better housing to the poor in declining areas. The programs assume that more and better housing will help transform the city from a socioeconomic trap into a revitalized center of upward economic mobility. But one must ask whether these housing programs are in fact drawing more poor into the city, worsening the conditions of job competition, crime, social alienation, and the like. If so, they actually contribute directly to the forces that cause housing abandonment and decay. In Lowell, there is no question that the major impact of public housing programs has been to open up low-income units into which the poor from outside the city can quickly move. The sharp increase in the number of poor in the city is compelling evidence of the negative side effects of subsidized and public housing construction.

Federal housing is cheap—construction often costs the city nothing. Yet subsidized housing is nontaxable, so the city's tax base is not increased. Meanwhile, the city must furnish police, fire, and other services to the housing; from a purely financial perspective, subsidized housing is a poor investment from the start. The Lowell Housing Authority pays the city of Lowell only 3 percent of its gross yearly income (renters, recall, pay 8 times that amount). Although exact figures are not available, the city spends at least $10.00 on LHA properties for every $1.00 received. Lowell cannot afford to make such expenditures if it is to meet the other needs of its populace. Yet in 1971 the city had 1,600 units of subsidized housing (65 percent low-income, 35 percent elderly) and had plans for at least 200 more.

Subsidized housing has been built in Lowell because nobody foresaw the negative side effects of rising population, increased land prices, and increased unemployment. Federal funds provide an alluring short-run incentive for cities, but in reality the long-run costs to the city often far outweigh the benefits of subsidized construction. Lowell must soon answer its question of housing needs. The housing situation is nearly out of control in the city, while building subsidized housing may only be compounding the problems manifest in the city's decaying housing.

Another Promising Alternative: *Zoning*.   The time constraints of the project did not permit a thorough investigation of Lowell's current zoning policies. Yet very preliminary data suggest that Lowell's zoning policies may also be moving the city in unforseen directions. Lowell is the center of a growing metropolitan region. As such, its role as a primary source of jobs is critical. But, "Whatever the reasons, the fact remains that apartments are permitted only in the City of Lowell, in Dracut, and in Pepperell (2 of Lowell's surrounding towns)."[22] Throughout the metropolitan region,

> One acre zoning prevails, while Lowell is the only community permitting dwellings on less than 20,000 sq. ft. Furthermore, Lowell has absorbed most of the multi-family construction in the region and a great disparity exists between suburban and city housing patterns.[23]

Land-use statistics for Lowell indicate that while over 36 percent of the city's total land is residential, less than 7 percent is in commercial and industrial use.

These figures suggest a severe imbalance of housing and jobs in Lowell. Present zoning ordinances seem to indicate the desire of the city to be primarily residential, yet the directors of the City Development Authority indicated that the city should contain at least as many jobs as housing units.

Zoning regulations help to shape a city's future development. Unfortunately, the pressures induced by zoning can be unhealthy ones:

> Zoning has in the past divided land into blocks that are too large and too homogeneous. A large area with housing built all at one time and of a similar quality deteriorates as a whole into a substandard condition. If such an area is large enough, it is avoided by new construction and becomes a slum.
>
> Zoning also allocates too much area for residential use and not enough for industry; this is especially critical when the area begins to age, with the concurrent decline of employment and increase of population. The ratio of residence to industry was satisfactory when the area was first being developed but becomes inbalanced with age. Unless there is rezoning to reduce residence and increase industry, or unless land is held empty initially for later commercial use, the aging area lacks economic vitality to maintain all of its housing stock and the area begins to deteriorate.[24]

New zoning policies for Lowell can open the city to more flexibility in its future development. Zoning has critical city-wide impacts, yet it has traditionally been controlled by the self-interests of neighborhood groups who have not taken an overall perspective of the city and its long-term needs. Cities are dynamic, developing new needs and problems as they evolve. Zoning ordinances, however, are difficult to change and become quickly outdated. With tools such as the *Urban Dynamics* model, changes in zoning policy can be quickly and inexpensively tested. A more complete understanding of the city may lead us to conclude that quite different zoning policies are in order.

20.5 Conclusion

There is a great deal of room for improvement in urban decision making. The urban dynamics approach provides important ideas that not only explain many urban failures but also give directions for more appropriate public policy.

This paper has described how a number of present city policies, when examined from the general perspective of the *Urban Dynamics* model, show signs of inconsistency with the city's needs and objectives. The ongoing Lowell Dynamics research program at M.I.T. aims to refine the basic urban dynamics concepts into formal policy statements. The process will take considerable time, and it will involve expanding the original *Urban Dynamics* model to address a broader range of urban decision alternatives. Further research into the dynamics of Lowell should yield a strategy for meeting Lowell's deeply rooted problems as well as an urban management tool applicable to the problems of a great many other troubled cities.

Notes

1. George F. Kenngott, *The Record of a City* (New York: Macmillan Co., 1912), p. 7.

2. L. S. Bryant and J. B. Rae, *Lowell: An Early American Industrial Community* (Cambridge, Mass.: Technology Press, 1950), p. 24.

3. Kenngott, *Record of a City*, p. 7.

4. Ibid.

5. Frederick Coburn, *History of Lowell and Its People* (New York: Lewis Historical Publishing Company, 1920), p. 1.

6. Ibid., p. 2.

7. Ibid., p. 168.

8. Ibid.

9. Ibid., p. 352.

10. From an interview with the Model Cities director, June 1971.

11. Coburn, *History of Lowell*, p. 353.

12. Ibid., p. 306.

13. Ibid., p. 307.

14. Ibid., p. 352.

15. Ibid.

16. Jay W. Forrester, "Toward a National Urban Consensus," Reading 18 in this volume, Section 18.2.

17. Ibid., Section 18.5.

18. This view was expressed, for example, in an interview with the city solicitor, June 1971.

19. The 37 percent figure on housing assessments is typical of most Massachusetts cities. Several cities in the Commonwealth are, however, beginning to comply with the state law requiring that housing be assessed at 100 percent of its fair market value. Lowell will probably follow these cities and reassess, but not for the next few years, at least.

20. Forrester, Reading 18, Section 18.5.

21. Ibid.

22. Northern Middlesex Area Commission, *Zoning Policies: Implications for Housing, Land and Public Service Costs* (Lowell, 1971), p. 5.

23. Ibid., p. 8.

24. Forrester, Reading 18, Section 18.5.

Index

TOWARD GLOBAL EQUILIBRIUM: COLLECTED PAPERS, edited by Dennis L. Meadows and Donella H. Meadows

Contains 13 papers which describe individual research on dynamic issues evolving from the Club of Rome project. It presents detailed analyses of several important global problems, e.g. DDT and mercury pollution, natural resource depletion, solid waste disposal, etc., and provides policy suggestions which may alleviate these problems. It also examines the economic, political, and ethical implications of growth and the transition to equilibrium.

1973, 358 pp., ill., $18.00

DYNAMICS OF COMMODITY PRODUCTION CYCLES by Dennis L. Meadows

Develops a general model of the economic, biological, technological, and psychological factors which lead to instability in commodity systems. With appropriate parameter values, the model explains the hog, cattle and chicken cycles observed in the real world.

1970, 104 pp., ill., $14.75

All books published by Wright-Allen Press are available in Great Britain and Australasia through John Wiley & Sons.

John Wiley & Sons Ltd.
Baffins Lane
Chichester, Sussex
England

John Wiley & Sons
Australasia Pty. Ltd.
110 Alexander Street
Crow's Nest, N.S.W.
Australia